Lecture Notes in Computer Science   10661

Commenced Publication in 1973
Founding and Former Series Editors:
Gerhard Goos, Juris Hartmanis, and Jan van Leeuwen

Raghunath Nambiar · Meikel Poess (Eds.)

Performance Evaluation and Benchmarking for the Analytics Era

9th TPC Technology Conference, TPCTC 2017
Munich, Germany, August 28, 2017
Revised Selected Papers

Springer

Editors
Raghunath Nambiar
Cisco Systems, Inc.
San Jose, CA
USA

Meikel Poess
Server Technologies
Oracle Corporation
Redwood Shores, CA
USA

ISSN 0302-9743 ISSN 1611-3349 (electronic)
Lecture Notes in Computer Science
ISBN 978-3-319-72400-3 ISBN 978-3-319-72401-0 (eBook)
https://doi.org/10.1007/978-3-319-72401-0

Library of Congress Control Number: 2017961804

LNCS Sublibrary: SL2 – Programming and Software Engineering

Printed on acid-free paper

This Springer imprint is published by Springer Nature
The registered company is Springer International Publishing AG
The registered company address is: Gewerbestrasse 11, 6330 Cham, Switzerland

Preface

The Transaction Processing Performance Council (TPC) is a nonprofit organization established in August 1988. Over the years, the TPC has had a significant impact on the computing industry's use of industry-standard benchmarks. Vendors use TPC benchmarks to illustrate performance competitiveness for their existing products, and to improve and monitor the performance of their products under development. Many buyers use TPC benchmark results as points of comparison when purchasing new computing systems.

The information technology landscape is evolving at a rapid pace, challenging industry experts and researchers to develop innovative techniques for evaluation, measurement, and characterization of complex systems. The TPC remains committed to developing new benchmark standards to keep pace with these rapid changes in technology. One vehicle for achieving this objective is the TPC's sponsorship of the Technology Conference Series on Performance Evaluation and Benchmarking (TPCTC) established in 2009. With this conference series, the TPC encourages researchers and industry experts to present and debate novel ideas and methodologies in performance evaluation, measurement, and characterization.

This book contains the proceedings of the 9th TPC Technology Conference on Performance Evaluation and Benchmarking (TPCTC 2017), held in conjunction with the 43rd International Conference on Very Large Data Bases (VLDB 2017) in Munich, Germany, from August 28 to September 5, 2017.

The hard work and close cooperation of a number of people have contributed to the success of this conference. We would like to thank the members of TPC and the organizers of VLDB 2017 for their sponsorship; the members of the Program Committee and Publicity Committee for their support; and the authors and the participants, who are the primary reason for the success of this conference.

October 2017

Raghunath Nambiar
Meikel Poess

TPCTC 2017 Organization

General Chairs

Raghunath Nambiar   Cisco, USA
Meikel Poess   Oracle, USA

Program Committee

Chaitanya Baru	SDSC, USA
Daniel Bowers	Gartner, USA
Michael Brey	Oracle, USA
Alain Crolotte	Teradata, USA
Paul Cao	HPE, USA
Akon Dey	University of Sydney, Australia
Harumi Kuno	HPE, USA
Karthik Kulkarni	Cisco, USA
Dhabaleswar Panda	Ohio State University, USA
Tilmann Rabl	University of Toronto, Canada
Reza Taheri	VMware, USA

Publicity Committee

Raghunath Nambiar	Cisco, USA
Andrew Bond	Red Hat, USA
Paul Cao	HPE, USA
Meikel Poess	Oracle, USA
Reza Taheri	VMware, USA
Michael Majdalany	L&M Management Group, USA
Forrest Carman	Owen Media, USA
Andreas Hotea	Hotea Solutions, USA

About the TPC

Introduction to the TPC

The Transaction Processing Performance Council (TPC) is a nonprofit organization focused on developing industry standards for data-centric workloads and disseminating vendor-neutral performance data to the industry. Additional information is available at http://www.tpc.org/.

TPC Memberships

Full Members

Full Members of the TPC participate in all aspects of the TPC's work, including development of benchmark standards and setting strategic direction. The Full Member application can be found at http://www.tpc.org/information/about/app-member.asp.

Associate Members

Certain organizations may join the TPC as Associate Members. Associate Members may attend TPC meetings, but are not eligible to vote or hold office. Associate membership is available to nonprofit organizations, educational institutions, market researchers, publishers, consultants, governments, and businesses that do not create, market, or sell computer products or services. The Associate Member application can be found at http://www.tpc.org/information/about/app-assoc.asp.

Academic and Government Institutions

Academic and government institutions are invited join the TPC and a special invitation can be found at http://www.tpc.org/information/specialinvitation.asp.

Contact the TPC

TPC
Presidio of San Francisco
Building 572B (surface)
P.O. Box 29920 (mail)
San Francisco, CA 94129-0920
Voice: 415-561-6272
Fax: 415-561-6120
Email: info@tpc.org

How to Order TPC Materials

All of our materials are now posted free of charge on our website. If you have any questions, please feel free to contact our office directly or by email at info@tpc.org.

Benchmark Status Report

The TPC Benchmark Status Report is a digest of the activities of the TPC and its technical subcommittees. Sign-up information can be found at the following URL: http://www.tpc.org/information/about/email.asp.

TPC 2017 Organization

Full Members

Actian
Cisco
Dell
DataCore
Fujitsu
Hewlett Packard Enterprise
Hitachi
Huawei
IBM
Inspur
Intel
Lenovo
Microsoft
Nutanix
Oracle
Pivotal
Red Hat
SAP
Teradata
TTA
VMware

Associate Members

IDEAS International
University of Coimbra, Portugal
China Academy of Information and Communications Technology

Steering Committee

Michael Brey (Chair)	Oracle, USA
Andrew Bond	Red Hat, USA
Matthew Emmerton	IBM, USA
Raghunath Nambiar	Cisco, USA
Jamie Reding	Microsoft, USA

Public Relations Committee

Raghunath Nambiar (Chair)	Cisco, USA
Andrew Bond	Red Hat, USA
Paul Cao	HPE, USA
Meikel Poess	Oracle, USA
Reza Taheri	VMware, USA

Technical Advisory Board

Jamie Reding (Chair)	Microsoft, USA
Andrew Bond	Red Hat, USA
Paul Cao	HPE, USA
Matthew Emmerton	IBM, USA
Da-Qi Ren	Huawei, USA
Ken Rule	Intel, USA
Nicholas Wakou	Dell, USA

Technical Subcommittees and Chairs

TPC-C	Jamie Reding	Microsoft, USA
TPC-H	Meikel Poess	Oracle, USA
TPC-E	Matthew Emmerton	IBM, USA
TPC-DS	Meikel Poess	Oracle, USA
TPC-DI	Meikel Poess	Oracle, USA
TPCx-HS	Tariq Magdon-Ismail	VMware, USA
TPCx-BB	Bhaskar Gowda	Intel, USA
TPCx-V	Reza Taheri	VMware, USA
TPCx-HCI	Reza Taheri	VMware, USA
TPCx-IoT	Raghunath Nambiar	Cisco, USA
TPC-Pricing	Jamie Reding	Microsoft, USA
TPC-Energy	Paul Cao	HPE, USA

Working Group and Chair

TPC-AI: Raghunath Nambiar	Cisco, USA

Contents

Industry Standards for the Analytics Era: TPC Roadmap

Raghunath Nambiar[1](✉) and Meikel Poess[2]

[1] Cisco Systems, Inc., 275 East Tasman Drive, San Jose, CA 95134, USA
rnambiar@cisco.com
[2] Oracle Corporation, 500 Oracle Parkway, Redwood Shores, CA 94065, USA
meikel.poess@oracle.com

Abstract. The Transaction Processing Performance Council (TPC) is a non-profit organization focused on developing data-centric benchmark standards and disseminating objective, verifiable performance data to industry. This paper provides a high-level summary of TPC benchmark standards, technology conference initiative, and new development activities in progress.

Keywords: Industry standards · Database benchmarks

1 TPC Benchmark Timelines

Founded in 1988, the Transaction Processing Performance Council (TPC) is a non-profit corporation dedicated to creating and maintaining benchmarks which measure database performance in a standardized, objective and verifiable manner. As of November 2017, 21 full members and three associate members comprise the TPC.

To date the TPC has approved a total of sixteen different benchmarks. Of these benchmarks, twelve are currently active. TPC currently defines two benchmark classes: Enterprise and Express. See Fig. 1 for the benchmark timelines.

- Enterprise benchmarks are technology agnostic. They are specification based, typically complex, and have long development cycles. Their specifications are provided by the TPC, but their implementation is up to the vendor. The vendor may choose any commercially available combination of software and hardware products to implement benchmarks. Examples of enterprise benchmarks are: TPC-C, TPC-E, TPC-H, TPC-DS, TPC-DI, TPC-VMS
- Express benchmarks are kit based, typically based on exiting workloads have shorter development cycles. It is required to use TPC provided kits for the publication of express benchmarks. Examples of express benchmarks: TPCx-HS, TPCx-BB, TPCx-V, TPCx-IoT

© Springer International Publishing AG 2018
R. Nambiar and M. Poess (Eds.): TPCTC 2017, LNCS 10661, pp. 1–8, 2018.
https://doi.org/10.1007/978-3-319-72401-0_1

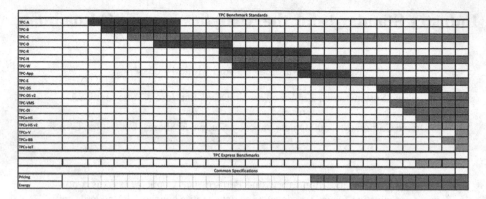

Fig. 1. TPC benchmark timelines

A high-level summary of current active standards are listed below:

1.1 Transaction Processing

TPC-C: Approved in July of 1992, TPC Benchmark C is an on-line transaction processing (OLTP) benchmark. TPC-C is more complex than previous OLTP benchmarks such as TPC-A because of its multiple transaction types, more complex database and overall execution structure. TPC-C involves a mix of five concurrent transactions of different types and complexity either executed on-line or queued for deferred execution. The database is comprised of nine types of tables with a wide range of record and population sizes. TPC-C is measured in transactions per minute (tpmC). While the benchmark portrays the activity of a wholesale supplier, TPC-C is not limited to the activity of any particular business segment, but, rather represents any industry that must manage, sell, or distribute a product or service.

TPC-E: Approved in February of 2007, TPC Benchmark E is an on-line transaction processing (OLTP) benchmark. TPC-E is more complex than previous OLTP benchmarks such as TPC-C because of its diverse transaction types, more complex database and overall execution structure. TPC-E involves a mix of twelve concurrent transactions of different types and complexity, either executed on-line or triggered by price or time criteria. The database is comprised of thirty-three tables with a wide range of columns, cardinality, and scaling properties. TPC-E is measured in transactions per second (tpsE). While the benchmark portrays the activity of a stock brokerage firm, TPC-E is not limited to the activity of any particular business segment, but rather represents any industry that must report upon and execute transactions of a financial nature.

1.2 Decision Support

TPC-H: The TPC Benchmark™H (TPC-H) is a decision support benchmark. It consists of a suite of business oriented ad-hoc queries and concurrent data modifications. The queries and the data populating the database have been chosen to have broad industry-wide relevance. This benchmark illustrates decision support systems that examine large volumes of data, execute queries with a high degree of complexity, and give answers to critical business questions. The performance metric reported by TPC-H is called the TPC-H Composite Query-per-Hour Performance Metric (QphH@Size), and reflects multiple aspects of the capability of the system to process queries. These aspects include the selected database size against which the queries are executed, the query processing power when queries are submitted by a single stream, and the query throughput when queries are submitted by multiple concurrent users. The TPC-H Price/ Performance metric is expressed as $/QphH@Size.

TPC-DS: The TPC Benchmark DS (TPC-DS) is a decision support benchmark that models several generally applicable aspects of a decision support system, including queries and data maintenance. The benchmark provides a representative evaluation of performance as a general purpose decision support system. A benchmark result measures query response time in single user mode, query throughput in multi user mode and data maintenance performance for a given hardware, operating system, and data processing system configuration under a controlled, complex, multi-user decision support work-load. The purpose of TPC benchmarks is to provide relevant, objective performance data to industry users. TPC-DS Version 2 enables emerging technologies, such as Big Data systems, to execute the benchmark [3, 4].

TPC-DI: Historically, the process of synchronizing a decision support system with data from operational systems has been referred to as Extract, Transform, Load (ETL) and the tools supporting such process have been referred to as ETL tools. Recently, ETL was replaced by the more comprehensive acronym, data integration (DI). DI describes the process of extracting and combining data from a variety of data source formats, transforming that data into a unified data model representation and loading it into a data store. The TPC-DI benchmark combines and transforms data extracted from an On-Line Transaction Processing (OTLP) system along with other sources of data, and loads it into a data warehouse. The source and destination data models, data transformations and implementation rules have been designed to be broadly representative of modern data integration requirements [5].

1.3 Big Data and Analytics

TPCx-HS v1: Big Data technologies like Hadoop has become an important part of the enterprise IT ecosystem. Introduced in 2014, the TPC Express Benchmark HS (TPCx-HS) Version 1 is industry's first ever standard for benchmarking big data systems. It was developed to provide an objective measure of hardware, operating system and commercial Apache Hadoop File System API compatible software distributions, and to provide the industry with verifiable performance, price-performance and availability metrics. Even though the modeled application is simple, the results are highly relevant to hardware and software dealing with Big Data systems in general. TPCx-HS stresses both the hardware and software stacks including the execution engine (MapReduce or Spark) and Hadoop Filesystem API compatible layers. This workload can be used to assess a broad range of system topologies and implementation of Hadoop clusters. The TPCx-HS benchmark can be used to assess a broad range of system topologies and implementation methodologies in a technically rigorous and directly comparable, in a vendor-neutral manner [6].

TPCx-HS v2: The Hadoop ecosystem is moving fast beyond batch processing with MapReduce. Introduced in 2016 TPCx-HS V2 is based on TPCx-HS V1 with support for Apache Spark - a popular platform for in-memory data processing that enables real-time analytics on Apache Hadoop. TPCx-HS V2 also supports MapReduce (MR2) and supports publications on traditional on premise deployments and clouds. More information about TPCx-HS v1 can be found at http://www.tpc.org/tpcx-hs/default.asp?version=1. The TPCx-HS v2 benchmark can be used to assess a broad range of system topologies and implementation methodologies in a technically rigorous and directly comparable, in a vendor-neutral manner.

TPCx-BB: TPCx-BB Express Benchmark BB (TPCx-BB) measures the performance of Hadoop-based Big Data systems. It measures the performance of both hardware and software components by executing 30 frequently performed analytical queries in the context of retailers with physical and online store presence. The queries are expressed in SQL for structured data and in machine learning algorithms for semi-structured and unstructured data. The SQL queries can use Hive or Spark, while the machine learning algorithms use machine learning libraries, user defined functions, and procedural programs [7].

1.4 Virtualization

TPC-VMS: Introduced in 2012, the TPC Virtual Measurement Single System Specification (TPC-VMS) leverages the TPC-C, TPC-E, TPC-H and TPC-DS Benchmarks by adding the methodology and requirements for running and reporting performance metrics for virtualized databases. The intent of TPC-VMS is to represent a Virtualization Environment where three database workloads are consolidated onto one server. Test sponsors choose one of the four benchmark workloads (TPC-C, TPC-E, TPC-H, or TPC-DS) and runs one instance of that benchmark workload in each of the 3 virtual machines (VMs) on the system under test. The 3 virtualized databases must have the same attributes, e.g. the same number of TPC-C warehouses, the same number of TPC-E Load Units, or the same TPC-DS or TPC-H scale factors. The TPC-VMS Primary Performance Metric is the minimum value of the three TPC Benchmark Primary metrics for the TPC Benchmarks run in the Virtualization Environment [8].

TPCx-V: The TPC Express Benchmark V (TPCx-V) benchmark measures the performance of a virtualized server platform under a demanding database workload. It stresses CPU and memory hardware, storage, networking, hypervisor, and the guest operating system. TPCx-V workload is database-centric and models many properties of cloud services, such as multiple VMs running at different load demand levels, and large fluctuations in the load level of each VM. Unlike previous TPC benchmarks, TPCx-V has a publicly-available, end-to-end benchmarking kit, which was developed specifically for this benchmark. It loads the databases, runs the benchmark, validates the results, and even performs many of the routine audit steps. Another unique characteristic of TPCx-V is an elastic workload that varies the load delivered to each of the VMs by as much as 16x, while maintaining a constant load at the host level [8].

1.5 Internet of Things (IoT)

TPCx-IoT: TPCx-IoT is the industry's first benchmark which enables direct comparison of different software and hardware solutions for IoT gateways. Positioned between edge architecture and the back-end data center, gateway systems perform functions such as data aggregation, real-time analytics and persistent storage. TPCx-IoT was specifically designed to provide verifiable performance, price-performance and availability metrics for commercially available systems that typically ingest massive amounts of data from large numbers of devices, while running real-time analytic queries. The workload is representative of activities typical in IoT gateway systems, running on commercially available hardware and software platforms. The TPCx-IoT can be used to assess a broad range of system topologies and implementation methodologies in a technically rigorous and directly comparable, in a vendor-neutral manner.

2 TPCTC Conference Series

To keep pace with rapid changes in technology, in 2009, the TPC initiated a conference series on performance analysis and benchmarking. The TPCTC has been challenging industry experts and researchers to develop innovative techniques for performance evaluation, measurement, and characterization of hardware and software systems. Over the years it has emerged as a leading forum to present and debate the latest and greatest in the world of benchmarking. The topics of interest included:

- Big data and analytics
- Complex event processing
- Database Optimizations
- Data Integration
- Disaster tolerance and recovery
- Emerging storage technologies (NVMe, 3D XPoint Memory etc.)
- Hybrid workloads
- Energy and space efficiency
- In-memory databases
- Internet of Things
- Virtualization
- Enhancements to TPC workloads
- Lessons learned in practice using TPC workloads
- Collection and interpretation of performance data in public cloud environments

2.1 Summary of the TPCTC Conferences Are Listed Below

The first TPC Technology Conference on Performance Evaluation and Benchmarking (TPCTC 2009), held in conjunction with the 35th International Conference on Very Large Data Bases (VLDB 2009) in Lyon, France from August 24th to August 28th, 2009 [9].

The second TPC Technology Conference on Performance Evaluation and Benchmarking (TPCTC 2010) was held in conjunction with the 36th International Conference on Very Large Data Bases (VLDB 2010) in Singapore from September 13th to September 17th, 2010 [10].

The third TPC Technology Conference on Performance Evaluation and Benchmarking (TPCTC 2011), held in conjunction with the 37th International Conference on Very Large Data Bases (VLDB 2011) in Seattle, Washington from August 29th to September 3rd, 2011 [11].

The fourth TPC Technology Conference on Performance Evaluation and Benchmarking (TPCTC 2012), held in conjunction with the 38th International Conference on Very Large Data Bases (VLDB 2012) in Istanbul, Turkey from August 27th to August 31st, 2012 [12].

The fifth TPC Technology Conference on Performance Evaluation and Benchmarking (TPCTC 2013), held in conjunction with the 39th International Conference on Very Large Data Bases (VLDB 2013) in Riva del Garda, Trento, Italy from August 26th to August 30st, 2013 [13].

The sixth TPC Technology Conference on Performance Evaluation and Benchmarking (TPCTC 2014), held in conjunction with the 40th International Conference on Very Large Data Bases (VLDB 2014) in Hangzhou, China, from September 1st to September 5th, 2014 [14].

The seventh TPC Technology Conference on Performance Evaluation and Benchmarking (TPCTC 2015), held in conjunction with the 41st International Conference on Very Large Data Bases (VLDB 2015) in Kohala Coast, USA, from August 31st to September 4th, 2015 [15].

The eighth TPC Technology Conference on Performance Evaluation and Benchmarking (TPCTC 2016), held in conjunction with the 42nd International Conference on Very Large Data Bases (VLDB 2016) in New Delhi, India, from September 5th to September 9th, 2016.

The ninth TPC Technology Conference on Performance Evaluation and Benchmarking (TPCTC 2017), held in conjunction with the 43nd International Conference on Very Large Data Bases (VLDB 2017) in Munich, India, from August 28th to September 1th, 2017.

TPCTC has had a significant positive impact on the TPC. TPC is able to attract new members from industry and academia to join the TPC. The formation of working groups on Big Data, Virtualization, Hyper-convergence, Internet of Things (IoT) and Artificial Intelligence were a direct result of TPCTC conferences.

3 Outlook

TPC remains committed to develop relevant standards in collaboration with industry and research communities and continue to enable fair comparison of technologies and products in terms of performance, cost of ownership.

Foreseeing the industry transition to digital transformation the TPC has created a working group to develop set of standards for hardware and software pertaining to Artificial Intelligence. Companies, research and government institutions who are interested in influencing the development of such benchmarks are encouraged to join the TPC [2].

Acknowledgements. Developing benchmark standards require a huge effort to conceptualize, research, specify, review, prototype, and verify the benchmark. The authors acknowledge the work and contributions of past and present members of the TPC.

References

1. Nambiar, R., Poess, M.: Reinventing the TPC: from traditional to big data to Internet of Things. In: Nambiar, R., Poess, M. (eds.) TPCTC 2015. LNCS, vol. 9508, pp. 1–7. Springer, Cham (2016). https://doi.org/10.1007/978-3-319-31409-9_1
2. Nambiar, R., Poess, M.: Keeping the TPC relevant! PVLDB 6(11), 1186–1187 (2013)
3. Nambiar, R., Wakou, N., Masland, A., Thawley, P., Lanken, M., Carman, F., Majdalany, M.: Shaping the landscape of industry standard benchmarks: contributions of the Transaction Processing Performance Council (TPC). In: Nambiar, R., Poess, M. (eds.) TPCTC 2011. LNCS, vol. 7144, pp. 1–9. Springer, Heidelberg (2012). https://doi.org/10.1007/978-3-642-32627-1_1
4. Nambiar, R., Poess, M.: The making of TPC-DS. In: VLDB 2006, pp. 1049–1058
5. Poess, M., Nambiar, R., Walrath, D.: Why you should run TPC-DS: a workload analysis. In: VLDB 2007, pp. 1138–1149
6. Poess, M., Rabl, T., Caufield, B.: TPC-DI: the first industry benchmark for data integration. PVLDB 7(13), 1367–1378 (2014)
7. Nambiar, R., Poess, M., Cao, P., Magdon-Ismail, T., Ren, D.Q., Bond, A.: Introducing TPCx-HS: the first industry standard for benchmarking big data systems. In: Nambiar, R., Poess, M. (eds.) TPCTC 2014. LNCS, vol. 8904, pp. 1–12. Springer, Cham (2015). https://doi.org/10.1007/978-3-319-15350-6_1
8. Baru, C., et al.: Discussion of BigBench: a proposed industry standard performance benchmark for big data. In: Nambiar, R., Poess, M. (eds.) TPCTC 2014. LNCS, vol. 8904, pp. 44–63. Springer, Cham (2015). https://doi.org/10.1007/978-3-319-15350-6_4
9. Bond, A., Johnson, D., Kopczynski, G., Taheri, H.R.: Profiling the performance of virtualized databases with the TPCx-V benchmark. In: Nambiar, R., Poess, M. (eds.) TPCTC 2015. LNCS, vol. 9508, pp. 156–172. Springer, Cham (2016). https://doi.org/10.1007/978-3-319-31409-9_10
10. Nambiar, R., Poess, M. (eds.): Performance Evaluation and Benchmarking. LNCS, vol. 5895. Springer, Heidelberg (2009). https://doi.org/10.1007/978-3-642-10424-4
11. Nambiar, R., Poess, M. (eds.): Performance Evaluation, Measurement and Characterization of Complex Systems. LNCS, vol. 6417. Springer, Heidelberg (2011). https://doi.org/10.1007/978-3-642-18206-8
12. Nambiar, R., Poess, M. (eds.): Topics in Performance Evaluation, Measurement and Characterization. LNCS, vol. 7144. Springer, Heidelberg (2012). https://doi.org/10.1007/978-3-642-32627-1

13. Nambiar, R., Poess, M. (eds.): Selected Topics in Performance Evaluation and Benchmarking. LNCS, vol. 7755. Springer, Heidelberg (2013). https://doi.org/10.1007/978-3-642-36727-4
14. Nambiar, R., Poess, M. (eds.): Performance Characterization and Benchmarking. LNCS, vol. 8391. Springer, Cham (2014). https://doi.org/10.1007/978-3-319-04936-6
15. Nambiar, R., Poess, M. (eds.): Performance Characterization and Benchmarking. Traditional to Big Data. LNCS, vol. 8904. Springer, Cham (2015). https://doi.org/10.1007/978-3-319-15350-6
16. Nambiar, R., Poess, M. (eds.): Performance Evaluation and Benchmarking: Traditional to Big Data to Internet of Things. LNCS, vol. 9508. Springer, Cham (2016). https://doi.org/10.1007/978-3-319-31409-9

PEEL: A Framework for Benchmarking Distributed Systems and Algorithms

Christoph Boden[1,2]([✉]), Alexander Alexandrov[1], Andreas Kunft[1],
Tilmann Rabl[1,2], and Volker Markl[1,2]

[1] Technische Universität Berlin, Berlin, Germany
{christoph.boden,alexander.alexandrov,andreas.kunft,tilmann.rabl,
volker.markl}@tu-berlin.de
[2] DFKI, Saarbrücken, Germany

Abstract. During the last decade, a multitude of novel systems for scalable and distributed data processing has been proposed in both academia and industry. While there are published results of experimental evaluations for nearly all systems, it remains a challenge to objectively compare different system's performance. It is thus imperative to enable and establish benchmarks for these systems. However, even if workloads and data sets or data generators are fixed, orchestrating and executing benchmarks can be a major obstacle. Worse, many systems come with hardware-dependent parameters that have to be tuned and spawn a diverse set of configuration files. This impedes portability and reproducibility of benchmarks. To address these problems and to foster reproducible and portable experiments and benchmarks of distributed data processing systems, we present *PEEL*, a framework to define, execute, analyze, and share experiments. PEEL enables the transparent specification of benchmarking workloads and system configuration parameters. It orchestrates the systems involved and automatically runs and collects all associated logs of experiments. PEEL currently supports Apache HDFS, Hadoop, Flink, and Spark and can easily be extended to include further systems.

1 Introduction and Motivation

During the last decade, the Big Data hype has led to the development of a plethora of novel systems for scalable data processing. Starting with the *MapReduce* paradigm [10] and its open-source implementation *Hadoop* [3], numerous successors have been proposed and implemented either as research prototypes or industry led open-source systems. Hadoop MapReduce was quickly embraced by practitioners, as it successfully abstracts away the complexity of scheduling a program's distributed execution on large clusters, managing the inter-machine communication as well as coping with machine failures by exposing a simple functional programming API to users. However, as focus shifted from rather simple extraction and aggregation jobs to the scalable execution of more complex workflows, such as inferring statistical models and machine learning algorithms, it

R. Nambiar and M. Poess (Eds.): TPCTC 2017, LNCS 10661, pp. 9–24, 2018.
https://doi.org/10.1007/978-3-319-72401-0_2

quickly became apparent that Hadoop was inherently inefficient at executing such workloads. While many machine learning algorithms can easily be formulated in the functional *MapReduce* programming model on a logical level [9], the acyclic data flow model underlying Hadoop's implementation and the intricacies of its distributed implementation lead to unsatisfactory performance. Particularly the fixed *Map-Shuffle-Reduce* pipeline and the inability to efficiently execute *iterative computations* turned out to be major drawbacks of Hadoop.

This led to numerous contributions from both the database and systems communities, which address these shortcomings. Systems such as Spark [4,16] or Stratosphere [5] (now called Flink [1,8]) were among the first systems to support efficient iterative computations, GraphLab [12] proposed an asynchronous graph-based execution model, which was subsequently distributed [11]. Pregel [13] and its open source implementation Giraph [2] provided a vertex-centric programming abstraction and Bulk Synchronous Parallel (BSP) based execution model.

While nearly all systems have been presented in scientific publications containing an experimental evaluation, it remains a challenge to objectively compare the performance of each system. Different workloads and implementations, usage of libraries, data sets and hardware configurations make it hard if not impossible to leverage the published experiments for such a comparison. Furthermore, it is a challenge to assess how much of the performance gain is due to a superior paradigm or design and how much is due to a more efficient implementation, which ultimately impairs the scientific process due to a lack of verifiability.

For this reason, it is imperative to enable and establish benchmarks for big data analytics systems. However, even if workloads and data sets or data generators are fixed, orchestrating and executing benchmarks can be a major challenge.

The principle goal of a system experiment as part of such a benchmark is to characterize the behavior of a particular system under test (SUT) for a specific set of values, configured as system and application parameters. The usual way to achieve this goal is to

1. define a workload application which takes specific parameters (e.g., input and output path),
2. run it on top of the SUT with a specific configuration (e.g., allocated memory, degree of parallelism (DOP)) and,
3. measure key performance characteristics (e.g., runtime, throughput, accuracy).

Achieving these goals for benchmark experiments on modern data management systems such as distributed data processing systems is significantly more complex than evaluating a traditional RDBMS. Figure 1 illustrates, that rather than having a single system under test running in isolation, novel data processing systems require several systems such as a distributed file system and a distributed data processing system to be executed jointly. Current trends actually advocate an architecture based on interconnected systems (e.g. HDFS, Yarn, Spark, Flink, Storm). Each of these systems has to be set up and launched with their own set of, potentially hardware-dependent, configurations.

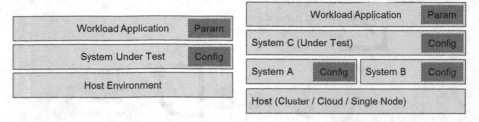

Fig. 1. The general setup: contrary to the setup when benchmarking traditional RDMB systems (left) where we evaluate only one System under Test (SUT), the landscape is more complicated when evaluating novel distributed data processing frameworks (right), as they usually require the interplay between multiple independent systems. Each of these systems has its own configurations with sets of parameters that have to be set, and potentially tuned.

Typically, one is not just interested in the insights obtained by a single experiment, but in trends highlighted by a suite of experiments where a certain system under test (SUT) configuration or application parameter value is varied and everything else remains fixed. When running a scale-out experiment with a varying number of nodes for example, the configuration of both the distributed file system as well as the distributed data processing system under test have to be changed, and the systems have to be appropriately orchestrated. This further complicates the benchmarking process. Additionally, hardware-dependent configurations hinder portability and thus reproducibility of benchmarks. When adjusting the systems is done manually, huge amounts of temporary files and generated data tend to clog up the disk space, as experiments may be run without proper tear-down of systems and cleaning of temporary directories. When such experiments are run on a shared cluster, as is often the case in an academic environment, this issue becomes even more severe.

Contribution: To address these problems and to enable and foster reproducible experiments and benchmarks of distributed data processing systems, we present *PEEL*[1], a framework to define, execute, analyze, and share experiments. On the one hand, PEEL automatically orchestrates experiments and handles the systems' setup, configuration, deployment, tear-down and cleanup as well as automatic log collection. On the other hand, PEEL introduces a unified and transparent way of specifying experiments, including the actual application code, system configuration, and experiment setup description. With this transparent specification, PEEL enables the sharing of end-to-end experiment artifacts, thus fostering reproducibility and portability of benchmark experiments. PEEL also allows for the hardware independent specification of these parameters, therefore enabling portability of experiments across different hardware setups. Figure 2 illustrates the process enabled by our framework. Finally, we make PEEL available as open-source software on GitHub.

---

[1] https://github.com/peelframework/peel.

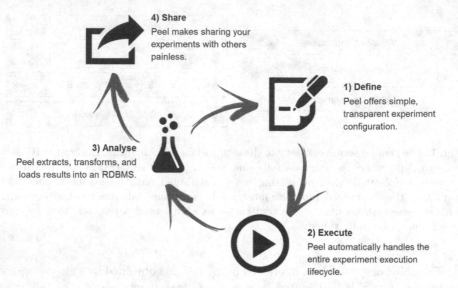

Fig. 2. The Peel process: Peel enables the transparent specification of workloads, systems configurations, and parameters to be varied. It also automatically handles the distributed orchestration and execution as well as sharing of these experiment bundles. After successfully running all experiments in a bundle, PEEL automatically extracts, transforms and loads relevant measurements from collected log files and makes them available in an RDBMS.

2   Outline

The rest of this paper is structured as follows: In Sect. 3 we introduce the running example of a supervised machine learning workload, which we will use to explain the details of defining an experiment. Section 4 introduces experiment definitions. Next, Sect. 5 describes the basics of a bundle. Section 6 discusses the approach of a unified, global experiment environment configuration and Sect. 7 illustrates how PEEL bundles can be deployed and executed on cluster environments, before Sect. 8 provides an overview, how results can be gathered and analyzed within the framework. Finally, we describe how PEEL can be extended with additional systems in Sect. 9.

3   Running Example: Benchmarking a Supervised Machine Learning Workload

As a running example, we will consider a supervised machine learning workload. This workload is part of an extensive machine learning benchmark for distributed data flow systems [7] (please see the paper for further details and experimental results).

More concretely, we train a logistic regression model for *click-through rate prediction* using a batch gradient descent solver. Click-through rate prediction for online advertisements forms a crucial building block in the multi-billion dollar online advertising industry and logistic regression models have their merit for this task [14,15]. Such prediction models are trained on hundreds of terabytes of data with hundreds of billions of training samples, which happen to be very high dimensional. For this reason, we are interested in evaluating the scaling behavior of the systems not just with respect to growing data set sizes and increasing number of compute nodes but also with respect to increasing model dimensionality as suggested in [7].

For the experiments, we use a subset of the *Criteo Click Logs*[2] data set. This dataset contains feature values and click feedback for millions of ad impressions drawn from a portion of Criteo's traffic over a period of 24 days. Since this data set contains categorical features, we use feature hashing as a pre-processing step. Feature hashing (also called the hashing trick) vectorizes the categorical variables by applying a hash function to the feature values and using the hash values as indices. It thus maps the sparse training data into a space with fixed

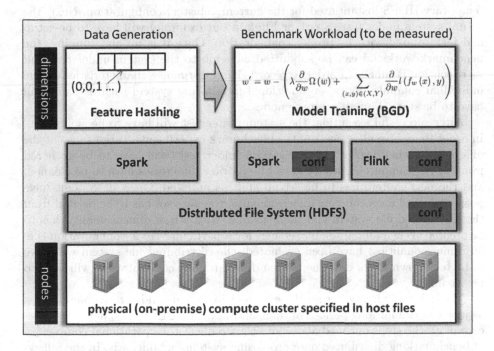

Fig. 3. An illustration of the running example: we evaluate *batch gradient decent* training of a supervised learning model as a workload on Apache Spark and Apache Flink as *systems under test*. The individual experiments depend on two parameters: the number of physical compute *nodes* and the dimensionality of the training data set (*dimensions*), which specify how the benchmark workload shall be executed. The data generation job is executed on a system independent of the system under test.

---

[2] http://labs.criteo.com/downloads/download-terabyte-click-logs/.

dimensionality, which can be controlled by a parameter. This feature hashing will be executed as a pre-processing job on Spark.

Figure 3 illustrates the running example. We want to evaluate *batch gradient decent* training of a supervised learning model as a workload on Apache Spark and Apache Flink as a *system under test*. Only for this part do we want to time the execution and record the system performance characteristics of the individual compute nodes involved. In order to evaluate the scalability of the systems with respect to a varying number of compute nodes as well as a varying dimensionality of the training data (and thus also the model to be trained) the two parameters: *nodes* and *dimensions* have to be varied accordingly.

For each particular configuration of physical compute nodes, a new distributed file system (HDFS) has to be set up. Next the raw criteo data, which is ingested from some external storage, has to be transformed to feature vectors of the desired dimensionality via feature hashing. Any system may be used for this step - independent of the actual system under test. In the example, we choose to run a Spark Job, which writes out the experimentation data into the temporary HDFS instantiated for the current (cluster) configuration. Next, the actual system under test (Spark or Flink in our example) will have to be setup and instantiated with its proper configuration. Once it is up and running, the benchmark workload can be submitted as a job to the system under test and its execution is timed. In order to record the performance characteristics on the individual compute nodes, an additional monitoring system such as *dstat* will have to be started on all compute nodes.

After successful execution, the system under test will have to be shut down. In order to archive all aspects of the benchmark experiments, various logs of the different systems involved (dstat, system under test) will have to be gathered from all the compute nodes. Next, all temporary directories have to be cleaned, and the next system has to be set up and instantiated. Once all systems have been evaluated for a concrete dimensionality, the data set has to be deleted from the distributed file system and the next one, with a new dimensionality, has to be created. When all parameter settings for a particular Node configuration (i.e. all dimensionalities) have been evaluated, the distributed file system will have to be torn down and a new one, with a different node configuration, will have to be set up.

Manually administering all these steps is a tedious and error-prone process as jobs can run for long periods of time, and may fail. PEEL automatically takes care of all the steps outlined above and thus reduces the operational complexity of benchmarking distributed data processing systems significantly. In the following sections, we will explore how a workload like the supervised learning example has to be specified in PEEL in order to benefit from this automation.

4   Experiment Definitions

Experiments are defined using a Spring dependency injection container as a set of inter-connected beans. Figure 4 displays the available bean types as a

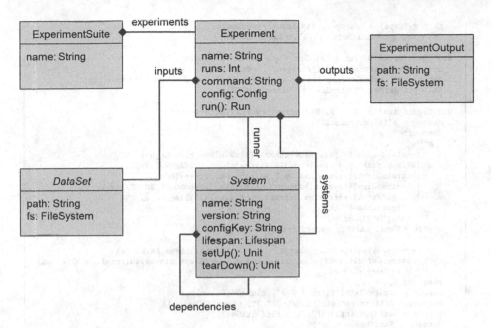

Fig. 4. A domain model of the PEEL experiment definition elements.

domain model. Beans definitions can be done either in XML or in annotated Scala classes. Scala is used for all examples in this paper. The beans required to define an experiment realize the system experiments domain introduced in the Motivation section.

We discuss the individual beans in light of our example of running *batch gradient descent* training of a logistic regression model for click-through rate prediction. Listing 1.1 shows the complete experiment definition of the definition of our example.

Listing 1.1. The main experiment definition of our running example.

```scala
class ExperimentsDimensionScaling extends ApplicationContextAware {
  var ctx: ApplicationContext = null
  def setApplicationContext(ctx: ApplicationContext): Unit = {
    this.ctx = ctx
  }

  def sparkFeatureHashing(i: String, numF: Int, perc: Double): SparkJob = new SparkJob(
    timeout = 10000L,
    runner = ctx.getBean("spark-1.6.2", classOf[Spark]),
    command =
      s"""
        |--class dima.tu.berlin.generators.spark.SparkCriteoExtract \\
        |$${app.path.datagens}/peel-bundle-datagens-1.0-SNAPSHOT.jar \\
        |--inputPath=$1 \\
        |--outputPath=$${system.hadoop-2.path.input}/train/$numF/$perc \\
        |--numFeatures=$numFeatures \\
        |--percDataPoints=$perc \\
      """.stripMargin.trim
  )
  def `bgd.output`: ExperimentOutput = new ExperimentOutput(
```

```
21      path = "{system.hadoop-2.path.input}/benchmark/",
22      fs = ctx.getBean("hdfs-2.7.1", classOf[HDFS2])
23    )
24    def 'bgd.input'(D: Int): DataSet = new GeneratedDataSet(
25      src = sparkFeatureHashing("/criteo/", numFeatures, perc),
26      dst = s"$${system.hadoop-2.path.input}/train/" + numFeatures + "/" + perc,
27      fs = ctx.getBean("hdfs-2.7.1", classOf[HDFS2])
28    )
29    def 'bgd.flink'(D: Int, N: String) = new FlinkExperiment(
30      name    = s"flink.train.$D",
31      command =
32        s"""
33          |--class dima.tu.berlin.benchmark.flink.mlbench.NewLogReg \\
34          |$${app.path.apps}/peel-bundle-flink-jobs-1.0-SNAPSHOT.jar \\
35          |--trainDir=$${system.hadoop-2.path.input}/train/$D \\
36          |--outputDir=$${system.hadoop-2.path.input}/benchmark/$N/$D/flink/ \\
37          |--degOfParall=$${system.default.config.parallelism.total} \\
38          |--dimensions=$D \\
39        """.stripMargin.trim,
40      config = ConfigFactory.parseString(
41        s"""
42          |system.default.config.slaves        = $${env.slaves.$N.hosts}
43          |system.default.config.parallelism.total = $${env.slaves.$N.total.parallelism}
44        """.stripMargin.trim),
45      runs    = 3,
46      runner = ctx.getBean("flink-1.0.3", classOf[Flink]),
47      systems = Set(ctx.getBean("dstat-0.7.2", classOf[Dstat])),
48      inputs = Set('bgd.input'(D), classOf[DataSet])),
49      outputs = Set('bgd.output')
50    )
51    def 'bgd.spark'(D: Int, N: String) = new SparkExperiment(
52      name    = s"spark.train.$D",
53      command =
54        s"""
55          |--class dima.tu.berlin.benchmark.spark.mlbench.RUN \\
56          |$${app.path.apps}/peel-bundle-spark-jobs-1.0-SNAPSHOT.jar \\
57          |--trainDir=$${system.hadoop-2.path.input}/train /$D \\
58          |--outputDir=$${system.hadoop-2.path.input}/benchmark/$N/$D/spark \\
59          |--numSplits=$${system.default.config.parallelism.total} \\
60        """.stripMargin.trim,
61      config = ConfigFactory.parseString(
62        s"""
63          |system.default.config.slaves        = $${env.slaves.$N.hosts}
64          |system.default.config.parallelism.total = $${env.slaves.$N.total.parallelism}
65        """.stripMargin.trim),
66      runs    = 3,
67      runner = ctx.getBean("spark-1.6.2", classOf[Spark]),
68      systems = Set(ctx.getBean("dstat-0.7.2", classOf[Dstat])),
69      inputs = Set('bgd.input'(D), classOf[DataSet])),
70      outputs = Set('bgd.output')
71    )
72    def 'bgd.dimensions.scaling': ExperimentSuite = new ExperimentSuite(
73      for {
74        Dims <- Seq(10, 100, 1000, 10000, 100000, 1000000)
75        Nodes <- Seq("top020", "top010", "top005")
76        Exps <- Seq('bgd.spark'(Dims, Nodes), 'bgd.flink'(Dims, Nodes))
77      } yield Exps
78    )
79  }
80  @Bean(name = Array("bgd.dimensions.scaling"))
```

Experiment: The central class in the domain model shown in Fig. 4 is *Experiment*. In our example definition in Listing 1.1 we specify two Experiments: one for Flink (lines 29–50) and one for Spark (lines 51–71). Each experiment specifies the following properties: the experiment name, the command that executes the experiment's job, the number of runs (repetitions) the experiment is executed, the inputs required and outputs produced by each run, the runner system that carries the execution, other systems, upon which the execution of the experiment depends (e.g. *dstat* in line 47 for monitoring the resource usage on the compute nodes) as well as the experiment-specific environment config which is discussed in Sect. 6.

System: The second important class in the model is *System*. It specifies the following properties: the system name, usually fixed per System implementation, e.g. flink for the Flink system or spark for the Spark system, the system version (e.g. 1.0.3 for Flink or 1.6.2 for Spark), a configKey under which config parameters will be located in the environment configuration, usually the same as the system name, a Lifespan value (one of *Provided, Suite, Experiment*, or *Run*) which indicates when to start and stop the system and a list of systems upon which the current system depends.

ExperimentSuite: A series of related experiment beans are organized in an *ExperimentSuite*. In our example listing, we define an ExperimentSuite in lines 72–78. Recall that our original motivation was to compare the scale-out characteristics of Spark and Flink with respect to both: scaling the nodes and scaling the model size. To accomplish this, we vary two parameters: *Dims* which specifies the dimensionality of the training data and *Nodes*, which refers to a list of hosts the experiment should run on. The for-comprehension creates a cartesian product of all parameter values and the two experiments. With this, we ensure that we only generate a new data set whenever either the node configuration or the desired dimensionality changes, but not for each experiment separately. Experiments typically depend on some kind of input data, represented as abstract *DataSet* elements associated with a particular *FileSystem* in our model. The following types are currently supported:

– *CopiedDataSet* - used for static data copied into the target FileSystem;
– *GeneratedDataSet* - used for data generated by a Job into the target FileSystem.

In the example we rely on a `GeneratedDataSet` to trigger the Spark job for feature hashing (lines 24–28). In addition, each experiment bean is associated with an *ExperimentOutput* which describes the paths the data is written to by the experiment workload application (lines 20–23). This meta-information is used to clean those paths upon execution.

5   Bundle Basics

A *bundle* packages together the configuration data, datasets, and workload jobs required for the execution of a particular set of experiments. Table 1 provides an overview of the top-level elements of such a bundle. It is self-contained and can be pushed to a remote cluster for execution as well as shared for reproducibility purposes. The main components of a bundle can be grouped as follows:

Table 1. The top-level elements of a bundle. (Non-fixed paths can be customized.)

Default path	Config parameter	Fixed	Description
./apps	app.path.apps	Yes	Workload applications
./config	app.path.config	Yes	configurations and experiment definitions.
./datagens	app.path.datagens	No	Data generators
./datasets	app.path.datasets	No	Static datasets
./downloads	app.path.downloads	No	Archived system binaries
./lib	app.path.log	Yes	Peel libraries and dependencies
./log	app.path.log	Yes	Peel execution logs
./results	app.path.results	No	State and log data from experiment runs
./systems	app.path.systems	No	Contains all running systems
./utils	app.path.utils	No	Utility scripts and files
./peel.sh	app.path.cli	Yes	The Peel command line interface

At the center of a bundle is the *PEEL command line tool (PEEL CLI)*, which provides the basic functionality of PEEL. While running, the Peel CLI spawns and executes OS processes. It can be used to start and stop experiments, and to push and pull bundles to and from remote locations. The *log* folder contains the `stdout` and `stderr` output of these processes, as well as a copy of the actual console output produced by PEEL itself. The *config* folder contains *.conf files written in HOCON[3] syntax which defines the environment configuration, as well the actual experiments defined in scala. The *apps* folder contains the binaries of the experiment workload applications. The *datasets folder* contains static, fixed-sized datasets required for the experiments. The datagens folder contains programs for dynamic generation of scalable datasets required for the experiments. The *downloads* folder contains system binary archives for the systems in the experiment environment. The archives are per default extracted in the *systems* folder. The *results* folder contains all the data collected from attempted and successful Peel experiment runs in a hierarchy following `$suite/$expName.run$NN` naming convention. Finally, the *utils folder* contains utility scripts (e.g., SQL queries and gnuplot scripts) that can be used next to or in conjunction with Peel CLI commands. A PEEL bundle is the unit to be shared when making available benchmarks that utilize the framework.

6   Environment Configurations

Environments are instantiated with a concrete set of configuration values (for the systems) and parameter values (for the experiment application). A number of problems can arise with a naïve approach for manual configuration (per system and experiment) of the environments:

---

[3] https://github.com/typesafehub/config/blob/master/HOCON.md.

Syntax Heterogeneity. Each system (HDFS, Spark and Flink) has to be configured separately using its own special syntax. This requires basic understanding and knowledge in the configuration parameters for all systems in the stack. (For example, the number of processing slots is called `spark.executor.cores` in Spark and `taskmanager.numberOfTaskSlots` in Flink.)

Variable Interdependence. The sets of configuration variables associated with each system are not mutually exclusive. Thus, care has to be taken that the corresponding values are consistent for the overlapping fragment (e.g., the slaves list in all systems should be the same).

Value Tuning. For a series of related experiments, all but a very few set of values remain fixed. These values are suitably chosen based on the underlying host environment characteristics in order to maximize the performance of the corresponding systems (e.g., memory allocation, degree of parallelism, temp paths for spilling).

PEEL associates one global environment configuration to each experiment. In doing this, it promotes:

– configuration reuse through layering
– configuration uniformity through a hierarchical syntax

At runtime, experiments are represented by experiment beans. Each experiment bean holds a *HOCON* config that is first constructed and evaluated based on the layering scheme and conventions discussed below, and then mapped to the various concrete config and parameter files and formats of the systems and applications in the experiment environment.

In our running example, this means that for varying the number of nodes between three different configurations (20, 10, and 5 nodes) - each of the six experiments (3x SparkBGD + 3x FlinkBGD) will have an associated config property - a hierarchical map of key-value pairs which constitute the configuration of all systems and jobs required for that particular experiment. This is illustrated in Fig. 5.

Configuration Layers. The configuration system is built upon the concept of layered construction and resolution. Peel distinguishes between three layers of configuration:

– **Default.** Default configuration values for Peel itself and the supported systems. Packaged as resources in related jars located in the bundle's `app.path.lib` folder.
– **Bundle.** Bundle-specific configuration values. Located in `app.path.config`. Default is the *config* subfolder of the current bundle.
– **Host.** Host-specific configuration values. Located in the $HOSTNAME subfolder of the `app.path.config` folder.

For each experiment bean defined in an experiment suite, an associated configuration will be constructed according to the entries in Table 2 (higher in the list means lower priority).

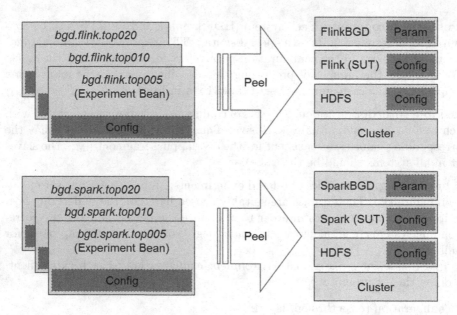

Fig. 5. Mapping the environment configurations for the six Batch Gradient Decent experiments

Table 2. Hierarchy of configurations which are associated with an experiment bean (higher in the list means lower priority).

Path	Description
`reference.peel.conf`	Default Peel config
`reference.$systemID.conf`	Default system config
`config/$systemID.conf`	Bundle-specific system config (opt)
`config/hosts/$hostname/$systemID.conf`	Host-specific system config (opt)
`config/application.conf`	Bundle-specific Peel config (opt)
`config/hosts/$hostname/application.conf`	Host-specific Peel config (opt)
Experiment bean *config* value	Experiment specific config (opt)
System	JVM system properties (constant)

First comes the *default* configuration, located in the `peel-core.jar` package. Second, for each system upon which the experiment depends (with corresponding system bean identified by `systemID`), PEEL tries to load the default configuration for that system as well as bundle- or host-specific configurations.

Third, bundle- and host-specific `application.conf`, which is a counterpart and respectively overrides bundle-wide values defined in `reference.peel.conf`.

Above follow the values defined the `config` property of the current experiment bean. These are typically used to vary one particular parameter in a sequence of experiments in a suite (e.g. varying the number of workers and the DOP).

Finally, a set of configuration parameters derived from the current JVM System object (e.g., the number of CPUs or the total amount of available memory) are appended.

7   Execution Workflow

In the previous Sections we explained the internals and the code required to configure the environment and define the experiments in a PEEL bundle. In this section, we will explain how to make use of the commands provided by the Peel CLI in order to deploy and run the experiments in a bundle.

As a first step, the bundle has to be assembled from the sources with `mvn deploy`. For large-scale applications, the environment where the experiments need to be executed typically differs from the environment of the machine where the bundle binaries are assembled. In order to start the execution process, the user therefore needs to first deploy the bundle binaries from the local machine to the desired host environment. The Peel CLI offers a special command for this. In order to push the peel-bundle to the remote cluster, one has to run: `./peel.sh rsync:push remote-cluster-name`. The command uses rsync to copy the contents of the enclosing Peel bundle to the target environment. The connection options for the rsync calls are thereby taken from the environment configuration of the local environment. The remote environment has to be specified in the `application.conf`.

As explained above, PEEL organizes experiments in sequences called *experiment suites*. The easiest option is to start an entire suite via `./peel.sh suite:run` which will automatically step through the entire execution lifecycle for each experiment:

- **Setup Experiment.** Ensure that the required inputs are materialized (either generated or copied) in the respective file system. Check the configuration of associated descendant systems with *provided* or *suite* lifespan against the values defined in the current experiment config. If the values do not match, it reconfigures and restarts the system. Set up systems with *experiment* lifespan.
- **Execute Experiment.** For each experiment run which has not been completed by a previous invocation of the same suite: Check and set up systems with *run* lifespan, execute experiment run, collect log data from the associated systems and clear the produced outputs.
- **Tear Down Experiment.** Tear down all systems with *experiment* lifespan.

Next to simply running a Full Suite which automatically executes all experiments specified, each of the above steps can be executed individually. This is particularly useful when developing and debugging a benchmark, as it allows to validate that each step is executed correctly.

Since PEEL also keeps track of failed experiments, one can simply re-run an entire suite in order to re-attempt the execution of the failed experiments. PEEL will automatically skip all experiments, which have already been successfully run.

8   Results Analysis

The results of all experiments are stored in a folder structure which contains log file data collected from the systems involved in the experiment. In order to make sense of the data, Peel ships with an extensible ETL pipeline that extracts relevant data from the log files, transforms it into a relational schema, and loads it into a database. One can then analyze various aspects of the obtained results by querying the underlying result schema with SQL statements.

The experiment suite defined by the running example in Sect. 3 will produce results similar to Table 3. (for detailed experimental results please see [7])

Table 3. Exemplary table listing the results of experiment runs.

Experiment	Nodes	Dimensions	Runtime in ms
flink.train	top023	10	165612
flink.train	top023	100	265034
flink.train	top023	1000	289115
flink.train	top023	10000	291966
flink.train	top023	100000	300280
flink.train	top023	1000000	315500
spark.train	top023	10	128286
spark.train	top023	100	205061
spark.train	top023	1000	208647
spark.train	top023	10000	219103
spark.train	top023	100000	222236
spark.train	top023	1000000	298778
...	...	...	...

Backends. Peel supports multiple relational database engines as a possible back-end for your experiment data. The decision which backend to use depends on the scope and complexity of the use case.

H2. The H2 backend is the easy and quick option for beginners. If the experiment logs are small, this is the best way to go as it requires zero overhead for setup. With the default H2 connection h2, PEEL will initialize and populate a results database in a file named h2.mov.db located in the ${app.path.results} folder.

MonetDB. If the experiments generated a lot of data or more advanced analytics on the extracted database instance are required, we recommend using a column store like MonetDB.

Analysis. To visually explore and analyze the results of the experiments, one can connect the database schema produced by Peel with a reporting tool like JasperReports, an OLAP cube analysis tool like Pentaho, or a visual data exploration tool like Tableau.

9   Extending Peel

Currently, PEEL supports various versions of the following systems out of the box: Hadoop MapReduce, Spark, Flink, HDFS, dstat and Zookeeper. However, the framework can easily be extended. Adding support for a new system is uncomplicated and only requires the definition of system specific sub-classes for the System and Experiment base-classes that were discussed in Sect. 4. The communication between the framework and the systems is typically done by calling scripts via external processes with the abstractions provided in PEEL. Thus, the range of systems that can be supported is not strictly limited to JVM-based ones.

In order to add support for a new system, one simply has to define the startup and shutdown behavior of the system, the configuration files and their management, and the way log files are to be collected inside the system class. As was presented in the example definition in Listing 1.1, the experiment bean then defines how jobs for the system are started and which arguments are passed. For cluster configurations without a network file system, PEEL also provides utility functions to distribute the required system files among the cluster nodes, as well as the collection of log files.

10   Conclusion

In this paper we introduced PEEL as a Framework for benchmarking distributed systems and algorithms. PEEL significantly reduces the operational complexity of performing benchmarks of novel distributed data processing systems. It automatically orchestrates all systems involved, executes the experiments and collects all relevant log data. Through the central structure of a peel-bundle, a unified approach to system configurations and its experiment definitions, PEEL fosters the transparency, portability, and reproducibility of benchmarking experiments. Based on the running example of a supervised machine learning workload, we introduced all the major concepts of PEEL, including experiment definitions and its experimentation process. We have sucessfully used PEEL in practice to orchestrate the experiments published in [6, 7] and hope that it will be a useful tool for many in the benchmarking community, as PEEL is freely available as open-source software available at https://github.com/peelframework/peel.

Acknowledgments. This work has been supported through grants by the German Science Foundation (DFG) as FOR1306 Stratosphere, the German Ministry for Education and Research as Berlin Big Data Center BBDC (funding mark 01IS14013A) and by Oracle Labs.

References

1. https://flink.apache.org/
2. https://giraph.apache.org/
3. https://hadoop.apache.org/
4. https://spark.apache.org/
5. Alexandrov, A., Bergmann, R., Ewen, S., Freytag, J.-C., Hueske, F., Heise, A., Kao, O., Leich, M., Leser, U., Markl, V., Naumann, F., Peters, M., Rheinländer, A., Sax, M.J., Schelter, S., Höger, M., Tzoumas, K., Warneke, D.: The stratosphere platform for big data analytics. VLDB J. **23**(6), 939–964 (2014)
6. Alexandrov, A., Kunft, A., Katsifodimos, A., Schüler, F., Thamsen, L., Kao, O., Herb, T., Markl, V.: Implicit parallelism through deep language embedding. In: Proceedings of the 2015 ACM SIGMOD International Conference on Management of Data, Melbourne, Victoria, Australia, 31 May–4 June, 2015, pp. 47–61 (2015)
7. Boden, C., Spina, A., Rabl, T., Markl, V.: Benchmarking data flow systems for scalable machine learning. In: Proceedings of the 4th Algorithms and Systems on MapReduce and Beyond, BeyondMR 2017, pp. 5:1–5:10. ACM, New York (2017)
8. Carbone, P., Katsifodimos, A., Ewen, S., Markl, V., Haridi, S., Tzoumas, K.: Apache Flink^{TM}: stream and batch processing in a single engine. IEEE Data Eng. Bull. **38**(4), 28–38 (2015)
9. Chu, C.-T., Kim, S.K., Lin, Y.-A., Yu, Y., Bradski, G., Ng, A.Y., Olukotun, K.: Map-reduce for machine learning on multicore. In: Proceedings of the 19th International Conference on Neural Information Processing Systems, NIPS 2006, pp. 281–288. MIT Press, Cambridge (2006)
10. Dean, J., Ghemawat, S.: MapReduce: simplified data processing on large clusters. In: OSDI, pp. 137–150 (2004)
11. Low, Y., Bickson, D., Gonzalez, J., Guestrin, C., Kyrola, A., Hellerstein, J.M.: Distributed graphlab: a framework for machine learning and data mining in the cloud. Proc. VLDB Endow. **5**(8), 716–727 (2012)
12. Low, Y., Gonzalez, J.E., Kyrola, A., Bickson, D., Guestrin, C.E., Hellerstein, J.: Graphlab: a new framework for parallel machine learning. arXiv preprint arXiv:1408.2041 (2014)
13. Malewicz, G., Austern, M.H., Bik, A.J., Dehnert, J.C., Horn, I., Leiser, N., Czajkowski, G.: Pregel: a system for large-scale graph processing. In: Proceedings of the 2010 ACM SIGMOD International Conference on Management of Data, SIGMOD 2010, pp. 135–146. ACM, New York (2010)
14. McMahan, H.B., Holt, G., Sculley, D., Young, M., Ebner, D., Grady, J., Nie, L., Phillips, T., Davydov, E., Golovin, D., Chikkerur, S., Liu, D., Wattenberg, M., Hrafnkelsson, A.M., Boulos, T., Kubica, J.: Ad click prediction: a view from the trenches. In: KDD 2013. ACM (2013)
15. Richardson, M., Dominowska, E., Ragno, R.: Predicting clicks: estimating the click-through rate for new ads. In: WWW 2007. ACM (2007)
16. Zaharia, M., Chowdhury, M., Das, T., Dave, A., Ma, J., McCauley, M., Franklin, M.J., Shenker, S., Stoica, I.: Resilient distributed datasets: a fault-tolerant abstraction for in-memory cluster computing. In: NSDI 2012 (2012)

Senska – Towards an Enterprise Streaming Benchmark

Guenter Hesse[(⊠)], Benjamin Reissaus, Christoph Matthies, Martin Lorenz,
Milena Kraus, and Matthias Uflacker

Hasso Plattner Institute, University of Potsdam, 14482 Potsdam, Germany
{guenter.hesse,benjamin.reissaus,christoph.matthies,martin.lorenz,
milena.kraus,matthias.uflacker}@hpi.de

Abstract. In the light of growing data volumes and continuing digitization in fields such as Industry 4.0 or Internet of Things, data stream processing have gained popularity and importance. Especially enterprises can benefit from this development by augmenting their vital, core business data with up-to-date streaming information. Enriching this transactional data with detailed information from high-frequency data streams allows answering new analytical questions as well as improving current analyses, e.g., regarding predictive maintenance. Comparing such data stream processing architectures for use in an enterprise context, i.e., when combining streaming and business data, is currently a challenging task as there is no suitable benchmark.

In this paper, we give an overview about performance benchmarks in the area of data stream processing. We highlight shortcomings of existing benchmarks and present the need for a new benchmark with a focus on an enterprise context. Furthermore, the ideas behind *Senska*, a new enterprise streaming benchmark that shall fill this gap, and its architecture are introduced.

Keywords: Benchmarking · Benchmark development
Data stream processing · Stream processing · Internet of Things

1 Introduction

Due to the ever increasing velocity and volume of data that is being produced nowadays, completely new challenges and opportunities arise.

Terms like Smart Factories, Industry 4.0, and Internet of Things (IoT) have gained traction to describe some of such new developments which bring new possibilities in how business can be done.

Industrial manufacturing is a particularly interesting domain in this context. An example for a factory where a high volume of data is captured with high velocity is the GE battery production plant in New York (state). There are 10,000 different data attributes recorded, some as often as every 250 ms [23]. Modern manufacturing equipment, e.g., injection molding machines, can generate up to terabytes of sensor data, daily [13]. Such data provides detailed

© Springer International Publishing AG 2018
R. Nambiar and M. Poess (Eds.): TPCTC 2017, LNCS 10661, pp. 25–40, 2018.
https://doi.org/10.1007/978-3-319-72401-0_3

information about the current state of machines and allows timely reactions to events, such as failures or changes in environment. When it comes to unlocking further efficiency improvements through IoT technologies such as sensors, highly-optimized production facilities are one of the key areas [17]. Combining gathered IoT data with existing transactional or business data, e.g., supplier information or information about machine operators, can lead to a better understanding of the holistic value chain. This combination of machine or sensor data and business data, which allows answering new analytical questions or existing ones in greater detail, can be described as vertical integration. A practical example of applying these ideas would be a printing machine, where the humidity is regulated depending on current sensor measurements (streaming data) as well as the currently used colors and paper (business or historical data) in order to optimize print quality.

Compared to transactional data, IoT or sensor data, as examples of streaming data, differ in aspects such as velocity and volume. A brief comparison of both these kinds of data is shown in Table 1. In order to efficiently handle sensor and general data streams as well as their analysis, new technologies were created.

Table 1. Comparison of sensor data and business data

Characteristic	Sensor data	Business data
Volume and velocity	Up to multiple terabytes by a single machine, daily [13]	Multiple terabytes in total, e.g., for a 20 years old SAP ERP installation at a leading Canadian energy company [21]
Data quality	Measurement errors, lost data	Correctness crucial for business
Data manipulations	No updates	Updates exist
References	Strong time and location reference	Strong business process reference
Value for enterprises	Usually not crucial for daily business	Essential for daily business

A particularly interesting example for a group of systems that can be leveraged for analyzing high frequency data sources are Data Stream Processing Systems (DSPSs). These systems analyze streams of data on the fly using continuous queries. Therefore, the generation of output is dependent on the underlying data streams, i.e., on the arrival of new data points. Moreover, the order of incoming data records is considered, meaning a potential out-of-order arrival at the DSPS may need to be handled in order to produce correct results. Compared to traditional Database Management Systems (DBMSs), the concepts employed in DSPSs differ in some aspects, e.g., with respect to queries, which usually do not run continuously on DBMSs. Storing data only for as long as it is needed for analysis not only benefits performance and data throughput, but also saves storage costs. As an extension to DBMSs, those benefits of DSPSs can be leveraged in enterprise applications. When analyzing data streams in DSPSs, data can be combined with data from business application databases, allowing for new business ideas and far-reaching optimizations of existing processes.

A multitude of new DSPSs were developed in recent years, such as Apache Flink, Apache Storm, Apache Spark Streaming, Apache Samza, Twitter Heron and Apache Apex [8,11,15]. Contrary to these recently developed systems, Aurora [3] and STREAM [5], for instance, were already presented in the early 2000's.

Although a broad variety of systems allows for more choice, picking the system or architecture that best suits a given use case becomes more of an issue. As shown, there is already a wide choice in the group of DSPSs, whose usage represents just one way of analyzing data streams. An alternative approach could be storing data streams in a database and analyzing them afterwards.

Due to the lack of satisfying real-world application benchmarks assessing data stream processing architectures, including the combination of streaming and transactional data for analyses, this is currently a certainly challenging task. We aim to tackle this issue by developing an application benchmark focussed on data stream processing architectures in an enterprise context, *Senska* - an Enterprise Streaming Benchmark (ESB). In this paper we present the following contributions:

- Illustration and motivation of the need for a new application benchmark for data stream processing
- The design objectives of Senska and their underlying concepts
- A first draft of the overall Senska architecture - design decisions are explained and selected components are presented in more detail

The remainder of this paper is structured as follows: Sect. 2 presents related work in the area of benchmarking and highlights the need for a new data stream processing benchmark. Section 3 introduces *Senska*, the Enterprise Streaming Benchmark, including the design objectives, its architecture, the developed query list, and limitations. Section 4 concludes, giving an overview of Senska and illustrating areas for future work.

2   Related Work

As mentioned in [12], only few benchmarks for data stream processing architectures are available compared to the number of benchmarks for DBMSs. A brief comparison of selected benchmarks is shown in Table 2, which is based on the overview shown in [12].

The *Linear Road* Benchmark by Arasu et al. [7] is one of the most, if not the most popular application benchmark focussing on data stream processing. It includes a benchmarking toolkit comprising a data generator, a data sender as well as a result validator. With an execution of a benchmark implementation, a variable tolling system for a metropolitan area covering multiple expressways is simulated. The amount of accumulated tolls is dependent on multiple aspects of the traffic situation on these expressways.

The data sender emits the streaming data into the system under test (SUT). This input data contains four different record types, from which position reports are by far the most abundant records. The remaining data consist of three record types that express explicit user requests that always expect an answer from the system. Depending on the overall situation on highways, car position reports may require the SUT to create an output or not.

With regard to the benchmark workload, Linear Road defines four different queries with corresponding output types. For complexity reasons, the implementation of the lastly presented query was even skipped in the two implementations described in [7]. Besides streaming data, historical data covering ten weeks of tolling history is generated and partly has to be used in order to produce correct answers.

As a benchmark result, Linear Road defines one overall metric called L-Rating. The L-Rating indicates how many expressways a system can handle without violating the defined maximum response times for each query. The number of highways is a configurable parameter for the data generation step that is influencing the amount of input data.

The second benchmark presented in Table 2 is *StreamBench* [16]. It aims at benchmarking distributed DSPSs and can be categorized as a micro benchmark, i.e., it measures atomic operations, such as the execution of a projection rather than those of more complex applications such as in Linear Road. Thus, when a system's performance for real-world scenarios or applications is to be evaluated, micro benchmark results only have limited validity. However, if, e.g., two distinct filter operators are to be compared, micro benchmarks have advantages over application benchmarks due to their simplicity. Measurements contain only the relevant parts without much overhead, which eases interpreting results.

StreamBench defines seven queries in total. They cover queries with single and multiple computational steps. Moreover, some queries require to keep a state in order to produce correct results while others do not. Only one query uses numerical data, while all others work on textual data. Overall, the seven queries cover a variety of functionalities, although some typical streaming operations like window functions are not taken into account.

Additionally, StreamBench defines four workload suites, which influence the way the benchmark is executed. The suite has an impact on, e.g., data scales, executed query set, the existence of an intentional node failure, or employed benchmark result metrics.

StreamBench makes use of two different real-world data sets. One of these contains textual data while the other one comprises numerical information. Generally, real-world data sets are always desirable as they represent real scenarios best and help increasing the benchmark's relevance. The two data sets used in StreamBench serve as seeds for data generation. Thus, synthetic data is used and reality is not represented entirely. Nevertheless, entirely using real-world data in a benchmark is certainly an ambitious aim as, e.g., scaling input data can easily become a challenge if the available data set is too small.

Contrary to Linear Road, StreamBench employs a message broker, which is used for decoupling data generation and consumption. This approach is similar to the benchmark architecture proposed in this paper, which is described in Sect. 3. In particular, Apache Kafka [14] is used as broker in StreamBench. Again, that is similar to the benchmark described in the present paper. A benchmark tool for data ingestion, such as the presented data sender that comes with Linear Road, is not described by the authors of StreamBench.

StreamBench defines different result metrics dependent on the workload suite. These include latency and throughput. The latter describes the average number of processed records per second and the amount of processed data in bytes per second. Both variants are calculated in total as well as per node. Moreover, three additional metrics are introduced: a durability index (uptime), a throughput penalty factor (assessing throughput change for node failure), and a latency penalty factor (assessing latency change for node failure). To the best of our knowledge, result validation with respect to query outcome is not supported by a dedicated benchmark tool.

The third benchmark shown in Table 2 is called *RIoTBench* [20] and focuses on benchmarking distributed DSPSs. It defines multiple micro benchmark scenarios as well as four application benchmark use cases, which represent combined

Table 2. Comparative overview of data stream processing system benchmarks

	Linear road	StreamBench	RIoTBench
Benchmark type	Application	Micro	Micro and application
Considered SUT	DSPS or DBMS	Distributed DSPS	Distributed DSPS
Domain	Smart City (variable tolling)	Log processing and network traffic monitoring	Smart City, Smart Energy, Health (IoT in general)
Input data	Synthetic (including historical data)	Synthetic (real-world data used as seed)	Synthetic (scaled real-world data sets)
Benchmark result metrics	One self-defined metric (throughput under latency restriction): L-Rating	Throughput or throughput-related, latency or latency-related, system availability	Latency, throughput, jitter (difference between expected and actual output rate), resource utilization
Query result validation	Validation tool provided	No tool provided	No tool provided

micro benchmarks. These cover Extract, Transform and Load (ETL) processes, statistics generation, model training, and predictive analytics scenarios.

As input data, RIoTBench uses scaled real-world data sets from different IoT domains, namely, smart city, smart energy and health. A data sender tool for ingesting data into the SUT or an application for query result validation are not provided by the benchmark.

Next to latency, throughput as well as CPU and memory utilization, RIoT-Bench measures *jitter* as a metric. It is defined as the difference between expected and actual output rate during a certain time interval.

Summarizing, we see the need for a new application benchmark for assessing data stream architectures in an enterprise context for several reasons. First, currently only two major application benchmarks for data stream processing exist and only one of them considers characteristics of distributed systems in its metrics.

Second, historical data is not or only barely taken into account in all of the presented benchmarks. We believe that this is a crucial aspect in many enterprise contexts since, in order to achieve the greatest added value, streaming data needs to be combined with historical business data. As a consequence of that gap in benchmarks, questions relating to business use cases, including interfaces or efficient combination of live and historical data, are currently challenging to answer. Additionally, the majority of current streaming benchmarks lack tool support, e.g., for result validation or data ingestion, which complicates implementing these benchmarks and retrieving objective results.

3   Senska: Enterprise Streaming Benchmark

Due to the lack of satisfying ways to comprehensively compare stream processing architectures for enterprise scenarios, we aim to develop Senska, an enterprise streaming benchmark, which aims to fill this gap. In this section, the design objectives, the architecture, the query set, and limitations of Senska are illustrated.

3.1   Design Objectives

The design objectives beyond Senska follow the four criteria defined by Gray [10], namely relevance, portability, scalability and simplicity, which should be fulfilled by domain-specific benchmarks. These criteria are the basis for several publications that provide guidelines in the area of benchmark development, which illustrates their impact [9]. Although these aspects defined by Gray were already published in the early 90s, we still consider them valid for state-of-the-art benchmarks.

The chosen domain for Senska is industrial manufacturing since it represents a natural fit for an enterprise application requiring data stream processing capabilities, see Sect. 1.

Relevance. The benchmark architecture, including data characteristics as well as the defined queries, will represent real-world scenarios and system environments as realistically as possible.

With respect to *data*, this ideally entails only employing real-world data in the benchmark. If no fitting data set can be found, synthetic data which is as close to real-world data as possible, will be generated. This can be achieved through generating data based on previously collected real-world data sets which alone would not be sufficient, similar to how, e.g., StreamBench tackles this issue, see Sect. 2.

Requirements in the context of input data exist, e.g., with regard to privacy concerns, size, or attribute variety. So in order to be a fitting data set, it should, e.g., be possible to publish the data as part of the benchmark, and its size as well as attribute variety should be appropriate in order to represent real-world environments.

Regarding data input rate, we aim to support multiple options in order to allow users to adapt Senska to their situation and be able to react to technology developments or environmental changes that might lead to increasing input rates in real-world environments.

Another area where relevance shall be considered are *queries*, i.e., the logic that is going to be executed by the system under test. This relevance in the sense of closeness to real-world scenarios shall be reached by validating the queries with industry partners from the corresponding benchmark domain, namely industrial manufacturing and similar industry sectors. This shall lead to a high acceptance of the benchmark and thus, to a higher credibility of its results as well as a higher motivation for implementing the benchmark. Although the benchmark focuses on a single domain, query characteristics, i.e., used functions, e.g., filtering or aggregating certain values of a data stream, are applicable to other areas and thus benchmark results can be beneficial for users from different domains. Moreover, Senska architecture and tools could be used for defining a new benchmark belonging to another domain, i.e., a query set with new data input that is be used for measurements.

Portability. The benchmark definition shall be as much OS and system independent as possible. This enables implementing the benchmark for as many different environments as possible. Thus, a potentially large number of implementations can be reached, which helps gaining insights into a system's or environment's performance. Furthermore, a high number of implementations contributes to a high relevance and result credibility.

Senska aims to ensure portability by not restricting the choice of OS or the choice of used technologies for benchmark implementation. Although DSPSs might seem as a natural fit for data stream processing, it could potentially be exchanged with any other system or implementation that is able to answer the defined queries. With respect to the benchmark toolkit, compatibility with many OSs and platforms will be reached by using a JVM language.

Scalability. The benchmark shall be able to handle smaller as well as bigger systems with regard to scale-up and scale-out architectures. Therefore, Senska will take the number of resources available into account when calculating benchmark results. Moreover, the provided tools, e.g., for data ingestion, are designed to handle scale-out architectures. This means no restrictions regarding number of nodes or CPU will exist in Senska and thus, there are no limits regarding scalability from the benchmark-side.

Simplicity. The benchmark shall be simple to understand and to use in order to encourage people implementing it as well as to ensure credibility with respect to benchmark results. By providing a set of tools that are developed with the objective of increasing simplicity, people implementing Senska shall be supported as much as possible. This toolset comprises scripts for setting up the needed systems for data ingestion and validation, as well as applications for data ingestion, results validation, and benchmark metrics calculation. Additionally, an optional component for monitoring the environment will be included that can help identifying issues and getting an overview of key performance indicators.

3.2 Architecture

Figure 1 shows a high-level overview of our idea of an architecture for benchmarks with focus on data stream processing. Knowing about this simplified view helps getting an understanding of the idea beyond Senska's architecture. It shows three main components: the *data feeder*, *system under test* and the *result validator*.

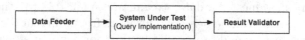

Fig. 1. General architecture for stream processing benchmarks in fundamental modeling concepts (FMC)

The data feeder or sender is responsible for ingesting data into the SUT. The used term SUT is defined as "the system to be evaluated" [18]. In the context of Senska or stream processing benchmarks in general, the SUT processes incoming data and responds according to the defined queries. Produced results are ideally evaluated by a result validator in order to ensure correctness of the query implementations. This component could also calculate benchmark result metrics, e.g., latency or throughput. Besides calculating such metrics after running the benchmark, selected aspects might already be monitored when during each run in order to, e.g., react to failures or unintended behavior as soon as possible.

A more detailed overview of Senska's architecture is illustrated in Fig. 2. All components are described in the following.

Input Data. Input data is represented through one or more files in CSV or similar format and represents sensor data from a manufacturing context. It acts as input for the system with respect to streaming data. In the best case, data will be entirely real-world data. If no suitable data set can be identified, synthetic data has to be used. Concretely, a data generation tool will be needed that takes care of creating the input data, preferably based on an existing real-world data set in order to keep characteristics. For the use within initial development of Senska, we use a data set from manufacturing context[1] published within the context of the DEBS Grand Challenge[2]. The challenge was conducted as part of the 2012 *Conference on Distributed Event-Based Systems*. In particular, the data set contains monitoring data, which was recorded by manufacturing equipment sensors. It includes about 32.4 million records, which result in an uncompressed file size of about 5.5 GB. As the end of the file can be reached quickly with high throughputs, we restart from the beginning when coming to that point in order to be able to run the benchmark for a certain period of time. That is an approach which is already proposed in, e.g., StreamBench [16].

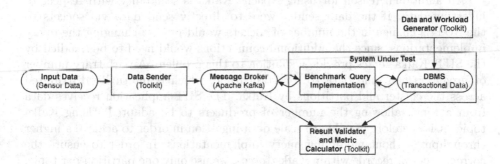

Fig. 2. Architecture of Senska in FMC

Data Sender. As part of the provided toolkit, the Senska data sender reads the input data and ingests it into the message broker component. The sending interval, i.e., the delay between sending consecutive records, is configurable. Although it is closer to reality to send records according to the timestamp they may contain, this might not be sufficient to satisfy configured data ingestion rates, i.e., to benchmark the SUT with certain data input rates. So it might not be possible to test, e.g., how much throughput an SUT can reach or how an SUT would behave with a doubled number of input records per second. Moreover, as reality and amounts of produced of data are rapidly changing, this flexibility allows staying up-to-date with a changing environment and prevents the benchmark from becoming outdated because of unrealistic data input rates.

---

[1] ftp://ftp.mi.fu-berlin.de/pub/debs2012/.
[2] http://www.csw.inf.fu-berlin.de/debs2012/grandchallenge.html.

The data sender, which is under development, is written in Scala and thus runs within a JVM on most common platforms. This compatibility with most OSs is the major reason for choosing Scala or a JVM language in general. As with all the tools in the toolkit, an open-source version of the data sender will be published with the first version of Senska.

Message Broker. The message broker represents a central part of Senska's architecture. It acts as interface between data sender and SUT. Furthermore, it is storage for query results in the defined setup. The message broker component in Senska is realized through Apache Kafka [14]. An overview about Kafka in the context of Senska is illustrated in Fig. 3.

One reason for using Apache Kafka within Senska is its usage in enterprise software architectures. Among others, a common way of using Kafka is as interface to a DSPS. Thus, its role in Senska reflects reality and so adds relevance to the benchmark. Such usages of Kafka in combination with a DSPS were presented by, e.g., Bouygues Telecom [4] and Zalando [22].

An additional reason for using Apache Kafka is scalability with respect to ingesting data. If the data sender were to directly send data via sockets to the SUT, a change in the number of sockets would require changing the query implementations, since the additional connections would need to be handled by the SUT. Kafka *topics* provide a solution to this problem. An arbitrary number of *producers* can send data to a certain topic, which is internally distributed across the cluster and partitions by Kafka. The SUT application receives data from a topic, allowing the number of producers to be adapted. Using Kafka topics it is therefore possible to scale data ingestion in order to achieve a higher throughput without modifying query implementations. In order to ensure the correct order of records within Kafka topics, we use only one partition per topic, which can be seen in Fig. 3.

Another reason for using Apache Kafka is latency measurements. In order to achieve latency results that are as correct and comparable as possible, we leverage Kafka's timestamp functionality. The timestamps before entering the SUT and after leaving the DSPS are taken into account for latency calculations. By doing so, it is possible to keep those calculations independent from the SUT and thus, no implementation modifications are needed and system-dependent differences or variations in terms of time measurements can be preempted.

Particularly, there are two types of timestamps Kafka offers to store with the messages, *create time* and *log append time* [2]. Create time is measured when a message is created and set by the Kafka producer that sends data to the cluster, and log append time is set by the broker when a message is appended to the Kafka log. In order to keep the measurements application-independent and so to avoid, e.g., unintentional application optimizations for reducing latency, we use log append time. Latency is computed by subtracting the output timestamp, i.e., log append time of the result record, from the input timestamp, i.e., log append time of the corresponding or last relevant input record. The downside of this approach is the included overhead time that is needed for transferring

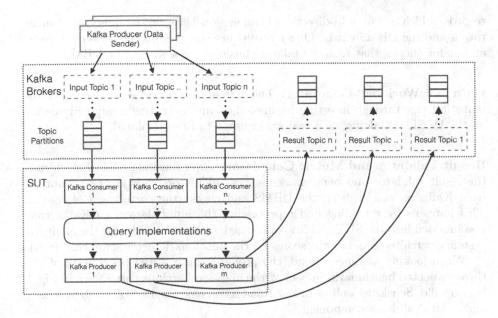

Fig. 3. Usage of Apache Kafka within Senska

messages from the broker to the SUT and back, which does not reflect the actual computation time of the SUT.

Although the exact processing times needed by the SUT are not measured by doing so, we do not consider this as an issue for the benchmark. Since all benchmarked systems follow the same approach, the overhead is included in all measurements and so results remain comparable in similar environments, i.e., if influencing parts, such as the network connection bandwith between Kafka and SUT, stay constant. Thus, we believe that the presented latency measurement approach is an objective way of calculating latencies in the context of Senska. It allows benchmarking any implementation that is able to retrieve and send data to and from Kafka. As times are taken independently outside of implementations, results are comparable and can not be unintentionally distorted by different time measurement mechanisms.

System Under Test. The SUT comprises two main components: the benchmark query implementation and a DBMS. The queries defined by Senska and can be implemented using any technology, e.g., a DSPS or DBMS features such as stored procedures. The only requirement on the technology used for the implementation is the ability to communicate with a DBMS and with the message broker, i.e., with Apache Kafka. Historical or transactional data is consumed from a DBMS on demand, i.e., whenever a query requires this data. As the speed of the DBMS can influence the responsive time of queries, it belongs to the SUT. Some queries might require updating one or multiple historical data

records, which is why a bi-directional connection between the query implementation and the DBMS exists. Query results are returned to the message broker,
except for queries that require updating business data within the DBMS.

Data and Workload Generator. The data and workload generator simulates
realistic usage through inserting business data and executing analytical queries
on the DBMS. By doing so, a real-world usage can be simulated.

Result Validator and Metric Calculator. After finishing a benchmark run,
the result validator and benchmark metrics calculator reads the query output
from Kafka as well as from the DBMS and checks the correctness of results.
This happens by rereading and reprocessing the input data from Kafka that
was ingested into the SUT. Additionally, the benchmark results for the analyzed
system or architecture, i.e., the scores for the benchmark metrics, are calculated.

When looking at Linear Road, the probably most noted benchmark of the
three presented benchmarks in Sect. 2, the high-level architecture shown in Fig. 1
is also valid. Senska as well as Linear Road have, next to the SUT, a data sender
and a data validator component.

A look to Senska's architecture in Fig. 2 reveals some differences, though.
Linear Road also uses input data files that are sent by a data sender, but there
is no message broker included. So the Linear Road data sender could directly
send the input to the SUT. Furthermore, historical data in Linear Road are plain
files that needs to be handled by the SUT. Thus, a DBMS is not required as
in Senska. Contrary to Linear Road, there is a workload generator for historical
data in Senska.

Similarly to Senska, a query result validator is provided as part of Linear
Road. A data generator component is also included in Linear Road, which creates
streaming and historical data. In Senska, there is a data generator for business
data and, depending on the search of suitable real-world input data sets and as
mentioned before, there might be a generator for streaming data, too.

3.3 Queries

When defining benchmark queries, relevance and simplicity need special consideration. The former one not only includes the closeness of queries to real-world
scenarios, but also the coverage of important stream processing functionality.

For ensuring the latter one, we use the core set of operations for complex
event processing (CEP) systems presented by [19] as a basis for functionality
that should be covered by the queries. Although this list of operations is defined
for CEP systems, it is applicable to data stream processing in general. Thus, we
slightly modified to the original list to our needs and benchmark specifics, e.g.,
by adding the aspect of combining streaming with DBMS data.

1. Windowing
2. Transformation
3. Aggregation/Grouping
4. Merging (Union)
5. Filtering (Selection/Projection)

6. Sorting/Ranking
7. Correlation/Enrichment (Join)
8. Machine Learning
9. Combination with DBMS data

Table 3 shows an excerpt of the first queries defined in Senska. Next to the use cases behind each query, the covered functionalities are given, referencing the above stated list. Moreover, a query definition and a description are shown. Queries are defined similar to CQL continuous query language [6].

Table 3. Excerpt of Senska query set

#	Use Case	Tested Aspects	Query Definition	Description
1	Check Sensor Status	1;2;3	SELECT AVG(VALUE), MIN(VALUE), MAX(VALUE) FROM STREAM_1 RANGE 20 SECONDS	Calculate sensor statistics (avg, min, max) for, e.g., last 20sec.
2	Predict Sensor Values	1;8	SELECT PREDICTION(VALUE, 20 SECONDS) FROM STREAM_1 RANGE 300 SECONDS	Calculate expected values for, e.g., the next 20sec, for a sensor based on data of, e.g., last 300sec.
3	Identify Error I	1;5	SELECT COUNT(VALUE) > 5 FROM STREAM_1 WHERE VALUE > 40 RANGE 60 SECONDS	Log if sensor value exceeds defined limit for a certain number of times within a determined timeframe.
4	Identify Error II	1;5;7	SELECT * FROM STREAM_1 AS s1, STREAM_2 AS s2 WHERE s1.VALUE > 40 AND s2.VALUE < 10 RANGE 60 SECONDS	Log if two sensor values exceeds defined limit within a determined timeframe.
5	Check Machine Power	7;9	SELECT * FROM STREAM_1 AS s, DB_TABLE_1 AS t WHERE s.MACHINE_ID = t.MACHINE_ID AND s.POWER = 0 AND (s.TS > t.DOWNTIME_END OR s.TS < t.DOWNTIME_START)	Log if the machine is in an unscheduled phase of being turned off or in stand-by (assumption: there is always the next downtime stored in DB_TABLE_1)

Except for 4. Merging (Union) and 6. Sorting/Ranking, all functionalities of the presented operation list are covered. We aim to test these currently missing functions with the complete query set.

Currently, there is a first viable example benchmark implementation for the first query shown in Table 3, which only processes streaming data. For data processing, a DSPS is used. As shown in Fig. 2, a data sender ingests the data into a Kafka cluster, which is the interface to the benchmark implementation. A result validator and metric calculator checks result correctness and computes latency for the queries.

3.4 Limitations

One limitation of Senska is its domain, namely industrial manufacturing. Senska, as every domain-specific benchmark, is focussed on a single application field, which can differ from other areas such as e-commerce software architectures. Differences may exist with respect to, e.g., data or query characteristics. Due to such varieties, there might be other benchmarks representing certain domain-specific circumstances better than Senska does. Nevertheless, queries defined by Senska cover functionalities, e.g., windowing or filtering, that can also be relevant to other domains.

Moreover, Senska only considers a limited data variety for simplicity reasons. To be more concrete, neither multimedia nor graph data is part of the benchmark and thus, capabilities of processing such data that a SUT might have will not be rewarded by Senska. So for scenarios where processing of such data is crucial Senska might not be the best choice of benchmark. Nevertheless, Senska will be open for extensions, which allows integrating such aspects.

A third limitation comes with the use of Apache Kafka as central part of Senska's architecture. As a consequence, a SUT must be able to retrieve and send data from and to Kafka. Since there are many clients available for Kafka that is not considered as a major drawback [1]. Besides, an architecture containing a message broker in general or Apache Kafka in particular might not be satisfying for everyone. Reasons can be, e.g., the wish to test another message broker or to test an architecture without message broker, which could mean retrieving streaming data within the SUT directly via one or multiple socket connection(s).

4 Conclusion

Within this paper, related work and the need for a new application benchmark for stream processing in an enterprise context is presented. The concept for such a new benchmark, namely Senska, is illustrated. Senska focusses on industrial manufacturing as domain and provides a toolkit for data ingestion into the SUT as well as query result validation and benchmark metrics calculation. While some queries can be answered solely using streaming data, other queries require access to historical transactional data in order to produce correct results.

By developing Senska, it is aimed to fill the gap that exists in the area of benchmarking enterprise architectures with focus on data stream processing. As a next step, we want to publish a first version of the benchmark together with an example implementation of the benchmark queries. Major future tasks are the search for a suitable input data set, and, if needed, the development of a data generator for scaling or generating streaming data. The example implementation has to be finished and the result validator adapted correspondingly. Additionally, the metric set as well as the tool responsible for its calculation have to be extended in order to cover all relevant aspects. Besides, the components related to business data have to be developed. Concurrently, the ideas shall be consistently be discussed with industry partners in order to validate design decisions with respect to relevance.

References

1. Apache Kafka - clients. https://cwiki.apache.org/confluence/display/KAFKA/Clients. Accessed 24 Apr 2017
2. Documentation - Kafka 0.10.2 documentation. https://kafka.apache.org/documentation/. Accessed 24 Apr 2017
3. Abadi, D.J., Carney, D., Çetintemel, U., Cherniack, M., Convey, C., Lee, S., Stonebraker, M., Tatbul, N., Zdonik, S.: Aurora: a new model and architecture for data stream management. VLDB J. **12**(2), 120–139 (2003). http://dx.doi.org/10.1007/s00778-003-0095-z
4. Abdessemed, M.A.: Real-time data integration with apache flink & kafka @bouygues telecom (2015). http://www.slideshare.net/FlinkForward/mohamed-amine-abdessemed-realtime-data-integration-with-apache-flink-kafka. Accessed 06 Apr 2017
5. Arasu, A., Babcock, B., Babu, S., Datar, M., Ito, K., Nishizawa, I., Rosenstein, J., Widom, J.: Stream: The stanford stream data manager (demonstration description). In: Proceedings of the 2003 ACM SIGMOD International Conference on Management of Data, SIGMOD 2003, pp. 665–665. ACM, New York (2003). http://doi.acm.org/10.1145/872757.872854
6. Arasu, A., Babu, S., Widom, J.: The CQL continuous query language: semantic foundations and query execution. VLDB J. **15**(2), 121–142 (2006). http://dx.doi.org/10.1007/s00778-004-0147-z
7. Arasu, A., Cherniack, M., Galvez, E., Maier, D., Maskey, A.S., Ryvkina, E., Stonebraker, M., Tibbetts, R.: Linear road: a stream data management benchmark. In: Proceedings of the Thirtieth International Conference on Very Large Data Bases, VLDB 2004, VLDB Endowment, vol. 30, pp. 480–491 (2004). http://dl.acm.org/citation.cfm?id=1316689.1316732
8. Dunning, T., Friedman, E.: Streaming Architecture: New Designs Using Apache Kafka and MapR Streams. O'Reilly Media, Sebastopol (2016)
9. Folkerts, E., Alexandrov, A., Sachs, K., Iosup, A., Markl, V., Tosun, C.: Benchmarking in the cloud: what it should, can, and cannot be. In: Nambiar, R., Poess, M. (eds.) TPCTC 2012. LNCS, vol. 7755, pp. 173–188. Springer, Heidelberg (2013). https://doi.org/10.1007/978-3-642-36727-4_12
10. Gray, J.: The Benchmark Handbook - For Database and Transaction Processing Systems. The Morgan Kaufmann Series in Data Management Systems. Morgan Kaufmann, Massachusetts (1993)
11. Hesse, G., Lorenz, M.: Conceptual survey on data stream processing systems. In: Proceedings of the 2015 IEEE 21st International Conference on Parallel and Distributed Systems (ICPADS), ICPADS 2015, pp. 797–802. IEEE Computer Society, Washington, DC (2015). http://dx.doi.org/10.1109/ICPADS.2015.106
12. Hesse, G., Matthies, C., Reissaus, B., Uflacker, M.: A new application benchmark for data stream processing architectures in an enterprise context: doctoral symposium. In: Proceedings of the 11th ACM International Conference on Distributed and Event-based Systems, DEBS 2017, pp. 359–362. ACM, New York (2017). http://doi.acm.org/10.1145/3093742.3093902
13. Huber, M.F., Voigt, M., Ngomo, A.N.: Big Data architecture for the semantic analysis of complex events in manufacturing. In: Informatik 2016, 46. Jahrestagung der Gesellschaft für Informatik, 26–30 September 2016, Klagenfurt, Österreich, pp. 353–360 (2016). http://subs.emis.de/LNI/Proceedings/Proceedings259/article173.html

14. Kreps, J., Narkhede, N., Rao, J., et al.: Kafka: a distributed messaging system for log processing. In: SIGMOD Workshop on Networking Meets Databases (2011)
15. Kulkarni, S., Bhagat, N., Fu, M., Kedigehalli, V., Kellogg, C., Mittal, S., Patel, J.M., Ramasamy, K., Taneja, S.: Twitter heron: stream processing at scale. In: Proceedings of the 2015 ACM SIGMOD International Conference on Management of Data, SIGMOD 2015, pp. 239–250. ACM, New York (2015). http://doi.acm.org/10.1145/2723372.2742788
16. Lu, R., Wu, G., Xie, B., Hu, J.: Stream bench: towards benchmarking modern distributed stream computing frameworks. In: Proceedings of the 2014 IEEE/ACM 7th International Conference on Utility and Cloud Computing, pp. 69–78. UCC 2014. IEEE Computer Society, Washington, DC (2014). http://dx.doi.org/10.1109/UCC.2014.15
17. Manyika, J., Chui, M., Bisson, P., Woetzel, J., Dobbs, R., Bughin, J., Aharon, D.: The internet of things: mapping the value beyond the hype, June 2015.   http://www.mckinsey.com/ /media/McKinsey/Business%20Functions/McKinsey%20Digital/Our%20Insights/The%20Internet%20of%20Things%20The%20value%20of%20digitizing%20the%20physical%20world/The-Internet-of-things-Mapping-the-value-beyond-the-hype.ashx. Accessed 01 Mar 2017
18. Menasce, D.A.: Tpc-w: a benchmark for e-commerce. IEEE Internet Comput. 6(3), 83–87 (2002)
19. Mendes, M.R.N., Bizarro, P., Marques, P.: A performance study of event processing systems. In: Nambiar, R., Poess, M. (eds.) TPCTC 2009. LNCS, vol. 5895, pp. 221–236. Springer, Heidelberg (2009). https://doi.org/10.1007/978-3-642-10424-4_16
20. Shukla, A., Chaturvedi, S., Simmhan, Y.: Riotbench: A real-time iot benchmark for distributed stream processing platforms. CoRR abs/1701.08530 (2017). http://arxiv.org/abs/1701.08530
21. Southekal, P.H.: Data for Business Performance: The Goal-Question-Metric (GQM) Model to Transform Business Data into an Enterprise Asset (2017)
22. Vieru, M., López, J.: Flink in zalando's world of microservices (2016). http://www.slideshare.net/ZalandoTech/flink-in-zalandos-world-of-microservices-62376341. Accessed 06 Apr 2017
23. Weiner, S., Line, D.: Manufacturing and the data conundrum - too much? too little? or just right? https://www.eiuperspectives.economist.com/sites/default/files/Manufacturing_Data_Conundrum_Jul14.pdf (2014). Accessed 01 Mar 2017

Towards a Scalability and Energy Efficiency Benchmark for VNF

Norbert Schmitt[(⊠)], Jóakim von Kistowski, and Samuel Kounev

University of Würzburg, 97074 Würzburg, Germany
{norbert.schmitt,joakim.kistowski,samuel.kounev}@uni-wuerzburg.de

Abstract. Network Function Virtualization (NFV) is the transfer of network functions from dedicated devices to high-volume commodity servers. It opens opportunities for flexibility and energy savings. Concrete insights on the flexibility of specific NFV environments require measurement methodologies and benchmarks. However, current benchmarks are not measuring the ability of a virtual network function (VNF) to scale either horizontally or vertically. We therefore envision a new benchmark that measures a VNF's ability to scale while evaluating its energy efficiency at the same time. Such a benchmark would enable the selection of a suitable VNF for changing demands, deployed at an existing or new resource landscape, while minimizing energy costs.

1 Introduction

Data centers in the United States consumed an estimate of 61 billion kWh annually in 2006, according to a Berkeley National Laboratory reported to congress [1]. By 2013, the energy consumption has risen to an estimated 93 billion kWh. National Resource Defense Council (NRDC) [2] projected the power consumption to climb to 140 billion kWh by 2020. Roughly 5–10% [1] of this consumed energy is used by networking equipment with its power demand expected to increase proportionally with the increasing server power demand.

The rise of cloud computing, enabling new products such as Software as a Service (SaaS), calls for increased flexibility in terms of service locality and network configuration abilities. The introduction of software defined networking (SDN) allows for greater flexibility in the network configuration. Yet the network infrastructure is mostly relying on dedicated appliances with limited flexibility in locality and scalability.

With growing data centers, the demand for performance in network equipment increases as well. Yet typical service demands are not constant over time but highly variable [3] and large amounts of resources remain unused when the system is not under peak load. Virtualization allows the on demand allocation of required resources to a certain task without a decrease in Quality of Service (QoS) or Quality of Experience (QoE). With the introduction of Network Function Virtualization (NFV) by the European Telecommunications Standards Institute (ETSI) [4], this trend towards virtualization is applied in the network

© Springer International Publishing AG 2018
R. Nambiar and M. Poess (Eds.): TPCTC 2017, LNCS 10661, pp. 41–54, 2018.
https://doi.org/10.1007/978-3-319-72401-0_4

domain by replacing dedicated appliances with high-volume commodity servers. NFVs based on commodity servers might not be more energy efficient than dedicated hardware devices when under peak load due to the optimized hardware within the dedicated network appliances. However, peak load only accounts for a fraction of the total time the service is available. Combined with the ability to scale both horizontally and vertically, NFV opens up opportunities for energy saving and reduced operational costs.

In this paper we describe our vision for scalability and energy efficiency benchmarking for virtual network functions (VNFs). Different techniques for auto-scaling in a cloud environment exist [5] today and research is still ongoing. The introduction of NFV also introduced the ability to scale network functions horizontally and vertically. This enables network functions to be used in auto-scaling scenarios in cloud environments. Yet, the differences in scalability of different or competing VNFs in an NFV environment remains unknown. Different implementations of an otherwise identical network function could behave differently when scaled. We therefore envision a new benchmark suite that rates a VNF's ability to scale horizontally and vertically.

While performance is a key characteristic, energy efficiency gains importance with the rising demand in flexible networking equipment. An energy efficiency aware benchmark could show opportunities for energy saving and subsequently reductions in operational costs. Our main goal for a new VNF benchmark is the rating of scalability, performance and energy efficiency of VNF implementations to select and deploy energy efficient VNFs without a decrease in QoS or QoE. Thus, we not only rate the performance of a VNF when scaled, but combine it with its energy efficiency for the performance demand.

The remainder of this paper is structured as follows: At first, we give an outline of the current state of the art. In Sect. 3, we formulate the problem statement of our envisioned scalability and energy efficiency benchmark. Section 4 describes our vision for a new benchmark followed by an approach to realize such a benchmark in Sect. 5. This includes preliminary methodology and setup of the benchmark. Finally, Sect. 6 provides a conclusion and an outlook for the next tasks towards our vision.

2   State of the Art

Huppler motivates the importance of efficiency benchmarks in his work [9] with many examples of benchmarks, including the Green500 ranking for supercomputers and TPC-Energy [26]. The latter is also the focus of [10], which introduces the new metric of energy proportionality. Energy proportionality is designed to represent a system's ability to adapt to changes in demand. This underlines the need for different load levels in energy efficiency benchmarking, also described in the SPEC Power Methodology [8] that is used for the Standard Performance Evaluation Corporation (SPEC) Server Efficiency Rating Tool (SERT) [28], ChauffeurWDK [29] and SPECpower_ssj2008 [27].

There is also a variety of existing virtualization benchmarks like the Standard Performance Evaluation Corporation (SPEC) VIRT_SC 2013 [23],

TPC-VMS [24] and TPCx-V [25]. However, these benchmarks are measuring the performance of a workload together with the virtualization technique and software stack. In contrast, we intend for our benchmark to be independent of the virtualization technique, software stack and hardware, to increase its range of possible applications and making different VNF implementations directly comparable.

Lange et al. [14] also states VNFs are more regularly used in higher abstraction levels, especially when used inside cloud environments. In addition, complexity and concurrency increase as well, due to the abstraction and interactions with other network functions. Subsequently the complexity of performance benchmarks for VNFs will also rise in complexity. Yet, our focus is not on the sole performance of VNF. A methodology for performance benchmarking network devices was already published as RFC 2544 [16] in 1999 and extended by RFC 6201 [17] and RFC 6815 [18]. In [15], the authors analyzed the performance of a single VNF (virtual router) and identified four performance bottlenecks. The relevance of these bottlenecks for other VNF types is questionable as only a single type was evaluated.

The expired RFC draft [20] made an early effort towards a VNF performance benchmarking methodology. It is listing required documentation and reporting, such as CPUs, caches, storage system, hypervisor and others. It also categorizes benchmarks in a 3×3 matrix for deployment, operation and de-activation of VNFs. A second, also expired, RFC draft [19] provides a testbed setup for VNF benchmarking. Yet, it also focuses only on performance.

In [6], Herbst et al. describe elasticity as the autonomic provisioning and deprovisioning of resources, such that the provided resources always match the demand as closely as possible. For a system to be elastic, it must be either horizontally or vertically scalable. A horizontally scalable system provisions and deprovisions more virtual or physical machines to a task to accommodate changes in resource demand. A vertically scalable system must be able to allocate more computing resources (i.e., CPU cores, memory size and network I/O) to an existing machine. An elastically managed system can be in three states, shown in Fig. 1. If the resource demand (red) is higher than the resources currently supplied (blue), the system is in an underprovisioned state U_n for the duration A_n. In case the resource supply is higher than the demand, the system is overprovisioned O_n for time B_n and has more resources than needed. If the system is neither overprovisioned nor underprovisioned, it is in an optimal state for a given demand.

3   Challenges

For a new scalability and energy efficiency benchmark, specifically built for VNF benchmarking, we identify four main challenges based on Sect. 2. While the performance of a VNF can also be dependend on its location, our benchmark should measure the performance of a VNF itself. Its score should not reflect the solution to placement problems, such as the ones shown in [21,22]. The challenges

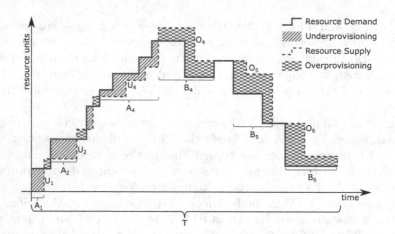

Fig. 1. Resource over- and underprovisioning [6] (Color figure online)

we want to address stem mainly from the variety of application domains a VNF can be deployed in and from the ever increasing abstraction and complexity:

1. As mentioned, VNF implementations should be directly comparable. Therefore the performance of the VNF must be isolated from the underlying software stack, virtualization and hardware. This includes research on metrics that can represent a VNFs performance independently from these factors. Yet, it should be taken into consideration that full isolation might not be possible. In this case, a fixed reference virtualization technique could be selected to keep the benchmark's relevance and fairness.
2. We intend to empirically show the correctness of our benchmark. Therefore a selection of VNFs must be made that not only shows that the benchmark works but is also representative to a wide variety of possible VNFs under test. As VNFs can differ significantly depending on the domain, different evaluation groups could be formed. For example a Carrier Grade Network address translator (CGN) might be relevant to an Internet Service Provider (ISP) but less relevant to a video streaming service provider. Finding suitable VNFs is therefore necessary for empirical evaluation and can also aid in showing the benchmark's generality or limitations.
3. VNFs come in many types, all needing a special setup and configuration for traffic generation and validation. VNFs can have different numbers of sources (s) and receivers (r), as shown in Fig. 2. These range from simple configurations with a single source and receiver to VNFs that require multiple sources or receivers. A $n : m$ relationship between sources and receivers is also possible as a combination of the two rightmost examples in Fig. 2. VNFs could also alter the traffic flow in form of a firewall, which blocks packets, or a Network Address Translator (NAT), changing the packet header information. The list is not exhaustive nor final and a VNF might not exclusively belong

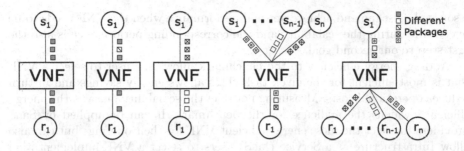

Fig. 2. Different VNFs with different needs for configuration and validation

to a single category. Yet, it shows the complexity in potential setups that must be handled by the benchmark.

4. Regarding vertical scaling, it is not known in advance which step size for resources should be used when scaling. For horizontal scaling, it is a question of how many resources should be allocated to each instance. This could be left to the benchmark user or defined by the benchmark methodology. If left to the user, the step size and allocation size might get optimized to his or her use case and might reduce comparability of results. If it is defined by the methodology, it is questionable if all possible VNFs can be represented and would further increase the challenge of finding relevant VNFs or VNF groups with predefined step sizes, able to indicate a VNF's behavior when scaled.

4 The Vision of a Scalability and Energy Efficiency Benchmark

Our envisioned benchmark includes two main goals. The first is measuring the vertical and horizontal *scalability* of a VNF. The second goal is measuring a VNF's *energy efficiency* when scaled. To make the benchmark versatile for a wide audience, it should be able to handle a large variety of VNFs with different needs on traffic generation and validation. We envision a benchmark that is agnostic to the VNF that is under test and can be freely configured. For our benchmark we focus on the following resource types as they can largely influence scalability, performance and power consumption and therefore energy efficiency: *(i)* number of CPU cores, *(ii)* size of main memory, *(iii)* filesystem I/O bandwidth and *(iv)* network bandwidth. Other metrics that are not mentioned can also be taken into consideration, depending on future research.

Measuring a VNF's ability to scale allows selecting the best performing VNF for an existing infrastructure by matching it to the available resource landscape. If for example only a single but powerful system is available, a vertically scalable VNF implementation could be deployed, while an environment with many but less powerful machines might be better suited for a horizontally scalable VNF. The user can therefore deploy a VNF implementation that suits its available resource landscape and achieve optimal performance when the VNF needs to be scaled. Measuring the scalability and the corresponding performance is also the first step to our second goal.

Adding energy efficiency to the benchmark allows the user to select a VNF that is most efficient for the given task. This allows energy savings and in turn reduces operational costs. Measuring not only the scalability but also the energy efficiency widens the audience for the benchmark. It can be applied by SaaS providers to select the most energy efficient VNF for their offerings but can also allow Infrastructure as a Service (IaaS) users to select a VNF implementation that is scalable within the provided resource landscape. An example use case is shown in Fig. 3. Three different VNF implementations with identical functions are measured and the results are stored in a database. The scalability demand by the customer and the efficiency demand are shown as the horizontal line. While VNF 1 satisfies the customers demand, it is not suited for the service provider. VNF 3 on the other hand is the best solution for the provider but

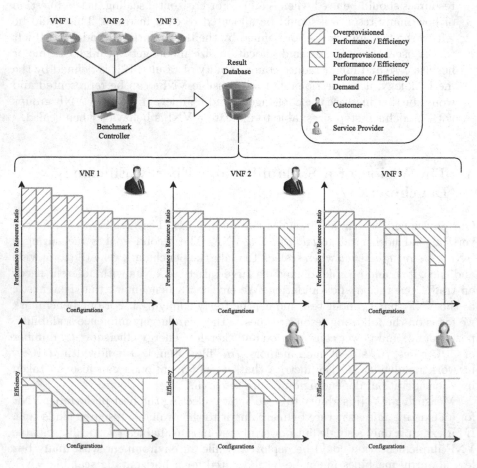

Fig. 3. Scalability and energy efficiency example use case

not for the customer. Yet, service provider and customer can both agree on the second implementation as a compromise. This shows, that results from such a benchmark can also be used to reach agreements between providers and consumers for a VNF that suits both needs, the customer's need for satisfactory performance and the provider's for minimizing cost.

5 Planned Approach

We have planned the following approach to achieve our vision of a scalability and energy efficiency benchmark for VNF. It consists of a benchmark methodology based on existing power and energy efficiency benchmarks and tools. We also show a preliminary benchmark setup for our approach. The term configuration used in the following section describes the amount of instances of a VNF for horizontal scaling and the number of different setups in the form of allocated network bandwidth, CPU count, main memory, filesystem I/O and network bandwidth for vertical scaling.

5.1 Methodology

Our methodology consists of two distinct parts and aims to comply with key characteristics for benchmarks, described in [7]. First, we describe the energy efficiency methodology, followed by the scalability methodology.

Energy Efficiency. For our work, we base our energy efficiency methodology on the SPEC Power Methodology [8]. Existing work has shown that this methodology ensures high accuracy for power measurements [12] and supports the characterization of system power over multiple load levels [13]. The goal is the power measurement in a steady-state at multiple load levels. DC Power is measured at the Server's power inlet. Loads used by the benchmark must have the characteristics of transactional benchmarking loads. In the context of performance benchmarking, we consider any load that consists of work packets with a clearly defined and measurable start and end time to be transactional. Transactionality of loads enables multiple benchmark features, such as throughput measurements, load calibration, and more. The System Under Test (SUT) is first calibrated to determine its maximum throughput. To achieve calibration, load is generated at a level that is guaranteed to exceed the SUT's capacity and the SUT's throughput is measured. The recorded throughput, averaged over multiple calibration intervals, is assumed to be the maximum (100%) load level achievable by the SUT. Lower load levels below 100% are reached by adding random exponentially distributed waiting times between transactions. The mean delay is chosen so that the target transaction rate corresponds to the load level. Figure 4 shows an example of an efficiency measurement according to [8] with the calibration and three load levels. All measurement intervals as well as the calibration have a pre- and post-measurement phase to allow the SUT to reach steady-state before measurements begin.

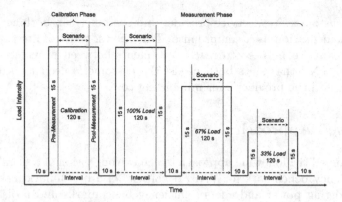

Fig. 4. Energy efficiency benchmark phases [11]

Figure 5 shows an example result from an energy efficiency measurement of a control plane VNF (SDN controller) for four different load levels, demonstrating the practical applicability of the envisioned approach. Results from measurements with our methodology should also include reporting requirements on which configuration was tested under what load. The figure shows that the VNF under test consumes different amounts of power for each of the load levels. As performance of the load levels varies by design, the resulting energy efficiency (the ratio of performance over power) differs as well.

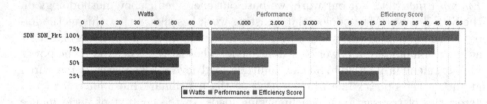

Fig. 5. Example result from an energy efficiency measurement with four load levels

The environmental conditions of the benchmark can have a significant impact on the power consumption of electrical devices. E.g., a hot environment would need more powerful cooling systems drawing more power. As a result, it is necessary not only to measure the power consumption but also the environmental temperature. The temperature for air cooled server systems is measured not more than 50 mm from the air inlet as described in [8].

Scalability. We currently plan to express a VNF's scalability as the ratio between its maximum performance and used resources. For horizontal scaling, *used resources* is the number of instances deployed and running. Vertical scaling uses CPU count, main memory, I/O bandwidth and network bandwidth as the scaled resource. In addition, a combination of resources might be possible, such that main memory and CPU count are scaled at the same time. Yet, benchmarking all possible resource combinations could increase the number of configurations and subsequently the benchmarks runtime significantly. Hence, we see the need to let the benchmark user select the resources that are scaled under well defined rules to achieve optimal results for the VNF under test. The resources selected must then be documented and combined with the benchmark results to keep them comparable. The benchmark should also include the scalability results for the four resources mentioned in Sect. 4 as a baseline to all benchmark runs.

As energy efficiency is measured simultaneously with scalability, the correct distribution of load levels across the different configurations becomes an important factor. We identified three different possibilities to distribute the load levels over all configurations as shown in Fig. 6:

(A) The first option is to distribute all measured load levels equally across all possible configurations and calibrate only once at the configuration with the highest performance. In the example in Fig. 6, each possible configuration has an equal number of load levels that are determined by the single calibration C_0. This keeps the benchmark runtime low, as only a single calibration has to be performed. Yet, this option has some drawbacks. First, if the number of configurations is not fixed in the benchmark, the number of load levels varies as well. This reduces the comparability between different VNF implementations that are measured with a different number of configurations. Even if the number of configurations is fixed, it cannot be guaranteed by the benchmark that the load levels for a specific configuration are representative. Second, in the example, the peak load for the second configuration is not measured. Neither by L_2 nor L_3. Also L_4 overloads the third configuration and possibly invalidating the measurement for this load level.

(B) The second option is to have a fixed number of load levels per configuration and calibrate each configuration. The load levels are distributed according to the SPEC measurement methodology [8], based on the calibration for the specific configuration. While this option avoids the second problem of not measuring peak load or overload of a configuration, this option also has drawbacks. In the example shown in Fig. 6, each configuration has three load levels, full load, 66% and 33%. For the first configuration, L_1 is below the maximum performance of the second configuration and L_2 is near the full load of configuration three. These load levels are not necessary for elasticity (see Sect. 2) as the system should adapt to the performance demand and will not operate in an overprovisioned state, elongating the benchmark's runtime unnecessarily.

(C) The third option is to distribute a fixed number of load levels between the calibrated full load of the current configuration and the next smaller (less peak performance) configuration. In our example (Fig. 6), the load levels for the first configuration are distributed between the calibration C_0 and C_1. For the second configuration the load levels are between C_1 and C_2. The configuration with the lowest maximum performance will distribute

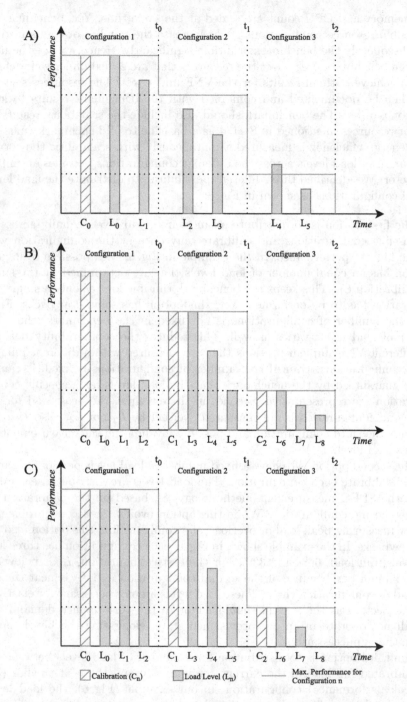

Fig. 6. Options for scalabilty and energy efficiency load level distribution across multiple configurations

its load levels between its calibration (C_2 in the example) and the idle state (L_8). This removes unnecessary load levels and increases the relevance with more load levels. Yet, it introduces an idle measurement at the lowest configuration.

Of the three introduced options for load level distribution among different system configurations. We discourage the first option *(A)* with the most drawbacks in favor of either option *(B)* or *(C)*. Between *(B)* and *(C)*, we see the latter as the most promising option with the least drawbacks that does not include possibly unnecessary measurements that, in return, might not be relevant to the benchmark user.

5.2 Setup

The envisioned setup of our benchmark consists of at least the following components: *(i)* experiment controller, *(ii)* load generator, *(iii)* traffic receiver and validator, *(iv)* power analyzer, *(v)* temperature analyzer and *(vi)* SUT. Optionally, a meter controller can also be used for managing the dedicated power and temperature measurement devices. Each component can be seen in Fig. 7.

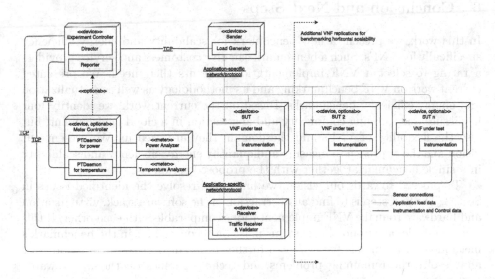

Fig. 7. Envisioned benchmark setup

The experiment controller starts and stops the measurements. It collects all data from the involved components and compiles the final report. Communication takes place in a dedicated control network so measurements are not disturbed.

The load generator produces traffic that matches the load level that should be measured and network related configuration, such as packet size, packet content and protocol that must be used to stress the VNF under test. It also distributes the traffic to all instances of VNFs deployed for measurement. Even though a dedicated load balancer is possible, we discourage using a load balancer not delivered together with the benchmark to keep the benchmark reproducible. An optimized load balancer could skew the results in favor of a specific VNF implementation, especially if the load balancer and its configuration is not publicly available for other users to reproduce and verify the results.

After the traffic has passed through the SUT, it must be validated to check if the VNF performed the operation according to specification. This is done at the traffic receiver and validator component. Both, the load balancer and validator, must be configurable to match the VNF that is under test appropriately.

Power and temperature measurements are performed with dedicated measurement devices deployed at the test site. They are either connected directly to the experiment controller or an optional meter controller if required.

The setup of the SUT varies. It depends on how many instances are deployed and on how many hypervisors or physical machines they are distributed. This changes over the course of a benchmark run as the system is scaled. Therefore, we do not specify any general setup restrictions.

6   Conclusion and Next Steps

In this work, we present a new benchmark for scalability and energy efficiency specifically for VNFs. Such a benchmark can give customers and service providers a rating to select a VNF implementation that fits their need. We presented current work on VNF benchmarking and its methodology as well as virtualization and energy efficiency benchmarks. Based on the current work, we identify four key issues due to rising complexity and abstraction in a cloud environment, but also the flexibility of VNFs and the domain they are used in. We present our vision and the approach to measure and quantify energy efficiency and scalability in a single benchmark together with the proposed setup.

To proceed towards our vision, we first must resolve the identified issues in Sect. 3. The first step is to find an abstraction of the software stack, virtualization and hardware to make VNF implementations comparable with each other. If this is not possible, all supporting systems must be accounted for in the benchmark's methodology. From this basis we can further proceed to build our methodology and resolve the remaining problems and technical issues on the way towards our vision.

References

1. Brown, R., Masanet, E., Nordman, B., Tschudi, B., Shehabi, A., Stanley, J., Koomey, J., Sartor, D., Chan, P., Loper, J., Capana, S., Hedman, B., Duff, R., Haines, E., Sass, D., Fanara, A.: Report to Congress on Server and Data Center Energy Efficiency: Public Law 109–431 (2007)

2. Whitney, J., Delforge, P.: Scaling Up Energy Efficiency Across the Data Center Industry: Evaluating Key Drivers and Barriers. Data Center Efficiency Assessment (2014)
3. von Kistowski, J., Herbst, N., Kounev, S.: Modeling variations in load intensity over time. In: Proceedings of the third International Workshop on Large Scale Testing, LT 2014, pp. 1–4 (2014)
4. Chiosi, M., Clarke, D., Willis, P., Reid, A., Feger, J., Bugenhagen, M., Khan, W., Fargano, M., Cui, C., Deng, H., Benitez, J., Michel, U., Damker, H., Ogaki, K., Matsuzaki, T., Fukui, M., Shimano, K., Delisle, D., Loudier, Q., Kolias, C., Guardini, I., Demaria, E., Miverva, R., Manzalini, A., López, D., Salguero, F., Ruhl, F., Sen, P.: Network functions virtualisation - introductory white paper. In: SDN and OpenFlow World Congress (2012)
5. Lorido-Botran, T., Miguel-Alonso, J., Lozano, J.A.: A review of auto-scaling techniques for elastic applications in cloud environments. J. Grid Comput. 12(4), 559–592 (2014)
6. Herbst, N., Kounev, S., Reussner, R.: Elasticity in cloud computing: what it is, and what it is not. In: Proceedings of the 10th International Conference on Autonomic Computing, ICAC, San Jose, California, USA (2013)
7. von Kistowski, J., A. Arnold, J., Huppler, K., Lange, K.-D., L. Henning, J., Cao, P.: How to build a benchmark. In: Proceedings of the 6th ACM/SPEC International Conference on Performance Engineering, ICPE, Austin, Texas, USA (2015)
8. Power and Performance Benchmark Methodology V2.1. Standard Performance Evaluation Corporation (SPEC), Gainesville, USA (2012)
9. Huppler, K.R.: Performance per watt - benchmarking ways to get more for less. In: Nambiar, R., Poess, M. (eds.) TPCTC 2012. LNCS, vol. 7755, pp. 60–74. Springer, Heidelberg (2013). https://doi.org/10.1007/978-3-642-36727-4_5
10. Schall, D., Hoefner, V., Kern, M.: Towards an enhanced benchmark advocating energy-efficient systems. In: Nambiar, R., Poess, M. (eds.) TPCTC 2011. LNCS, vol. 7144, pp. 31–45. Springer, Heidelberg (2012). https://doi.org/10.1007/978-3-642-32627-1_3
11. von Kistowski, J., Becket, J., Lange, K.-D., Block, H., A. Arnold, J., Kounev, S.: Energy efficiency of hierarchical server load distributions strategies. In: 2015 IEEE 23rd International Symposium on Modeling, Analysis and Simulation of Computer and Telecommunications Systems (MASCOTS), Atlanta, USA (2015)
12. von Kistowski, J., Block, H., Beckett, J., Spradling, C., Lange, K.-D., Kounev, S.: Variations in CPU power consumption. In: Proceedings of the 7th ACM/SPEC International Conference on Performance Engineering, ICPE 2016, Delft, The Netherlands, pp. 147–158 (2016)
13. von Kistowski, J., Block, H., Beckett, J., Lange, K.-D., A. Arnold, J., Kounev, S.: Analysis of the influences on server power consumption and energy efficiency for CPU-intensive workloads. In: Proceedings of the 6th ACM/SPEC International Conference on Performance Engineering, ICPE 2015, Austin, Texas, pp. 223–234 (2015)
14. Lange, S., Nguyen-Ngoc, A., Gebert, S., Zinner, T., Jarschel, M., Köpsel, A., Sune, M., Raumer, D., Gallenmüller, S., Calre, G., Tran-Gia, P.: Performance benchmarking of a software-based LTE SGW. In: 2015 11th International Conference on Network and Service Management (CNSM), Barcelona, Spain (2015)
15. Falkner, M., Leivadeas, A., Lambadaris, I., Kesidis, G.: Performance analysis of virtualized network functions on virtualized systems architectures. In: 2016 IEEE 21st International Workshop on Computer Aided Modelling and Design of Communication Links and Networks (CAMAD), Toronto, Canada (2016)

16. Bradner, S., McQuaid, J.: RFC 2544: Benchmarking Methodology for Network Interconnected Devices. IETF (1999)
17. Bradner, S., McQuaid, J.: RFC 6201: Device Reset Characterization. IETF (2011)
18. Bradner, S., Dubray, K., McQuaid, J., Morton, A.: RFC 6815: Applicability Statement for RFC 2544: Use on Production Networks Considered Harmful. IETF (2012)
19. Rosa Ed., E., Szabo, R.: VNF Benchmarking Methodology (draft expired in September 2016). IETF (2016)
20. Morton, A.: Considerations for Benchmarking Virtual Network Functions and Their Infrastructure (draft expired in August 2015). IETF (2015)
21. Moens, H., De Turck, F.: VNF-P: a model for efficient placement for virtualized network functions. In: 2014 10th International Conference on Network and Service Management (CNSM), Rio de Janeiro, Brazil (2014)
22. Addis, B., Belabed, D., Bouet, M., Secci, S.: Virtual network functions placement and routing optimization. In: 2015 IEEE 4th International Conference on Cloud Networking (CloudNet), Niagara Falls, Canada (2015)
23. SPEC VIRT_SC 2013. The Standard Performance Evaluation Corporation (SPEC) (2013). https://www.spec.org/virt_sc2013/
24. Smith, W.D., Sebastian, S.: Virtualization Performance Insights from TPC-VMS. Transaction Processing Performance Council (2013)
25. Bond, A., Johnson, D., Kopczynski, G., Taheri, H.R.: Profiling the performance of virtualized databases with the TPCx-V benchmark. In: Nambiar, R., Poess, M. (eds.) TPCTC 2015. LNCS, vol. 9508, pp. 156–172. Springer, Cham (2016). https://doi.org/10.1007/978-3-319-31409-9_10
26. TPC-Energy Specification. Transaction Processing Performance Council, Version 1.5.0 (2012). http://www.tpc.org/tpc_documents_current_versions/pdf/tpc-energy_v1.5.0.pdf
27. SPECpower_ssj2008. The Standard Performance Evaluation Corporation (SPEC) (2007). https://www.spec.org/power_ssj2008/
28. Server Efficiency Rating Tool 2. The Standard Performance Evaluation Corporation (SPEC) (2017). https://www.spec.org/sert2/
29. Chauffeur^{TM}WDK 2. The Standard Performance Evaluation Corporation (SPEC) (2017). https://www.spec.org/chauffeur-wdk/

Characterizing BigBench Queries, Hive, and Spark in Multi-cloud Environments

Nicolas Poggi[✉], Alejandro Montero, and David Carrera

Barcelona Supercomputing Center (BSC),
Universitat Politècnica de Catalunya (UPC-BarcelonaTech), Barcelona, Spain
npoggi@ac.upc.edu

Abstract. BigBench is the new standard (TPCx-BB) for benchmarking and testing Big Data systems. The TPCx-BB specification describes several business use cases—queries—which require a broad combination of data extraction techniques including SQL, Map/Reduce (M/R), user code (UDF), and Machine Learning to fulfill them. However, currently, there is no widespread knowledge of the different resource requirements and expected performance of each query, as is the case to more established benchmarks. Moreover, over the last year, the Spark framework and APIs have been evolving very rapidly, with major improvements in performance and the stable release of v2. It is our intent to compare the current state of Spark to Hive's base implementation which can use the legacy M/R engine and Mahout or the current Tez and MLlib frameworks. At the same time, cloud providers currently offer convenient on-demand managed big data clusters (PaaS) with a pay-as-you-go model. In PaaS, analytical engines such as Hive and Spark come ready to use, with a general-purpose configuration and upgrade management. The study characterizes both the BigBench queries and the out-of-the-box performance of Spark and Hive versions in the cloud. At the same time, comparing popular PaaS offerings in terms of reliability, data scalability (1 GB to 10 TB), versions, and settings from Azure HDinsight, Amazon Web Services EMR, and Google Cloud Dataproc. The query characterization highlights the similarities and differences in Hive an Spark frameworks, and which queries are the most resource consuming according to CPU, memory, and I/O. Scalability results show how there is a need for configuration tuning in most cloud providers as data scale grows, especially with Sparks memory usage. These results can help practitioners to quickly test systems by picking a subset of the queries which stresses each of the categories. At the same time, results show how Hive and Spark compare and what performance can be expected of each in PaaS.

1 Introduction

A benchmark captures the solution to a problem and guides decision making. For Big Data Analytics Systems (BDAS) BigBench has been recently standardized by the Transaction Processing Performance Council (TPC) as TPCx-BB. It has

© Springer International Publishing AG 2018
R. Nambiar and M. Poess (Eds.): TPCTC 2017, LNCS 10661, pp. 55–74, 2018.
https://doi.org/10.1007/978-3-319-72401-0_5

been originated from the need to expand previous decision support style benchmarks i.e., TPC H [21] and DS [22] into semi and non-structured data sources,
and it is the result of many years of collaboration between the database industry
and academia [2,5]. BigBench includes 30 business uses cases—queries—covering
merchandising, pricing optimization, product return, and customer questions.
It's implementation requires a broader set of data technologies than SQL i.e.,
Map/Reduce (M/R), user code (UDF), Natural Language Processing (NLP),
and Machine Learning; which expand and differentiates from previous SQL-only
benchmarks, as required by today's enterprise.

BigBench's original implementation was based on Apache Hadoop and Hive
with Map/Reduce (M/R) as execution engine and Mahout as Machine Learning
(ML) library [2]. However, due to the rapid development of the open source
Big Data ecosystem and BigBench online repository [10], it is now possible—
and convenient—to use e.g., Tez as execution engine and MLlib to lower the
query latency, or even to replace Hive altogether with Spark. However, there
is not only a large set of technologies that a user can choose from, but there
are multiple stable major versions of the frameworks. Moreover, Spark—and
MLlib—have been evolving rapidly over the last year, with major enhancements
in performance and API changes with v2. It is impart our intent to quantify
and understand the performance improvements of such changes from the base
implementation.

At the same time in recent years, new managed enterprise big data services have emerged in most cloud providers [13], facilitating software-defined
on-demand big data deployments. These services create compelling technical
reasons for migration to the cloud, such as elasticity of both compute and
storage, while maintaining a simplified infrastructure management i.e. via *virtualization*. Furthermore, with such services often using a *Pay-as-you-Go* or
even *Pay-as-you-Process* pricing model, they are economically attractive to customers [13]. Furthermore, cloud providers make the complex configuration and
tuning process [17] transparent to their clients, while providing features such as
data security and governance. On top of this, by having multiple customers, service providers can potentially improve their software-stack from user feedback, as
upgrading services more often than smaller companies [16]. As a result, the client
can benefit from the immediate availability of a tested and generically-optimized
platform with upgrade management.

The current cloud and open source Big Data ecosystem, leaves the enterprise facing multiple decisions that have can an impact both in the budget as
in the agility of their business. These include selecting both an infrastructure
and services provider, as well as the Big Data frameworks along their configuration tuning [17]. With this respect, BigBench becomes the clear choice to
contrast cloud providers and choose the appropriate data framework to make an
appropriate choice. However, as being a new benchmark, still little is understood
of the underlying implementation and expected performance of the queries. To
day, only a handful of official submissions are available [20], as well as a few
publications with detailed per query characterization [2,12].

The goal of this study is two-fold. First, it provides a first approach to Big-Bech query characterization to understand both Hive and Spark implementations. Second, it compares the out-of-the-box performance and data scalability from 1 GB to 10 TB of popular cloud PaaS solutions. Surveyed services include Azure HDinsight, Amazon Web Services EMR, and Google Cloud Dataproc, as well as an on-premises cluster as baseline. The work is the natural extension of the previous cloud SQL-on-Hadoop comparison, where the same cloud providers where compared using the TPC-H SQL benchmark [16] and only using Hive. The reason for not using Spark before, was that the versions, performance and configuration were not stable or comparable enough among providers. The study targets medium size clusters of 128-core each. In particular, we benchmark similar clusters in each provider consisting of 16 data nodes, with a total of 128 worker CPU cores and about 60 GB of RAM, using networked/block storage only. The master nodes where chosen with 16-cores each and more than 60 GB of RAM to sustain the concurrency tests.

Objectives and contributions:

1. A characterization of the different BigBench queries to better understand the use cases resource requirements and implementation differences of Hive and Spark.
2. Survey the popular entry level PaaS Hadoop solutions from main cloud providers and contrast offerings and data scalability using networked/block storage.
3. Compare the performance of the different versions of the Big Data Apache/Hadoop ecosystem, as well as the machine learning libraries.

Organization. The rest of the study is organized as follows. Section 2 presents the cloud providers and cluster hardware and software specs. Section 3 presents the background of the different technologies as well as the most relevant state-of-the art in the field. Section 4 presents the methodology used for the testing as well as the query characterization by resource usage for both Hive and Spark. While Sect. 5 presents the main query performance results at different data scales. Section 6 adds to discussion other tests performed with different versions of the frameworks. While Sect. 6 discusses the results and Sect. 7 provides a summary and the conclusions.

2   Providers and Systems-Under-Test (SUTs)

The Hadoop PaaS services from 3 major cloud providers are compared:

- HDInsight (HDI) from Microsoft Azure.
- Elastic Map Reduce (EMR) from Amazon Web services (AWS).
- Dataproc (GCD) from Google Cloud Platform.

The elasticity properties of the 3 providers have been previously studied [16] using a derived TPC-H benchmark implemented in Hive [11], along with Rackspace's Cloud Big Data (CBD) not included in this report. There were different reasons justifying the selection of each provider. HDI has been studied previously [15,17], and as such, their APIs are already well-integrated into the ALOJA platform (see Sect. 3). EMR was the first major Hadoop PaaS solution, and currently has one of the largest usage shares [13]. Both AWS and EMR are commonly used as bases of comparison in the literature [23,26,27]. GCD from Google Cloud has been included due to it being identified as a leading provider [13], as well as for being a new service (GA in 2016) which could potentially have a differentiated architecture.

HDInsight for HDI, we have used the D4v2 VM instances, which features 8-cores and 28 GB of RAM. The HDFS on all HDI instances is backed by the Azure Blob store (through the WASB driver). This means that it is an object-store over the network. As a consequence, the storage on HDI is decoupled from compute and can grow elastically, as well as be used from outside the HDFS cluster on other shared services and users. Local disks, backed by SSD drives on the D-series, are *ephemeral* and used for temporary or intermediate data only. The two included master nodes are of the D14v2 instance type, featuring 16-cores each and 112 GB of RAM. Deployment times in Azure took close to 20 min on most builds. The on-demand price for the cluster was $20.68 per hour, billed by the minute.

Elastic Map Reduce for EMR, the default m4.2xlarge instance was tested. Is an EBS-only instance. It comes with 8-cores and 32 GB of RAM. EBS stands for Elastic Block Store, Amazon's over-the-network storage. EBS has 4 different throughput (IOPS) plans, according to the technology backing the storage. The plans being high-performance or regular, for both SSDs and rotational drives; we chose the default regular SSDs (GPS2). The master node was the m4.4xlarge with 16-cores and 64 GB of RAM. Deployment times were faster than HDI at around 10 min. ERM is billed by the hour or fraction of hour, being the only provider maintaining this high billing. The cluster on-demand price was of $10.96 per hour.

Cloud Dataproc for GCD, we have evaluated the n1-standard-8 instance with 8-cores and 30 GB RAM, with the Google Cloud Storage (GCS)—the network based storage. In GCD, up to 4 SSDs can be added per node at creation time and the volumes are not *ephemeral* as in HDI, but used for HDFS. Deployment times were surprisingly fast for GCD, with cluster build times at around 1 min. The master node was of the n1-standard-16 with 16-cores and 60 GB of RAM, GCD has the option to include one or two master nodes, we choose one. GCD is billed by the minute. The cluster had an on-demand cost of $10.38 per hour.

2.1   Software Stack and Versions

While EMR, dating back to 2009, was the first major PaaS Hadoop solution, the other main providers have caught up in packaging Hadoop with other popular ecosystem services. Currently, all of the four providers tested ships with both *Hive* and *Spark* v2 for SQL-like analysis on top of Hadoop, as well as other services and tools i.e., Presto, HBase, Storm, Pig, etc.. There are differences in security and governance features, but these are not compared in this work. In relation to the software versions, Azure base their PaaS solutions on the Hortonworks Data Platform (HDP) [7], a popular Hadoop distribution that users might already be familiar with. HDI uses Ubuntu Linux 16.04 as Operating System (OS). During the main experimental period—June 2017—HDI added support for HDP version 2.6, which features Spark 2.1, but still runs on Hive v1. AWS uses a custom-built stack for EMR, as well as a custom Linux version called the Amazon Linux AMI, in this case v 2017.03. The EMR tests were run with the latest version available at the time of testing, EMR 5.5 featuring both Hive and Spark at v2. Like AWS, Google's Cloud Dataproc also uses a custom Hadoop distribution built using Apache BigTop (as EMR also does), and Debian Linux 8.4 OS. Tests were run on the *preview* version, as the current v1.1 only featured Spark 2.0, and we wanted to test the 3 of them with Spark 2.1. A comparison among Spark versions 1.6.3, 2.0, and 2.1 is provided in Sect. 6. Versions tested for the SUTs are the default ones offered at time of cluster deployment during June 2017. More information on the software versions can be found on the release notes of each provider. Relating to data center zones, we have tested HDI at *South Central US*, EMR at *us-east-1*, and GCD at *west-europe-1*.

Software Configuration Differences. While this work focuses on the out-of-the-box performance of PaaS services, the difference in execution times from Sect. 5 for SUTs with similar HW led us to compare configuration choices in detail as summarized by Table 1. Note that while the Java versions are 1.8, all providers used the OpenJDK versions, as opposed to Oracle's JDK as traditionally recommended. At the HDFS level, all providers used their object networked-based storage. As object stores are typically replicated besides by Hadoop, it was interesting to see that only GCD and CBD lowered the HDFS replication to 2 copies. Most block sizes were the default at 128 MB, while only EMR used the default *file buffer sizes*. EMR and CBD both compressed the map outputs by default, and each tuned the I/O factor and the I/O MBs.

While there were some differences at the Java/Hadoop level, tuning Hive had the most significant impact on performance. It was remarkable that GCD did not have the Tez execution engine enabled by default. Tez reduces the total BigBench running time by 2–3x as shown in Sect. 3.2. There were also differences in other Hive parameters among providers, such as using the *cost-based optimizer, vectorized execution* and bucket settings. The provider that enabled most performance improvements in Hive i.e., HDI, got the best results for similar HW. In the case of Spark, the main results all use versions 2.1. The main difference among providers is that GCD has twice the memory per executor, at

Table 1. Most relevant Hadoop-stack configurations for providers

Category	Config	EMR	HDI	GCD
System	OS	Linux AMI 2017.03	Ubuntu 16.04	Debian 8.4
	Java version	OpenJDK 1.8.0_121	OpenJDK 1.8.0_131	OpenJDK 1.8.0_121
HDFS	File system	EBS	WASB	GCS
	Replication	3	3	2
	Block size	128 MB	128 MB	128 MB
	File buffer size	4 KB	128 KB	64 KB
M/R	Output compression	SNAPPY	FALSE	FALSE
	IO Factor/MB	48/200	100/614	10 /100
	Memory MB	1536	1536	3072
Hive	Hive version	2.1	1.2	2.1
	Engine	Tez	Tez	M/R
Spark	Spark version	2.1.0.2.6.0.2-76	2.1	2.1.0
	Driver memory	5G	5G	5G
	Executor memory	4G	5G	10G
	Executor cores	4	3	4
	Executor instances	Dynamic	20	Dynamic
	dynamicAllocation enabled	TRUE	FALSE	TRUE
	Executor memoryOverhead	Default (384 MB)	Default (384 MB)	1,117 MB

10 GB. Another interesting difference is that HDI is still setting the number of executor instances statically, while both EMR and GCD use dynamic allocation. Dynamic allocation is a recent feature that we are exploring on our on-premises cluster currently to quantify the trade offs.

3 Background and Related Work

The motivation behind this work is to expand the cloud provider survey [16] from SQL-only TPC-H using Hive into BigBench. As well as expanding the work to include Spark and update the results to the current versions and larger cluster sizes—from 8 to 16 datanodes. The work is integrated into the ALOJA benchmarking and analysis platform [15,17], which can be used to reproduce the tests and provide access to the raw results from these tests. The ALOJA project is an open initiative from the Barcelona Supercomputing Center (BSC) to explore and automate the characterization of cost-effectiveness for big data deployments. Furthermore, in a previous study with Ivanov et al., in collaboration with the SPEC research group in big data benchmarking [6] led to the generation of a "Big Data Benchmark Compendium" [19], which surveys and classifies the most popular big data benchmarks. This work represents also an expansion of the survey by adding BigBench results for Hive and Spark.

TPCx-BB (BigBench) [5] BigBench is an end-to-end application level bench-mark specification standardized by TPC as TPCx-BB. It is the result of many years of collaboration between industry and academia. Covering most Big Data Analytical properties (3Vs) in 30 business use cases—queries—for a retailer company in the areas of merchandising, pricing optimization, product return, and customers. It is also able to scale the data from 1 GB to petabytes of data. The BigBench v1.2 reference Implementation resulted in:

- 14 declarative queries (SQL): 6, 7, 9, 11, 12, 13, 14, 15, 16, 17, 21, 22, 23, 24.
- 3 with user code (UDF): 1, 29, 30 (also uses M/R).
- 4 Natural Language Processing (NLP) 10, 18, 19, 27.
- 4 with data preprocessing with M/R jobs: 2, 3, 4, 8.
- 5 with Machine Learning jobs: 5, 20, 25, 26, 28.

Apache Hive [8] has become the *de facto* data-warehousing engine on top of Hadoop, providing data summarization, analysis, and most importantly, support for SQL-like queries. The Hive engine can be controlled using HiveQL, an SQL-like language designed to abstract the Map/Reduce (M/R) jobs involved in such queries for analysts. As an example, Hive queries have been gradually replacing the use of M/R in large companies such as Facebook and Yahoo! [24]. In Hive the default engine to manage task executions is Hadoop's M/R. However, in the latest versions Hive added support for different execution engines. Namely Tez [24] (from the Stinger project) is a popular drop-in replacement, which improves on the M/R model to provide lower latency and performance. The Hive configuration employed by the different SUTs is described further in Sect. 2.1. For ML, Hive relied originally on the Mahout library, however, it can also use the MLlib provided by Spark more actively developed as use in the main results of this work.

Apache Spark [25] similar to Hive, Spark is another popular framework gaining momentum [12]. Spark is a processing engine which provided increased performance over the original Map/Reduce by leveraging in-memory computation. Spark was originally created in 2009 by the AMPLab at UC Berkeley and was developed to run independently of Hadoop. The Spark project consists of several integrated components including: the Spark core as general execution engine and APIs, Spark SQL for analyzing structured data, Spark Streaming for analyzing streaming data, MLlib for Machine Learning, and GraphX for graph analytics. During the past year, the Spark API had suffered significant changes and improvements, many in the area of performance. Now stabilizing at v2, and with most cloud providers supporting the current versions, Spark becomes a natural choice as an integrated framework over Hive and Mahout.

3.1 Related Work

Most recent evaluations of Hadoop systems in the cloud are SQL-only [4, 16]. This is the first attempt to measure performance of cloud-based SUTs and make comparisons between the main providers using BigBench, which expands use cases from the SQL-only boundary and includes both Hive and Spark v2 results. There are already several tests of Amazon's EMR services in the literature: Sruthi [23] presents the performance and costs models of EMR (PaaS) vs. AWS (IaaS) using the Intel HiBench [9] benchmark suite, but only includes a minimal Hive-test benchmark based on Pavlo's CALDA [14] benchmark, concluding that PaaS solutions benefit from being provider-optimized. Zhang et al. [26,27] focuses on scheduling of jobs in EMR and on Hadoop configuration using micro-benchmarks similar to our previous work [17]. In Floratou et al. [3] describe the current problems associated with benchmarking SQL-on-Hadoop systems, and advocate the standardization of the process. We believe that BigBench [5] is the current reference benchmark for such systems. Relating to BigBench query results, to day there are only a handful of official submissions are available [20], as well as a few publications with detailed per query characterization [2,12]. More established benchmarks i.e., TPC-H have been thoroughly analyzed, in work including the query their *choke points* as in "TPC-H Analyzed" [1]. It is the intent to provide here a first look into BigBenche's *choke points*. This work expands on the available BigBench results by including Spark v2, along with detailed per query characterization, and cloud data scalability results.

3.2 Legacy Execution Engine and Machine Learning Frameworks

In a previous work [18], we have compared the performance of Hive with M/R vs. Tez as execution engine, as well as Mahout vs. MLlib v1. Figure 1(a) shows preliminary results comparing the Map/Reduce (M/R) execution engine to Tez in Hive at 100 GB. While Fig. 1(b) shows Hive using the Mahout Machine Learning

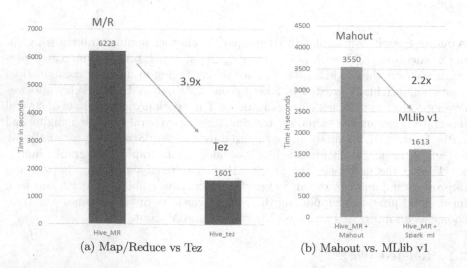

(a) Map/Reduce vs Tez   (b) Mahout vs. MLlib v1

Fig. 1. Comparison of legacy vs. current Hive execution engine and ML library at 100 GB

library vs. the newer MLlib from the Spark package. It can be seen that Tez can be up to 3.9x faster than the classical M/R. For this reason, all of the following tests are done with Tez when possible. Similarly, for Machine Learning, MLlib v1 from the Spark package can be at least twice as fast than the now legacy Mahout framework. For more details refer to [18].

4   Methodology and Query Characterization

The configuration of the tested PaaS services is left as the provider pre-configures them, so that the out-of-the-box performance can be measured without introducing bias towards a provider. This means that the HDFS configuration, default execution engine i.e. M/R or Tez, Hive, and OS are all left unmodified. Our intentions are not to produce the best results for the hardware as in our previous works [15,17], but instead to survey different instance combinations, and test the clusters as the provider intended for general purpose usage. We also expect each provider to optimize to their respective infrastructures, especially to their storage services. Where information i.e., underlying physical hardware, might not be readily available to implement in a custom IaaS fashion. By using defaults, the aim is to provide an indication of experience that an entry-level user might be expected to have on a given system without having to invest in additional fine-tuning. Specific configurations can be found at Sect. 2.1 and at the providers release page for further reference.

As test methodology, the 30 BigBench queries are run sequentially and at least 3 times for each SUT and scale factor, capturing running times. We test each SUT with scale factor 1, 10, 100, 1000 (1 TB), and 10000 (10 TB). The metrics we present are the execution times of each individual query or in together in the concurrency tests. Opposed to the final BigBech queries per minute (BBQpm) metric, only permitted in audited results. The tests were run in June 2017, and the reported pricing and specs correspond to this period. All of the instances are using the on-demand (non-discounted) pricing, which usually is the highest, but simplifies calculations. As a side note, prices should only be regarded as indicative; in [16] we have noted that in a 4-month test period, prices were changed at least 2 times for some providers, while also new versions of the software stack were released.

4.1   Query Characterization

As BigBench is a recent benchmark with constant changes and additions to the implementation, there is still little knowledge about the difference in queries besides the official submitted results [20] and the works of [2,12]. Per query knowledge can be useful to quickly benchmark a new SUT e.g., by *cherry-picking* queries that stresses different resources, or that are the most demanding ones. In this way, a user can perform a *smoke test*, or spot configuration problems more rapidly. Also, this knowledge is useful to validate results, optimize the

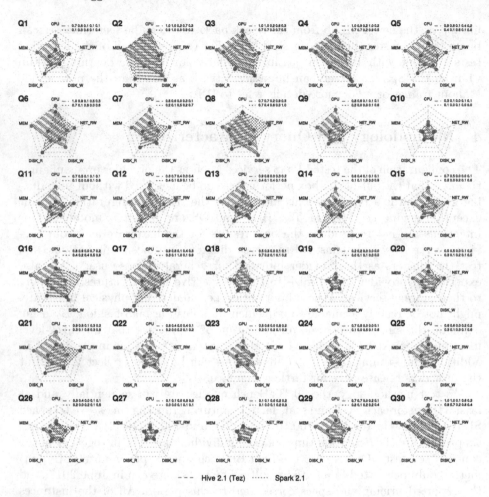

Fig. 2. Per query resource consumption radar chart of BigBench at 1 TB for Hive and Spark. Legend prints CPU, RAM, Disk R/W, and network normalized resource usage respectively. (Color figure online)

current implementation, or when adding new systems as in more established benchmarks [1].

Figure 2 presents a radar chart of the 30 BigBench queries by normalized system resource utilization, comparing Hive and Spark EMR at 1 TB. The system resources requirements represent the query's average utilization so that measurements are not dominated by query times. Results are normalized between 1 (maximum) and 0 (minimum) as they have different units. They include 5 separate metrics including CPU percentage utilization, MEM for main memory (RAM), Disk Read, Disk Write, and Network R/W. The network resource averages the R/W as the traffic is only internal and both values aggregate to the same amount. To obtain these numbers, performance metrics where captured in ALOJA using the *sysstat* package.

The chart can be read as follows: each query, in order is presented in its own subplot; each radar chart has the 5 resource dimensions (read counter-clockwise); the larger the area, the more resources consumed; Hive in red long dashes and Spark in blue short dashes. Additionally, the small legend on the upper left corner prints the values of each resource in order, and we be used to export the results (due to space limitations). The EMR SUT was selected to represent the resource consumption due to GCD using M/R, and as we saw in Sect. 3.2 the performance is not comparable to Tez. HDI was discarded as access to the storage is counted as network traffic, opposed to EMR and GCD. This resulted in the chart representing Hive 2.1 and Spark 2.1, both with MLlib v2.

Figure 2 shows visually the highest resource demanding queries, as well as the similarities and differences between Hive and Spark. The list of query categories can be found in Sect. 3. The queries with the highest resource usage in both systems are the M/R style of queries. Query 2 is the highest for Spark and second for Hive, while Q4 is the highest for Hive and second for Spark. Besides Q2 and Q4, Q30 is the next with highest resource requirements for both systems, while Q30 is in the UDF category, it also makes use of M/R style processing. So in general, the M/R queries need the highest resources and similar behavior in Hive and Spark. In contrast, the queries with the lowest requirements are the Natural Language Processing (NLP) group. They are implemented for both systems using the OpenNLP framework as UDFs.

The SQL-type queries is the second group with the highest requirements for some queries—also the most numerous, so they cover a wide range of values. Query 6 has the highest requirement on Hive—but not in Spark, while Q16 is the highest in Spark and second in Hive. In general, the SQL-type queries are the most dissimilar between Hive and Spark. Hive+Tez in general have a very high CPU requirement, while Spark reads more in average from the disks. This read from disk difference is particularly high for Q14 and Q17, the queries which requires a cross-join which is discussed further on Sect. 5 as limitation in Spark.

4.2 Hive vs. Spark Approaches

Comparing Hive to Spark, their configuration and execution approach in the 3 providers is quite distinct. While Hive and Tez are configured to use many but small containers, Spark is configured the opposite way. Spark favors *fat* containers, fewer containers, but with more CPUs and memory each. While Hive is typically setup in the traditional M/R way of independent and redundant containers, which could be potentially more scalable and fault-tolerant, but also requires higher disk writes as shown in Fig. 2. Tez also has a higher CPU utilization than Spark, which is not using all of the cluster resources when running single queries in the power tests. Spark in general has a higher network usage (shuffling data) and more intensive in disk reads. Surprisingly it uses less memory than Hive, but this is explained as not all of the available containers per node are used in single query runs.

Even though the different configuration approaches, about half of the queries have similar behavior in both systems. These queries being: 2, 4, 3, 10, 18, 19,

20, 22, 25, 26, 27, 28, 29, and 30; while queries 8, 9, 13, 15, 16, 21, 23 share some similarities. As mentioned, the SQL queries are the most differentiated, including queries: 1, 5, 6, 7, 11, 12, 14, 17, 24.

In the ML category, while the query times are significantly different, Hive is also using the MLlib v2 library from Spark. So both systems have very similar resource requirements. The ML query with the highest resource needs is Q5, which performs a logistic regression. Query 5 is analyzed in more detail bellow and the difference between Hive and Spark as seen in the following section.

CPU Utilization for Query 5 at 1 TB Example. Figures 3(a) and (b) shows the average CPU utilization percentage for Hive-on-Tez and Spark respectively

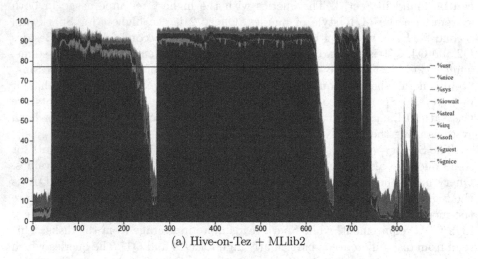

(a) Hive-on-Tez + MLlib2

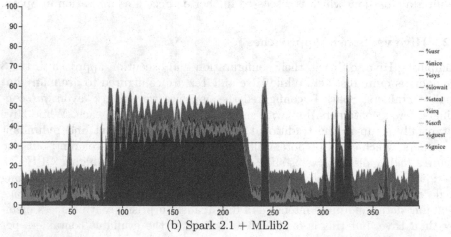

(b) Spark 2.1 + MLlib2

Fig. 3. CPU% utilization over time (s.) comparison for Hive and Spark for query 5 at 1 TB

for query 5 on HDI. Query 5 was chosen as it was found to have the highest resource requirements of the Machine Learning queries. For this query, Spark takes less than half the time as Hive. This is interesting as both are using the exact MLlib v2 library. While Tez is CPU bound in general, we can see that for Spark, the main bottleneck is the I/O wait. Taking a closer look into disk and network utilization, it was found that the I/O wait in Spark is caused by the network, as the disk requirements are much lower than Hive's. For this query, Spark is more optimal on the storage subsystem. While this is an example, we are currently working in more in-depth comparison of the engines and queries. Especially, as lower query times can lead to differentiated resource bottlenecks, i.e., CPU I/O wait.

5   Power Tests from 1 GB to 10 TB

This section presents the execution times of the 3 providers when increasing the data scale factor from 1 GB by factors of ten up to 10 TB. The main comparison is centered at the 1 TB scale, while a brief comparison is made for all the scale factors for all of the queries. Finally, the results at 10 TB for the SQL-queries is presented, and the errors found on the scaling process.

Execution Times at 1 TB. Figure 4 presents the total time for the *power runs* at 1 TB for both Hive and Spark v2 for the different providers in a bar chart. Each bar is subdivided into the different query categories: SQL, M/R, ML, and UDF. The Y-axis shows the number of seconds employed by each section and in total. Results are separated by provider first, EMR, GCD, and HDI; internally by Hive and Spark respectively.

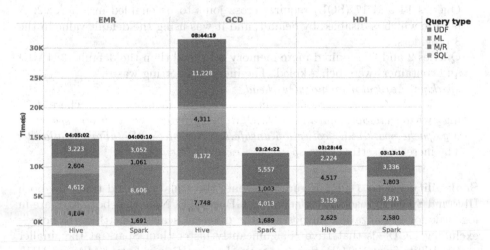

Fig. 4. Execution times for a power test at 1 TB by provider and framework (Hive vs. Spark)

Results show that Spark is slightly faster than Hive in both HDI—which gets the fastest results—and EMR. In GCD, Spark gets the second best result while the Hive results is more than two times the slowest result across providers taking more than 8 h for the full run. The reason for Hive in GCD being at least twice as slow is due to GCD not using Tez as the execution engine, and using the legacy Map/Reduce engine. This result is consistent with previous work [16].

Besides the GCD Hive result, the rest take between 3 and 4 h for the full run. While results look similar, especially when comparing Hive vs. Spark in EMR and HDI, times for the different categories of queries differ significantly. In EMR, only the UDF queries take similar times, while Spark is more than twice as fast in the SQL queries, but almost twice as slow in the M/R ones. For the ML queries, in all providers Spark gets the best times, being at least twice as fast than in Hive. Another result that highlights it the long execution time for the M/R portion in EMR with Spark, taking more than twice the time in the rest of the providers. Having a closer look at the M/R portion, it is query 2 the one that takes most of the time in EMR.

The difference across providers by query type, shows that tuning the configuration from the defaults can lead to significant improvements in execution times. In this case, while HDI gets the best times for both Hive and Spark, the ML queries in EMR with Hive take about half the time, while GCD's ML is the fastest with Spark. In the case of query 2 for EMR, in a later experiment increasing Sparks memory, the resulting times where then similar to both HDI and GCD.

Errors Found During the 1 TB Tests. Up to 1 TB, everything was run with the out-of-the-box configuration in Hive, except for some queries in Spark at 1 TB:

- Queries 14 and 17 (SQL) requires cross joins to be enabled in Spark v2. A feature which is disabled by default, and it was using the default value in the 3 providers.
- Queries 2 and 30 required more memory overhead than the default (384 MB) and containers were being killed. The increased setting was: *spark.yarn.executor.memoryOverhead*.
- Queries 3, 4, and 8 required more executor memory, and where failing with *TimSort java.lang.OutOfMemoryError: Java heap space at org.apache.spark.util. collection.unsafe.sort.UnsafeSortDataFormat.allocate.* The increased setting was: *spark.yarn.executor.memory*.

Scalability up to 1 TB. Figure 5 presents the scalability and times for both Hive and Spark for each provider from 1 GB to 1 TB. Note that both axes are in log scale for visualization purposes of the different scales. One thing to note— excluding GCD—is that Hive is significantly faster than Spark at the smaller scales. While from 100 GB, Spark is very close to Hive in both EMR and HDI. This similarity on results could also mean that a common bottleneck is reached by both frameworks, and it is part of our ongoing study.

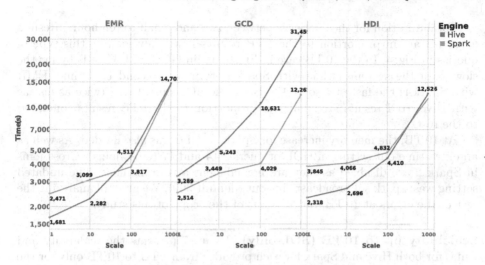

Fig. 5. Scalability from 1 GB to 1 TB for Hive and Spark by provider. Log-log scale.

5.1 Execution Times at 10 TB (SQL-only)

Figure 6 presents the results by query for only the declarative set of the queries—SQL-only—for both Hive and Spark. The reason for presenting the SQL-only queries is due to errors in query execution. While with some trial-and-error tuning we were able to run all of the queries in Hive in HDI and EMR, we were not able with this cluster sizes to run it successfully with Spark v2 across providers and Hive (M/R) in GCD. 10 TB seem to be the limits for the current cluster setup. However, with the SQL-only queries, we can already see some differences from 1 TB and across providers.

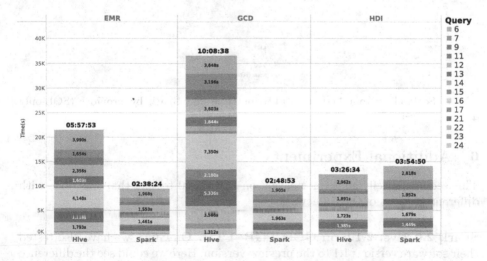

Fig. 6. Execution times of SQL-only queries (14) at 10 TB by provider and framework

Total duration for the queries is between two and a half to ten hours. Results at 10 TB are in proportion to the 1 TB results if we only look at this type of queries in Fig. 4. In the 10 TB case in Fig. 6, again GCD with Hive is by far the slowest of the systems, while with Spark obtains the second best time. EMR with Spark is the fastest also at 10 TB for the SQL only, being twice as fast as with Hive. HDI results are similar in proportion to the 1 TB results compared to the rest.

At 10 TB, the memory increase for Spark at 1 TB was also needed. As well as an extra time out setting in HDI for queries 14 and 17 (cross-joins). Cross joins in Spark 2 are disabled as they are not efficient at the moment. The updated setting was: spark.sql.broadcastTimeout (default 300). We are still analyzing the rest of the errors at 10 TB, but it is out of the scope of this study.

Scalability up to 10 TB (SQL-only). Figure 7 presents the scalability and times for both Hive and Spark for each provider from 1 TB to 10 TB only for the 14 SQL queries. Note that both axes are in log scale for visualization purposes of the different scales. It is interesting to see in the EMR case that Spark is twice as fast than Hive at 1 and 10 TB. While on HDI, they obtain similar results.

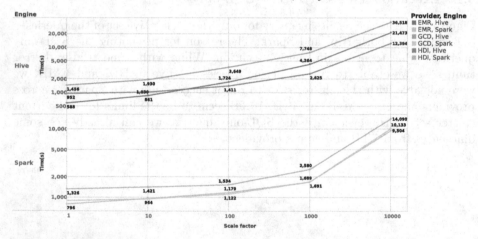

Fig. 7. Scalability from 1 GB to 10 TB for Hive and Spark by provider (SQL-only queries). Log-log scale.

6   Additional Experiments

This sections briefly adds information on additional testing that was done with different versions of the frameworks.

Spark 2.0.2 vs. 2.1.0 on GCD 1 GB–1 TB. On GCD, we have also tested their software versions 1.1 to the preview version. Here we could see the difference of Spark 2.0.2 to Spark 2.1.0 on exactly the same hardware. We found that Spark 2.1 is a bit faster at small scales, but slower at 100 GB and 1 TB specifically on the UDF/NLP queries.

Spark 1.6.3 vs. 2.1.0 MLlib 1 Vs 2.1 MLlib 2 on HDI 1 GB–1 TB. In HDI which uses the HDP distribution we could test Spark version 1.6.3 and Spark 2.1 on exactly the same cluster. We found that Spark 2.1 is always faster than 1.6.3 this case. In the HDI cluster we also compared MLlib v1 to v2. MLib v2 makes use of the newer dataframes API, opposed to RDDs in v1. We found v2 to be only slightly faster than V1.

Throughput Runs. Figure 8 shows the results for Hive and Spark for each provider as the number of concurrent streams (clients) are increased. Streams are increased from 1 (no concurrency) to 32 streams. At 32 streams we can see that the best numbers are obtained by Hive in HDI and EMR. We can also see a great variation of results in HDI with Spark, as with 16 streams is the slowest of the systems, but the fastest at 32 streams. This situation also highlights the variability of cloud results as we have studied previously in [16].

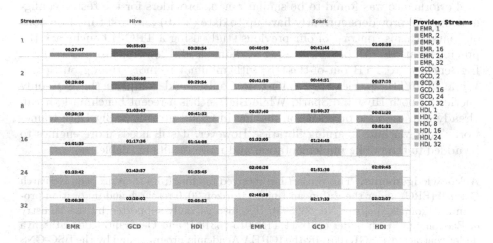

Fig. 8. Throughput runs from 1 to 32 streams at 1 GB scale in Hive and Spark by provider

7 Conclusions

This study presented first a characterization of the resource consumption by each BigBench query. As BigBench is a recent benchmark with constant changes to the implementations, there is still little knowledge about the difference in queries. Such knowledge can be useful to quickly benchmark a new SUT by *cherry-picking* queries that stresses different resources. Also, it is useful to validate results and compare future implementations. In particular, we have found that the M/R type queries utilizes the most resources, with query 2 having the highest utilization of all. For the UDF queries, query 30 is by far the most resource hungry, having the highest network and disk requirements. On the ML queries, query 5 has the highest resource requirements, while query 6 from the SQL-only group.

While Hive-on-Tez in general uses a *thin* container strategy as in classical M/R and Spark uses *fat* containers, results show that more than half of the queries share similar resource requirements. The SQL-only queries were the ones with more differences between the frameworks. On our preliminary tests we have also found that Hive-on-Tez improves the performance up to 4x over Hive-on-MapReduce as used in GCD. Spark MLlib has also improved the performance over the Mahout Machine Learning library, and MLlib v2 over v1 using the dataframes API in a moderate amount. The first BigBench implementation was for both M/R and Mahout can now be considered legacy and should be avoided. Spark 2.1 is faster than previous versions, however, Spark improvements are within the 30% range, and was not found to be as pronounced as in Web articles. Hive-on-Tez (+ MLlib for ML) are still faster than Spark at lower scales, but this difference narrows down at larger scales. We are currently investigating if due to a common hardware bottleneck of framework at scale, but Spark shows improved performance under concurrency.

Performance was found to be similar among providers for the tested configurations. All providers currently have up to date (2.1.0) and well tuned versions of Spark. This is contrast of our previous study using a TPC-H benchmark the previous year [16]. All providers using medium-sized, 128-core clusters could run BigBench up to 1 TB out-of-the-box with minimal memory tuning on Spark. While at 10 TB, queries start failing and only could complete the SQL-only queries for both Hive and Spark. While BigBench is a recent benchmark, it can already help us guide our decision making in Cloud providers, Big Data frameworks, and Machine Learning libraries. However, it still needs more engines to be added to the public implementation and more results available.

Acknowledgements. This project has received funding from the European Research Council (ERC) under the European Unions Horizon 2020 research and innovation programme (grant agreement No. 639595). It is also partially supported by the Ministry of Economy of Spain under contract TIN2015-65316-P and Generalitat de Catalunya under contract 2014SGR1051, by the ICREA Academia program, and by the BSC-CNS Severo Ochoa program (SEV-2015-0493).

References

1. Boncz, P., Neumann, T., Erling, O.: TPC-H analyzed: hidden messages and lessons learned from an influential benchmark. In: Nambiar, R., Poess, M. (eds.) TPCTC 2013. LNCS, vol. 8391, pp. 61–76. Springer, Cham (2014). https://doi.org/10.1007/978-3-319-04936-6_5
2. Cao, P., Gowda, B., Lakshmi, S., Narasimhadevara, C., Nguyen, P., Poelman, J., Poess, M., Rabl, T.: From BigBench to TPCx-BB: standardization of a big data benchmark. In: Nambiar, R., Poess, M. (eds.) TPCTC 2016. LNCS, vol. 10080, pp. 24–44. Springer, Cham (2017). https://doi.org/10.1007/978-3-319-54334-5_3
3. Floratou, A., Özcan, F., Schiefer, B.: Benchmarking SQL-on-Hadoop systems: TPC or Not TPC? In: Rabl, T., Sachs, K., Poess, M., Baru, C., Jacobson, H.-A. (eds.) WBDB 2015. LNCS, vol. 8991, pp. 63–72. Springer, Cham (2015). https://doi.org/10.1007/978-3-319-20233-4_7

4. Floratou, A., Minhas, U.F., Özcan, F.: SQL-on-Hadoop: full circle back to shared-nothing database architectures. In: Proceedings of VLDB Endowment (2014)
5. Ghazal, A., Rabl, T., Hu, M., Raab, F., Poess, M., Crolotte, A., Jacobsen, H.-A.: BigBench: towards an industry standard benchmark for big data analytics. In: Proceedings of the 2013 ACM SIGMOD International Conference on Management of Data, SIGMOD 2013, pp. 1197–1208. ACM, New York (2013)
6. S. R. B. D. W. Group (2016). https://research.spec.org/working-groups/big-data-working-group.html
7. Hortonworks Data Platform (HDP) (2016). http://hortonworks.com/products/hdp/
8. Apache Hive (2016). https://hive.apache.org/
9. Huang, S., et al.: The HiBench benchmark suite: characterization of the MapReduce-based data analysis. In: 22nd International Conference on Data Engineering Workshops (2010)
10. Intel: Big-data-benchmark-for-big-bench (2016). https://github.com/intel-hadoop/Big-Data-Benchmark-for-Big-Bench
11. Ivanov, T.: D2F TPC-H benchmark repository (2016). https://github.com/t-ivanov/d2f-bench
12. Ivanov, T., Beer, M.-G.: Performance evaluation of spark SQL using BigBench. In: Rabl, T., Nambiar, R., Baru, C., Bhandarkar, M., Poess, M., Pyne, S. (eds.) WBDB -2015. LNCS, vol. 10044, pp. 96–116. Springer, Cham (2016). https://doi.org/10.1007/978-3-319-49748-8_6
13. Gualtieri, M., Yuhanna, N.: Elasticity, automation, and pay-as-you-go compel enterprise adoption of hadoop in the cloud. The Forrester Wave: Big Data Hadoop Cloud Solutions, Q2 2016
14. Pavlo, A., Paulson, E., Rasin, A., Abadi, D.J., DeWitt, D.J., Madden, S., Stonebraker, M.: A comparison of approaches to large-scale data analysis. In: SIGMOD, pp. 165–178 (2009)
15. Poggi, N., Berral, J.L., Carrera, D., Vujic, N., Green, D., Blakeley, J., et al.: From performance profiling to predictive analytics while evaluating hadoop cost-efficiency in ALOJA. In: 2015 IEEE International Conference on Big Data (Big Data) (2015)
16. Poggi, N., Berral, J.L., Fenech, T., Carrera, D., Blakeley, J., Minhas, U.F., Vujic, N.: The state of SQL-on-Hadoop in the cloud. In: 2016 IEEE International Conference on Big Data (Big Data), pp. 1432–1443, December 2016
17. Poggi, N., Carrera, D., Vujic, N., Blakeley, J., et al.: ALOJA: A systematic study of hadoop deployment variables to enable automated characterization of cost-effectiveness. In: 2014 IEEE International Conference on Big Data (Big Data), Washington, DC, USA, 27–30 October 2014
18. Poggi, N., Montero, A.: Using BigBench to compare hive and spark versions and features
19. Ivanov, T., Rabl, T., Poess, M., Queralt, A., Poelman, J., Poggi, N., Buell, J.: Big data benchmark compendium. In: Nambiar, R., Poess, M. (eds.) TPCTC 2015. LNCS, vol. 9508, pp. 135–155. Springer, Cham (2016). https://doi.org/10.1007/978-3-319-31409-9_9
20. TPC: TPCx BB official submissions (2016). http://www.tpc.org/tpcx-bb/results/tpcxbb_perf_results.asp
21. Transaction Processing Performance Council: TPC Benchmark H - Standard Specification, Version 2.17.1 (2014)
22. Transaction Processing Performance Council: TPC Benchmark DS - Standard Specification, Version 1.3.1 (2015)

23. Vijayakumar, S.: Hadoop based data intensive computation on IAAS cloud platforms. UNF Theses and Dissertations, page Paper 567 (2015)
24. T. Yahoo Betting on Apache Hive and YARN (2014). https://yahoodevelopers.tumblr.com/post/85930551108/yahoo-betting-on-apache-hive-tez-and-yarn
25. Zaharia, M., Xin, R.S., Wendell, P., Das, T., Armbrust, M., Dave, A., Meng, X., Rosen, J., Venkataraman, S., Franklin, M.J., Ghodsi, A., Gonzalez, J., Shenker, S., Stoica, I.: Apache spark: a unified engine for big data processing. Commun. ACM **59**(11), 56–65 (2016)
26. Zhang, Z., Cherkasova, L., Loo, B.T.: Exploiting cloud heterogeneity for optimized cost/performance mapreduce processing. In: CloudDP 2014
27. Zhang, Z., et al.: Optimizing cost and performance trade-offs for MapReduce job processing in the cloud. In: NOMS 2014

Performance Characterization of Big Data Systems with TPC Express Benchmark HS

Manan Trivedi[✉]

Cisco Systems, Inc., 275 East Tasman Drive, San Jose, CA 95134, USA
matrived@cisco.com

Abstract. TPC Express Benchmark HS (TPCx-HS) is industry's first standard for benchmarking big data systems. There are many moving parts in a large big data deployment which includes compute, storage, memory and network collectively called the infrastructure, platform and application and in this paper, we characterize in detail how each of these components affect performance.

Keywords: Industry standards · Performance · Hadoop · Spark

1 Introduction

Performance is key to any application and more so to a big data deployment as it usually involves hundreds and thousands of nodes for both data storage and processing. This paper goes in to the detail on various bottlenecks to performance at each level and to what extent one could improve the performance by overcoming these bottle necks. Even a small percentage gain in performance can be a lot of capex reduction in a large deployment as fewer nodes can take on more tasks. The focus of this paper is on Hadoop performance characterization and goes into details of tuning and consideration of the storage – with Solid State Disks (SSD) and Hard Disk Drive (HDD), Networking - with 10 Gbit and 40 Gbit, application - Spark and MapReduce.

1.1 Hadoop Evolution

Apache Hadoop is a software framework used for distributed storage and processing of big data. The two main components of Apache Hadoop are the Hadoop Distributed File System (HDFS), and the MapReduce framework. HDFS implements a fault-tolerant distributed file system. MapReduce is a framework for the parallel processing of data stored in HDFS. The MapReduce architecture divides the task into many smaller jobs. The code for each of these jobs is pushed to each server where the data resides. The framework executes the code on each server in parallel; intermediate results are returned, then combined for the final result.

The first version of the MapReduce framework, MRv1, implemented an architecture that handled both the processing of jobs and the resource management across the cluster. This approach had a number of limitations:

- Single point of failure: If the server coordinating all the tasks, called the NameNode, fails, then all processing fails.

© Springer International Publishing AG 2018
R. Nambiar and M. Poess (Eds.): TPCTC 2017, LNCS 10661, pp. 75–92, 2018.
https://doi.org/10.1007/978-3-319-72401-0_6

- Scalability: The architecture is limited to approximately 4000 nodes.
- Lock-in: MRv1 requires the use of MapReduce, which is not the optimal choice for many workloads.

To address these limitations the open source community developed another approach to handle job processing and cluster management called MRv2 (also known as YARN). In MRv2, the responsibilities are handled by separate components. This addresses the issues of a single point of failure and scalability while also opening the framework to run other programming models besides MapReduce. This allows multiple applications to be run on the same cluster at the same time. YARN can assign and reassign resources for different concurrent applications to allow better utilization of the cluster's resources (Fig. 1).

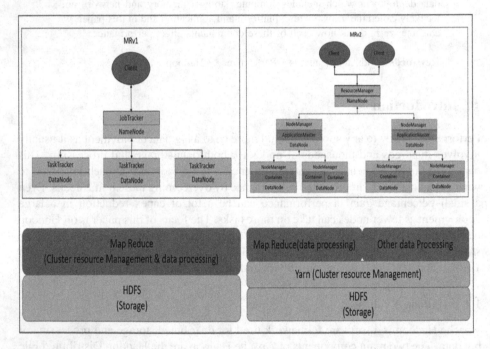

Fig. 1. MRv1 and MRv2 architecture

The ability to run new programming models on the cluster opens the door to address the issues with MapReduce. Parallel data processing as implemented by Apache Hadoop executes map and reduce phases that output intermediate data sets that are themselves input to the next map and reduce phase. There can be many such phases and MapReduce's key constraint is that it writes the intermediate data sets out to the disk, and then reads from the disk for the next phase. As such, MapReduce's speed is governed by the I/O bandwidth of the storage system.

To overcome the disk, I/O constraint of MapReduce the open source community developed Apache Spark. Apache Spark addresses the issue by reading the data into memory, storing and transforming it there before producing the final result. As the majority of operations are performed in memory at electronic speeds the system executes much faster. In addition, Apache Spark provides a rich set of functionality for in-memory processing that is both fault-tolerant and easier to program than MapReduce. It's in-memory approach enables applications for real-time processing of streaming data and interactive analysis.

Another solution to the disk I/O constraint issue comes from improvements in storage technology that have made SSDs a viable choice for data storage in big data systems. SSDs enable much faster read and write access as they do not have the same physical limitations of spinning disks and moving heads that hard disk drives have. Finally, advances in network technology have created faster throughput speeds which also benefit big data systems.

2   Introduction to TPCx-HS Benchmark

TPCx-HS is the industry's first standard for benchmarking big data systems [1–3]. It is designed to provide verifiable performance, price-to-performance, and availability metrics for hardware and software systems that use big data.

TPCx-HS can be used to assess a broad range of system topologies and implementation methodologies for Hadoop in a technically rigorous and directly comparable, vendor-neutral manner [5]. While the modeling is based on a simple application, the results are highly relevant to big data hardware and software systems.

TPCx-HS benchmarking has three steps:

- HSGen: Generates data and retains it on a durable medium with three-way replication
- HSSort: Samples the input data, sorts the data, and retains the data on a durable medium with three-way replication
- HSValidate: Verifies the cardinality, size, and replication factor of the generated data

The TPCx-HS specification mandates two consecutive runs to demonstrate repeatability, as depicted in Fig. 2, and the lower value is used for reporting.

TPCx-HS uses three main metrics:

- HSph@SF: Composite performance metric, reflecting TPCx-HS throughput, where SF is the scale factor
- $/HSph@SF: Price-to-performance metric
- System availability date

TPCx-HS also reports the following numerical quantities:

- TG. Data generation phase completion time, with HSGen reported in hh:mm:ss format
- TS: Data sort phase completion time, with HSSort reported in hh:mm:ss format
- TV: Data validation phase completion time, reported in hh:mm:ss format

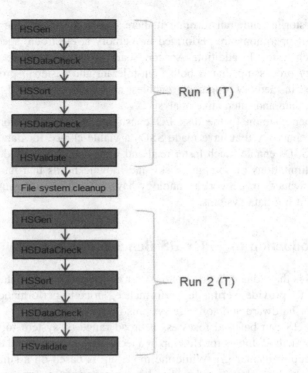

Fig. 2. TPCx-HS Benchmark processing

The primary performance metric of the benchmark is HSph@SF, the effective sort throughput of the benchmarked configuration. Here is an example (using the summation method):

$$HSph@SF = \left\lfloor \frac{SF}{(T/3600)} \right\rfloor$$

Here, SF is the scale factor, and T is the total elapsed time for the run-in seconds. The price-to-performance metric for the benchmark is defined as follows:

$$\$/HSph@SF = \frac{P}{HSph@SF}$$

Here, P is the total cost of ownership (TCO) of the system under test (SUT).

The system availability date indicates when the system under test is generally available as defined in the TPC-Pricing specification.

3 Performance Characterization

The tests were conducted a series of TPCx-HS to characterize the performance in various deployment scenarios. The test configuration consisted of Cisco UCS Integrated Infrastructure for Big Data cluster with 17 Cisco UCS C240 M4 Rack Servers. The Cisco UCS Integrated Infrastructure for Big Data is built using the following components:

- Cisco UCS 6300 Series Fabric Interconnect, provide high-bandwidth, low-latency connectivity for servers, with Cisco UCS Manager providing integrated, unified management for all connected devices. The Cisco UCS 6300 Series Fabric Interconnects are a core part of Cisco UCS, providing low-latency, lossless 40 GB Ethernet, Fibre Channel over Ethernet (FCoE), and Fibre Channel functions with management capabilities for systems deployed in redundant pairs. Cisco Fabric Interconnects offer the full active-active redundancy, performance, and exceptional scalability needed to support the large number of nodes that are typical in clusters serving big data applications.
- Cisco UCS C240 M4 Rack Server: Cisco UCS C-Series Rack Servers extend Cisco UCS in standard rack-mount form factors. The Cisco UCS C240 M4 Rack Server is designed to support a wide range of computing, I/O, and storage capacity demands in a compact design. It supports two Intel® Xeon® processor E5-2600 v4 series CPUs, up to 1.5 TB of memory, and 24 small-form-factor (SFF) disk drives plus two internal SATA boot drives and Cisco UCS Virtual Interface Card (VIC) 1387 adapters.

The Cisco UCS Integrated Infrastructure for Big Data cluster configuration consists of two Cisco UCS 6332 fabric interconnects, 17 Cisco UCS C240 M4 servers with two Intel Xeon processor E5-2680 v4 series CPUs, 256 GB of memory, and 24 SFF disk drives or 8 SFF 1.6 TB SATA SSD plus two internal SATA boot drives and Cisco UCS VIC 1387 adapters, as shown in Fig. 3. Table 1 lists the software versions used.

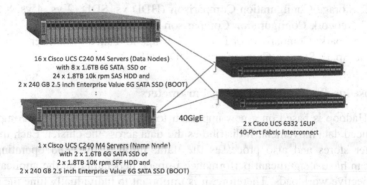

Fig. 3. Cisco UCS integrated infrastructure for big data cluster configuration

Table 1. Software versions

Layer	Component	Version or Release
Computing	Cisco UCS C240 M4 server	C240M4.2.0.13d.0.0812161132
Network	Cisco UCS 6332 fabric interconnect	3.1 (2b)
	Cisco UCS VIC 1387 firmware	4.1 (2d)
	Cisco UCS VIC 1387 driver	2.3.0.31
Software	Red Hat Enterprise Linux (RHEL) server	7.2 (x86_64)
	Cisco UCS Manager	3.1 (2b)
Hadoop	Cloudera Enterprise	Version 5.10.0

3.1   Cisco UCS Integrated Infrastructure for Big Data Cluster Configuration

- 16 × Cisco UCS C240 M4 Servers (Data Nodes) with:
- 8 × 1.6-TB 6-Gbps SATA SSD or
- 24 × 1.8-TB/1.2 TB 12-Gbps SAS 10 K-rpm SFF HDD
- 2 × 240-GB 2.5–in. Enterprise Value 6-Gbps SATA SSD (Boot)
- 2 × 40 Gigabit Ethernet
- 2 × Cisco UCS 6332 fabric interconnect
- 1 × Cisco Nexus® 9372PX Switch

4   Hardware and Software: Performance Characterization

In the following section, we will do an in-depth performance analysis with various permutations of these hardware and software constituents:

- Baseline Performance Tuning parameters (Infrastructure and Operating System)
- Performance tuning parameters of MRv2
- Performance characteristics comparison of MRv1 vs. MRv2
- MRv2 Storage Configuration Comparison (HDD vs. SDD, 2 vs. 4 vs. 8 SSD)
- MRv2 Network Configuration Comparison (10 g vs. 40 g)
- Apache Spark: Comparison of Default Settings to Tuned Parameters
- Apache Spark Storage Comparison: HDD vs. SSD

4.1   Baseline Performance Tuning Parameters

Apache Hadoop is based on a new approach to storing and processing complex data, with reduced data movement. It distributes the data across the cluster. Each machine in the cluster stores and also processes the data. Infrastructure and operating system tunings can have a significant performance impact, depending on the applications and their respective workloads. Therefore, it is important to individually tune the compute, network and storage parameters of the system to achieve optimal performance for the cluster.

Hadoop is a complex application designed to address many different types of workloads. Very often, the default settings are not optimized for the best performance, instead being defined to work out of the box on the minimum hardware required. Tuning the Hadoop settings can produce significant performance improvements [4].

The key areas for Hadoop performance tuning are: infrastructure (compute, network and storage), operating systems and Hadoop parameters. These parameters are covered in-depth in a previous paper I wrote titled "Performance Evaluation and Benchmarking" as part of Springer's Lecture Notes in Computer Science Series.

The focus of this paper is to study the MRv2 architecture and compare its performance to MRv1. We will use the MRv1 performance tuning and results from our earlier study published under: "Lessons Learned: Performance Tuning for Hadoop Systems."[1]

4.2 Apache Hadoop MRv2 Tuning

The default Apache Hadoop MRv2 settings are not optimized for performance. Instead, they are defined so the system works out of the box with the minimum hardware requirement. HDFS provides storage for all the data and is a core component of Apache Hadoop. Fine-tuning the settings here can produce significant performance improvements. The settings discussed in this section have been tested and will provide improved speed for heavy workloads. Here are the tuning parameters which we used to tune the cluster for MRv2.

The following are the parameters and tuned values for the test cases run in this paper (Tables 2 and 3).

- hdfs-site.xml
- mapred-site.xml

Table 2. hdfs-site.xml settings

Parameter	Value
dfs.blocksize	1 GB
dfs.datanode.failed.volumes.tolerated	4
dfs.datanode.handler.count	40
dfs.datanode.max.xcievers, dfs.datanode.max.transfer.threads	32000
dfs.namenode.handler.count	1400
dfs.namenode.service.handler.count	55
dfs.namenode.servicerpc-address	8022
Java Heap Size of NameNode in Bytes	16 GB
Java Heap Size of Secondary NameNode in Bytes	16 GB

---

[1] **Note:** These settings represent a starting point for tuning a big data system. The actual best values will vary based on the workload of the system.

Table 3. mapred-site.xml settings

Parameter	Value
Mapreduce.client.submit.file.replication	3
yarn.app.mapreduce.am.command-opts	-Djava.net.preferIPv4Stack=TRUE -Xmx2800m
io.file.buffer.size	128 KB
mapreduce.job.reduce.slowstart.completedmaps	0.85
mapreduce.job.reduces	895
mapreduce.task.timeout	3 min
mapreduce.map.java.opts	-Djava.net.preferIPv4Stack=true -XX:+UseParallelGC -XX:ParallelGCThreads=8 -XX:-UseAdaptiveSizePolicy -XX:+DisableExplicitGC
mapreduce.reduce.java.opts	−Djava.net.preferIPv4Stack=true -XX:+UseParallelGC -XX:ParallelGCThreads=8 -XX:-UseAdaptiveSizePolicy -XX:+DisableExplicitGC
mapreduce.task.io.sort.factor	100
mapreduce.task.io.sort.mb	1500 MB
mapreduce.reduce.shuffle.parallelcopies	30
yarn.nodemanager.heartbeat.interval-ms, yarn.resourcemanager.nodemanagers.heartbeat-interval-ms	160 ms
yarn.scheduler.fair.preemption	Resource Manager Default Group
zlib.compress.level	BEST_SPEED
yarn.app.mapreduce.am.resource.mb	3 GB
ApplicationMaster Java Maximum Heap Size	1 GB
mapreduce.map.memory.mb	2500 MB
mapreduce.reduce.memory.mb	3 GB
mapreduce.map.java.opts.max.heap	2300 MB
mapreduce.reduce.java.opts.max.heap	2800 MB
yarn.nodemanager.resource.memory-mb	246 GB
yarn.nodemanager.resource.cpu-vcores	56
yarn.scheduler.maximum-allocation-mb	246 GB
yarn.scheduler.maximum-allocation-vcores	56

4.3   MRv1 vs MRv2 (YARN)

MRv1, the first version of the Apache Hadoop framework makes use of a job tracker that creates a set of map and reduce tasks which are then managed by the appropriate task trackers on each node.

The next version of the MapReduce framework, MRv2, introduces YARN (Yet Another Resource Negotiator). YARN separates cluster resource management and MapReduce specific logic. The Resource Manager tracks and allocates available resources and an Application Master process is created for each application which is responsible for the entire life cycle of the MapReduce application.

To understand MRv2 performance compared to MRv1 we did an in-depth study of the performance of both frameworks by running a TPCx-HS benchmark. This led to the following observations:

- Overall, in terms of total time taken, MRv1 performed faster than MRv2.
- While MRV2 was faster in HSSort phase, and MRv1 was faster in the HSGen and HSValidate phases.

The test results here show the comparison of MRv1 vs. MRv2 at a 3-TB scale factor.

Result: MRv1 vs MRv2 (YARN).

This observed performance penalty is offset by the numerous benefits of the MRv2 framework in terms of scalability, fault-tolerance and support for simultaneously running multiple applications. The results in Table 4 show that MRv1 is performing 6% better than MRv2.

These results are based on one set of tuning parameters. These parameters will vary from workload to workload.

Cluster Detail: 16 data nodes each containing 8×1.6 TB Intel SSDs and 2×40 G Network connectivity (Fig. 4).

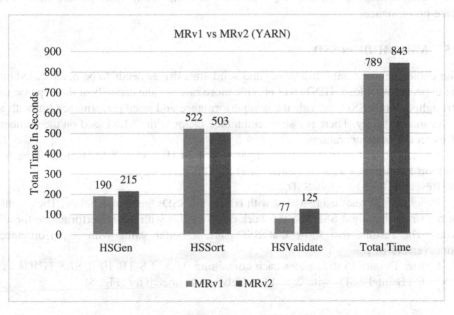

Fig. 4. MRv1 vs MRv2 (YARN)

Table 4 lists detailed response times for each benchmark phase.

Table 4. MRv1 vs MRv2 (YARN)

Phase	MRv1	MRv2
HSGen	190	215
HSSort	522	503
HSValidate	77	125
Total time	789	843
HSph@SF at 3-TB scale factor	13.52	12.71

4.4   MRv2 Storage Configuration Comparison

Apache Hadoop solves the big data problem by breaking the data up into smaller chunks and storing them across many servers. The processors of each of these individual servers are then used to operate on their locally stored data. This use of many smaller servers with direct attached storage is a key reason Apache Hadoop scales in such a linear fashion.

The use of this architecture means that the I/O bandwidth, i.e. how fast we can read and write data, is the key constraint for the system. Recent advances in storage technology have made solid state disks (SSDs) a viable choice for big data systems. However, the performance gains from using SSDs are so dramatic that they exceed the total available bandwidth of the internal throughput of the system. As a result, when comparing SSDs to HDDs, we have to look at both raw performance and price-performance.

4.5   MRv2 HDD vs SSD

The choice between hard disk drives and solid-state drives needs to be made based on the expected workload. HDDs will provide more raw storage capacity at the expense of throughput while SSDs provide the best performance and price-performance but with a lower total capacity. There is also an endurance factor with SSDs based on the number of expected write operations.

The test results here show the comparison of 24 HDDs vs. 8 SSDs using Apache Hadoop MapReduce version 2 (MRv2) at a 3-TB scale factor.

Result: MRv2 HDD vs SSD.

Results of the tests using MRv2 with HDDs vs. SSDs are shown below. The results demonstrate that eight SSDs do the work of 24 HDDs with better performance for all tasks. The results also show that SSDs are a better value with a performance improvement of 2%

Cluster Detail: 16 data nodes each containing 24 × 1.8 TB 10 K SAS HDDs vs. 8 × 1.6 TB Intel SSDs with 2 × 40 G Network connectivity (Fig. 5).

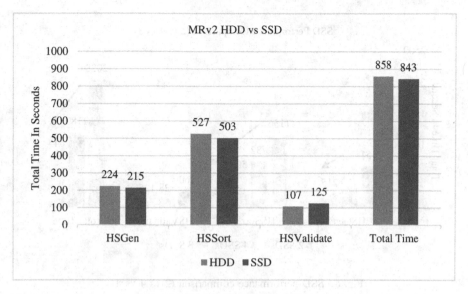

Fig. 5. MRv2 HDD vs SSD

Table 5 lists detailed response times for each benchmark phase.

Table 5. MRv2 HDD vs SSF

Phase	HDD (1.8 TB)	SSD (1.6 TB)
HSGen	224	215
HSSort	527	503
HSValidate	107	125
Total time	858	843
HSph@SF at 3-TB scale factor	12.47	12.71

4.6   SSD Performance Comparison (2 vs 4 vs 8)

One of the key advantages of Apache Hadoop is that it scales linearly with the more data nodes and more data disk drives.

This test compares the performance of 2 vs 4 vs 8 SSDs in each server, using Apache Hadoop MapReduce version 2 (MRv2) at a 3-TB scale factor.

Result: SSD Performance Comparison (2 vs 4 vs 8).

Results of the tests using MRv2 with 2 vs 4 vs 8 SSDs are shown below. The results demonstrate the linear scaling of performance using 8 SSDs. As shown in Fig. 6, on an individual server basis, Apache Hadoop performance improves with the number of drives per node.

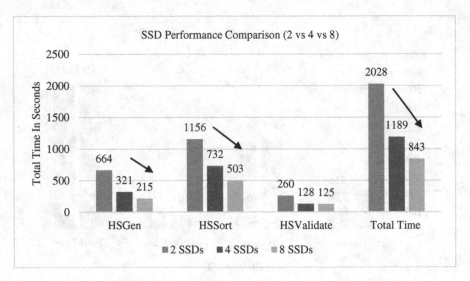

Fig. 6. SSD performance comparison (2 vs 4 vs 8)

Cluster Detail: 16 data nodes each containing 2, 4 and 8 × 1.6 TB Intel SSDs and 2 × 40G Network connectivity.

Table 6 lists detailed response times for each benchmark phase.

Table 6. SSD performance comparison (2 vs 4 vs 8)

Phase	2 SSDs	4 SSDs	8 SSDs
HSGen	664	321	215
HSSort	1156	732	503
HSValidate	260	128	125
Total time	2028	1189	843
HSph@SF at 3-TB scale factor	5.32	9.08	12.71

Test Result: End-to-End Write I/O Bandwidth Utilization.

TPCx-HS enables fair comparisons to be made between software and hardware systems. It also exercises various subsystems. Figure 7 shows disk write IO bandwidth utilization for 2, 4 and 8 SSDs using one of the node's end-to-end run. As we are seeing in the chart below 8 drives are performing 3 times faster than 2 drives. We are seeing it scaling linearly as the number of the SSDs increase.

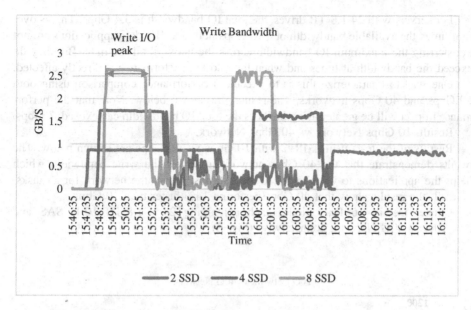

Fig. 7. End-to-End Write I/O bandwidth utilization comparison (2 vs 4 vs 8)

5 MRv2 Network Configuration Comparison

The impact of the network on big data systems is enormous. An efficient and resilient network is a crucial part of a good Apache Hadoop cluster because the network is what connects all the nodes. The network is used to load the data, read the data, and write the intermediate data sets and final output.

The impact of the failure of a network device is dire. Individual jobs and even entire applications may need to be restarted with the workloads pushed to remaining available nodes. The network must be well designed with fault-tolerance, redundancy and multiple paths between computing nodes. It must also be able to scale with the data.

The network can quickly become the constraining factor, and this is becoming more common as technologies like Apache Spark and SSDs proliferate. In response to this, faster networks have been developed. The current generation of 40G networks are aimed squarely at big data systems with local storage using SSDs or high throughput HDDs. Upgrading to the latest generation of Cisco UCS fabric interconnects, we increased the underlying fabric from 10 Gbps to 40 Gbps.

5.1 10G Network vs. 40G Network

Comparing network bandwidth to IO bandwidth can be confusing as networks are commonly measured in bits per second while IO bandwidth is measured in bytes per second. Converting the network measurements to bytes:

- Standard 10 Gbps networks = 1.25 Gbps
- New 40 Gbps networks = 5 Gbps

For servers with 24 1.8 TB drives, the total IO bandwidth is 5.4 Gbps. This is over four times the available bandwidth of a 10 Gbps network. Big data applications are not transferring the maximum IO bandwidth across the network all the time. But they do exceed the bandwidth at times and when they do the performance is directly affected.

One way to characterize this is to execute a performance comparison using both 10 Gbps and 40 Gbps networks. The results are shown below. Note that the performance impact will be greater using SSDs as the total IO bandwidth can exceed 7 Gbps.

Result: 10 Gbps Network vs 40 Gbps Network.

Results of the tests using MRv2 with 10 Gbps vs. 40 Gbps are shown below. The results demonstrate that the 40 Gbps network improves the write bandwidth which helps the applications to write and read the data faster over the network for all tasks. Overall, the results show that 40 Gbps performs 14% faster than 10 Gbps.

Cluster Detail: 16 Data Nodes each containing 24 × 1.8 TB 10 K SAS and 2 × 10G vs 40G Network connectivity (Fig. 8).

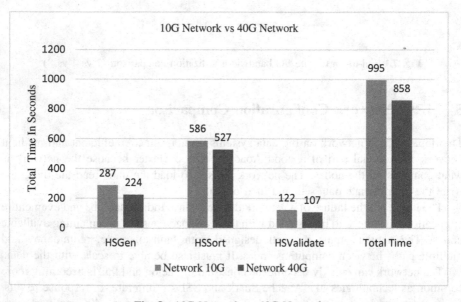

Fig. 8. 10G Network vs 40G Network

Table 7 lists detailed response times for each benchmark phase.

Table 7. 10G Network vs 40G Network

Phase	10G Network	40G Network
HSGen	287	224
HSSort	586	527
HSValidate	122	107
Total time	995	858
HSph@SF at 3-TB scale factor	10.85	12.47

6 Apache Spark

While MapReduce has become a standard for batch processing, Apache Spark is a better choice for real-time data processing and interactive analysis. Apache Spark was developed to overcome the disk I/O constraint of MapReduce. The model for processing distributed data in parallel uses many cycles of first mapping the data, then reducing it. Each of these cycles produces an intermediate output which is input to the next. MapReduce writes these intermediate sets of output to disk, which is then read from disk as input to the next cycle. Thus, the overall performance is gated by the relatively slow speed of disk I/O. Apache Spark addresses this disk I/O bottleneck by reading the data into memory and then performing all data operations in memory, eliminating the disk I/O constraint.

6.1 Apache Spark Tuning

Out of the box, Apache Spark is not optimized for performance. Instead, the default parameters are designed to work without modification on the minimum hardware requirements.

Tuning the parameter can yield significant performance improvements. The tuning parameters discussed in this section provide a guideline towards improved performance for real-time data processing workloads.

Table 8 is the list of Spark parameters which are tuned across the different test cases covered in this section.

Table 8. List of Spark tuning parameters

Parameter	Value
spark.shuffle.compress	true
spark.broadcast.compress	true
spark.io.compression.codec	org.apache.spark.io.SnappyCompressionCodec
spark.shuffle.spill.compress	true
spark.kryo. referenceTracking	false
spark.executor. extraJavaOptions	-XX:+PrintFlagsFinal -XX:+PrintReferenceGC -verbose:gc -XX:+PrintGCDetails -XX:+PrintGCTimeStamps -XX:+PrintAdaptiveSizePolicy -XX:+UnlockDiagnosticVMOptions -XX:+G1SummarizeConcMark
spark.shuffle.spillAfterRead	true
spark.kryoserializer.buffer	2000
spark.default.parallelism	2110

6.2 Comparison of Default Settings to Tuned Parameters

An interesting starting point is a comparison of out of the box performance vs performance with parameters tuned specifically for the System Under Test (SUT).

Result: Default Settings vs Tuned Parameters.

As a part of this experiment, we tuned the Spark for running the TPCx-HS benchmark on the cluster with below details.

Observation: Spark, with our tuned parameters performed significantly better: 63% performance improvement over default settings. Note that Apache Spark performs better when all the data fits in the memory, so with this cluster configuration, the 1 TB scale factor test performs better than 3 TB scale factor.

Although, in-memory processing provides significant advantages, it also adds an extra layer of consideration when tuning the system. The results below are based on one set of tuning parameters. The tunings will vary from workload to workload.

Cluster Detail: 16 Data Nodes each containing 8 × 1.6 TB Intel SSDs and 2 × 40G Network connectivity in both test scenarios (Fig. 9).

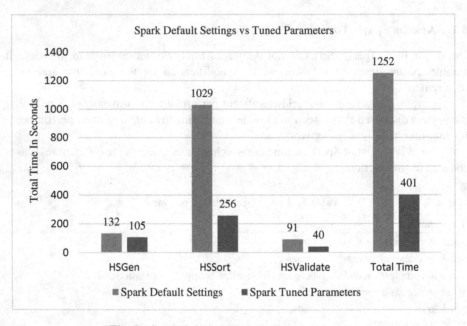

Fig. 9. Spark default settings vs Tuned parameters

Table 9 lists detailed response times for each benchmark phase

Table 9. Spark default settings vs. Tuned parameters

Phase	Spark default	Spark tuned
HSGen	132	105
HSSort	1029	256
HSValidate	91	40
Total time	1252	401
HSph@SF at 1-TB scale factor	2.85	8.97

Note: Spark test was performed with 1 TB scale factor using TPCx-HS

6.3 Apache Spark Storage Comparison: HDD vs SSD

Apache Spark reads the data into memory and processes is it there. This initial read of the data is constrained by disk I/O. However, if instead of HDDs you use SSDs you can further improve performance. But, by how much? Answering this question helps to understand if the additional cost of SSDs is worth it.

Further, if there is more data than will fit in memory, or the intermediate result sets exceed the amount of available memory, Apache Spark will "spill" the data to disk (conceptually equivalent to operating system "swapping"). When this happens, disk I/O as a constraint re-enters the performance equation.

Result: Spark HDD vs SSD

We have done a study of the performance comparison between HDDs and SSDs using Apache Spark by running the TPCx-HS benchmark on the test setup described below. This led to the following observation:

The observed performance shows that SSDs performed better with Spark than HDDs. Spark's processing engine is designed to use both in-memory and on-disk, so it performs operations when data does not fit in memory. This is where the high I/O performance of SSDs overcomes the slower read and write access of HDDs and Spark's performance is improved. As a result, with larger data sizes or scale factors SSDs performance will be better than HDDs.

Cluster Detail: 16 data nodes each containing 24 × 1.8 TB 10 K SAS HDDs vs. 8 × 1.6 TB Intel SSDs with 2 × 40G Network connectivity (Fig. 10).

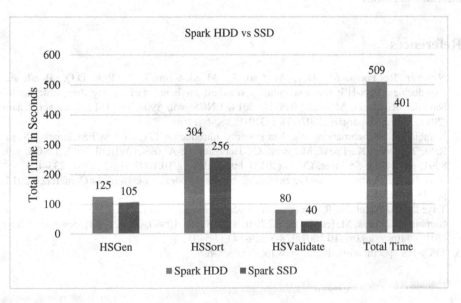

Fig. 10. Spark HDD vs SSD

Table 10 lists detailed response times for each benchmark phase.

Table 10. Spark HDD vs SSD

Phase	Spark HDD	Spark SSD
HSGen	125	105
HSSort	304	256
HSValidate	80	40
Total time	509	401
HSph@SF at 1-TB scale factor	7.07	8.97

Note: Test was performed with 1 TB scale factor using
TPCx-HS.

7 Conclusion

This paper provides a summary of lessons learned from performance tuning for the
TPCx-HS benchmark. The tuning parameters and test results have broad applicability
across Hadoop-based applications. In general, we clearly see improvements in performance as the technology advances to address the limitations of the previous generation. This paper quantifies those improvements providing the data needed to make
informed decisions.

References

1. Nambiar, R., Poess, M., Dey, A., Cao, P., Magdon-Ismail, T., Ren, D.Q., Bond, A.:
   Introducing TPCx-HS: the first industry standard for benchmarking big data systems. In:
   Nambiar, R., Poess, M. (eds.) TPCTC 2014. LNCS, vol. 8904, pp. 1–12. Springer, Cham
   (2015). https://doi.org/10.1007/978-3-319-15350-6_1
2. Nambiar, R.: Benchmarking big data systems: introducing TPC express benchmark HS. In:
   Rabl, T., Sachs, K., Poess, M., Baru, C., Jacobson, H.-A. (eds.) WBDB 2015. LNCS, vol.
   8991, pp. 24–28. Springer, Cham (2015). https://doi.org/10.1007/978-3-319-20233-4_3
3. Nambiar, R.: A standard for benchmarking big data systems. In: BigData Conference 2014,
   pp. 18–20 (2014)
4. Trivedi, M., Nambiar, R.: Lessons learned: performance tuning for hadoop systems. In:
   Nambiar, R., Poess, M. (eds.) TPCTC 2016. LNCS, vol. 10080, pp. 121–141. Springer, Cham
   (2017). https://doi.org/10.1007/978-3-319-54334-5_9
5. TPCx-HS specification. http://www.tpc.org/tpcx-hs/

Experiences and Lessons in Practice Using TPCx-BB Benchmarks

Kebing Wang[1](✉), Bianny Bian[1](✉), Paul Cao[2](✉), and Mike Riess[1](✉)

[1] Intel Corporation, Zizhu Science Park, Shanghai 200241, China
{kebing.wang,bianny.bian,mike.riess}@intel.com
[2] Hewlett Packard Enterprise,
11445 Compaq Center W Dr, Houston, TX 77070, USA
paul.cao@hpe.com

Abstract. The TPCx-BigBench (TPCx-BB) is a TPC Express benchmark, which is designed to measure the performance of big data analytics systems. It contains 30 use cases that simulate big data processing, big data storage, big data analytics, and reporting. We have used this benchmark to evaluate the performance of software and hardware components for big data systems. It has very good coverage on different data types and provides enough scalability to address data size and node scaling problems. We have gained lots of meaningful insights through this benchmark to design analytic systems. In the meantime, we also found we cannot merely rely on TPCx-BB to evaluate and design an end-to-end big data systems. There are some gaps between an analytics system and a real end-to-end system. The whole data flow of a real end-to-end system should include data ingestion, which moves data from where it is originated into a system where it can be stored and analyzed such as Hadoop. Data ingestion may be challenging for businesses at a reasonable speed in order to maintain a competitive advantage. However, TPCx-BB cannot help on performance evaluation of software and hardware for data ingestion. Big data is composed of three dimensions: Volume, Variety, and Velocity. The Velocity refers to the high speed in data processing: real-time or near real-time. With big data technology widely used, real-time and near real-time processing become more popular. There is very strict limitation on bandwidth and latency for real-time processing. TPCx-BB cannot help on performance evaluation of software and hardware for real-time processing. This paper mainly discusses these experiences and lessons in practice using TPCx-BB. Then, we provide some advices to extend TPCx-BB to cover data ingestion and real-time processing. We also share some ideas how to implement TPCx-BB coverage.

Keywords: TPCx-BB · End-to-end big data benchmark
Data ingestion · Real-time processing · Big data analytics

1 Introduction

Big data refers to technologies and initiatives that involve data that is too diverse, fast-changing or massive for conventional technologies, skills and infra-structure

© Springer International Publishing AG 2018
R. Nambiar and M. Poess (Eds.): TPCTC 2017, LNCS 10661, pp. 93–102, 2018.
https://doi.org/10.1007/978-3-319-72401-0_7

to address efficiently. To solve the challenges from volume/variety/velocity of big data, new technologies and architectures are invented. A typical system using new big data technologies generally contains 3 components: data ingestion, data storage, and data analytic as shown in Fig. 1.

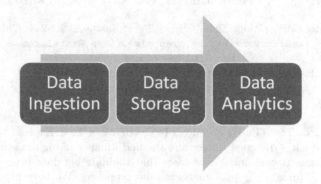

Fig. 1. Big data components

In a big data system, data comes from dynamic, disparate and distributed sources of differing formats, schemas, protocols, speeds and sizes such as machines, geo location devices, click streams, files, social feeds, log files and videos. Data ingestion is to collect, filter, transform and reliably move the data to a system where it can be stored and processed. Data ingestion may be continuous or asynchronous, real-time or batched or both depending upon the characteristics of the source and the destination. Data ingestion can be challenging for businesses at a reasonable speed in order to maintain a competitive advantage. Currently, popular software stacks used in data ingestion include Kafka [1], Flume [2], Kinesis [3], and Sqoop [4].

Big data storage can handle very large amount of structured/unstructured data, and be easily scaled to keep up with data growth. It must provide the bandwidth necessary to deliver data to analytic tools. HDFS [4], HBase [5], Cassandra [6], MongoDB [7] and Kudu [8] are widely used distributed software stacks for big data storage.

Big data analytics examine large amounts of data to uncover hidden patterns, correlations and other insights. Typical scenarios of big data analytics are real-time and batch cases as well as interactive accesses. Popular execution engines for big data analytics include MapReduce [9], Spark [10], Storm [11] and Tez [12]. Many libraries and tools building on these engines are used for interactive analytics, machine learning and graph processing, including Hive [13], MLlib [14], Mahout [15], GraphX [16].

With big data technologies grown significantly and widely adopted over past few years, users need a standard benchmark to evaluate and compare the performance of big data systems. The benchmark should cover the whole data flow and all usage scenarios of big data technologies. TPCx-BB [17] is an

Express Benchmark to measure the performance of big data systems. TPCx-BB is based on BigBench [18], which is an end-to-end big data analytics framework. TPCx-BB benchmark addresses the variety, velocity and volume aspects of big data systems containing structured, semi-structured and unstructured data. 30 queries of TPCx-BB cover different categories of big data analytics from business prospective.

However, TPCx-BB cannot help evaluate the performance of data ingestion and real-time processing in big data systems. Users cannot merely rely on TPCx-BB to evaluate and design an end-to-end big data system. Although TPC-DI [19] is a standard data ingestion benchmark, it mainly focuses batch mode and structured data ingestion, not including real-time mode and unstructured data ingestion. It is better that one benchmark can evaluate the whole data flow and entire framework of big data systems. So, we advise to extend TPCx-BB covering data ingestion and real-time processing.

The reminder of this paper is organized as the follows. Section 2 shares some experiences and lessons in practice using TPCx-BB. We suggest TPCx-BB extending data ingestion and real-time processing coverage, and provide some initial ideas how to implement these extensions in Sect. 3. Section 4 involves relative benchmarks investigation work. Finally, Sect. 5 discusses our future work.

2   Experience and Lessons in Practice Using TPCx-BB

We help many users to deploy big data clusters in past several years. We have used TPCx-BB to evaluate the performance of software and hardware components of big data systems. TPCx-BB has very good coverage on different data types and provides enough scalability to address data size and node scaling problems. We have gained lots of meaningful insights through this benchmark to design an analytic system.

At the meantime, some issues are also found in practice using TPCx-BB, especially when designing an end-to-end big data system. For example, there are two real use cases from our customers: one is a continuous video stream processing system, and the other is a health monitor system. Both cases are end-to-end solutions with big data technologies.

In the continuous video stream processing system as shown in Fig. 2, raw videos are continuously sent to data center through gateway. Big data cluster accepts the stream, encodes the videos, real-time analyzes the video, and also responses some interactive access for history data.

In the health monitor system, user has decided software stacks for the whole framework as shown in Fig. 3. Cardiac Event Records (CERs) collect patients' heart status and upload heart events to data center through smart phones and gateways. Kafka cluster receives cardiac event records, and then transfers them to spark streaming cluster for real-time analytics. If any potential healthy risk is identified by real-time analytics, real-time alert will be generated to inform patient and doctor. The events are also stored into HDFS. Later, doctor can do some batch analytics on patient's history data stored in HDFS, which can help form a treatment plan.

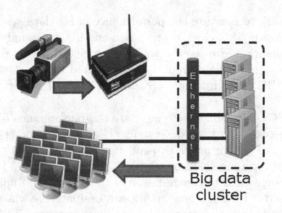

Fig. 2. Video stream processing system

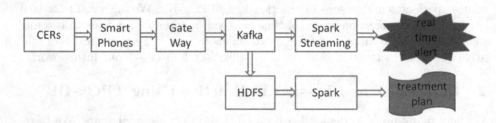

Fig. 3. Health monitor system

In both use cases, users want to use some standard benchmarks to get some insights on the workload characteristics of different software stacks, and some indications on cluster deployment, plan and optimization. While TPCx-BB was used for these use cases, several issues were found.

1. End to end data pipeline includes messaging, stream processing, ingestion and analytics. TPCx-BB only represents the analytics and cannot be used for messaging, stream processing and ingestion, because the workload characteristics of different software stacks are different.

   Figures 4 and 5 are processor frequency and core count scaling of 30 queries of TPCx-BB, and cluster settings are listed in Table 1. In Fig. 4, it can be found all queries are sensitive with CPU frequency, and scaling efficiency for power test of TPCx-BB is 93% from 1.2 GHz to 1.8 GHz, 88% from 1.2 GHz to 2.3 GHz. Figure 5 tells TPCx-BB is also sensitive with processor core count, and scaling efficiency for power test is 80% from 9C18T (9 Cores/18 Threads) to 18C36T, 50% from 9C18T to 36C72T. But, disk and network bandwidth scaling results are very different with processor. As shown in Figs. 6 and 7, only few long execution queries are sensitive with disk and network bandwidth, including query 2/4/30. Overall, performance of power test is only increased by 1%, when increasing network bandwidth from 10 GbE

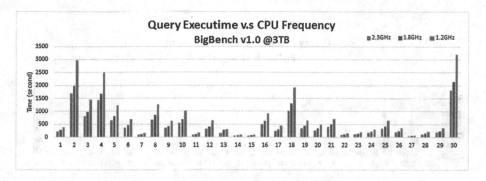

Fig. 4. TPCx-BB CPU frequency scaling

to 25 GbE or increasing disk bandwidth from 400 MB to 2500 MB.

While network and disk bandwidth are very important for data ingestion, we use Kafka as an example to show workload characteristics of data ingestion. Kafka is a popular distributed messaging queue, which is widely used as a critical software component of data ingestion. As shown in Fig. 8, Kafka throughput is increased by 4.2X and 6.9X, when 1 GbE network updating to 10 GbE and 25 GbE. In Fig. 8, cluster setting is the same with Table 1 except that node number is 3 not 9. The size of message sending to Kafka is 230 KB, and there are total 3 customers for this topic of messages.

Based on previous profiling data, TPCx-BB is processor intensive and modest request on network and disk I/O. But, data ingestion is generally network and disk I/O intensive. Due to the difference of workload characteristics between data ingestion and analytics parts, TPCx-BB cannot be used for representing the whole end-to-end data pipeline of big data systems.

2. Even for the analytics part, real-time analytics are not covered by TPCx-BB. Latency is a critical metric for real-time processing. In the use case of health monitor system, latency of real-time alert directly connects with patients' life, and any delay would put patients' life in risks. TPCx-BB doesn't consider the latency at all, and user cannot get any indication of latency from TPCx-BB, because it only focuses on batch analytics.

3. Different components of a big data system are usually running on the same physical cluster. For example, data ingestion, real-time and batch analytics often concurrently execute on cluster to share the resources. In the use case of health monitor system, spark streaming for real-time analytics and spark for batch analytics co-execute on the same cluster. In this usage scenario, user cannot just use analytics benchmarks to evaluate the whole system, because different components have different workload characteristics and different metrics for measurement.

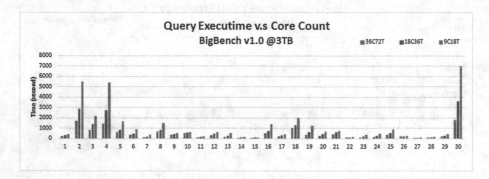

Fig. 5. TPCx-BB core count scaling

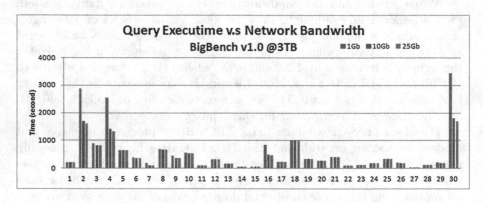

Fig. 6. TPCx-BB network scaling

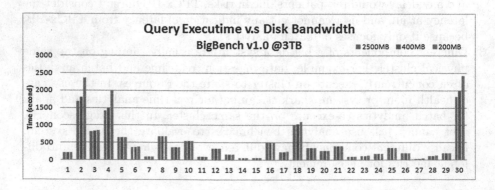

Fig. 7. TPCx-BB disk scaling

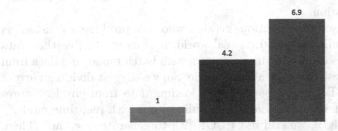

Fig. 8. Kafka network scaling

Table 1. Cluster settings

Node Count	1 master + 8 slaves(HP DL380 Gen9)
Processor	E5-2699 v3 @ 2.30 GHz
DRAM	256G DDR4-2133, 8 channels
Disk	Intel SSD DC 3700 2.0 TB
Network	Intel 25 GbE
Hadoop Version	CDH5.5

3 Suggestions for TPCx-BB Extension

Based on real experiences and lessons from TPCx-BB usages, we advise TPCx-BB extending to cover the whole data flow of end-to-end big data framework. And, we also provide some initial ideas how to implement the extensions.

1. Extend to involve data ingestion benchmark.
   Data ingestion may be real-time or batch depending upon the characteristics of the source and the destination. Load test of TPCx-BB can be looked as a

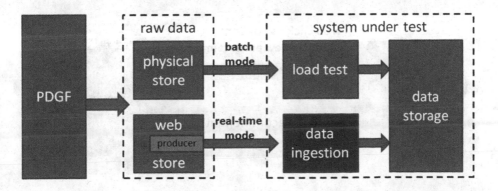

Fig. 9. New data ingestion

very simple batch mode of data ingestion. But, current TPCx-BB does not involve any sub-component that can measure the performance of real-time mode of data ingestion.

BigBench is based on a fictitious retailer who sells products to customers via physical and online stores. In a real world, it is more possible that data from physical stores is ingested into a system with batch mode, and data from online stores is ingested with real-time mode. So, we suggest dividing current load test of TPCx-BB into 2 parts: one is loading data from physical stores as before; the other is loading data from online store with real-time mode.

As shown in Fig. 9, we still use PDGF [20] to generate raw data. Then, raw data belonging to physical stores is loaded into data storage component with optimized storage formats (e.g., ORC or PARQUET) as before. But, raw data belonging to web store will not be ingested directly anymore. It will be emitted by new introduced component: producer, which wraps up and sends raw data to data warehouse. Producer can control stream input rate to data ingestion component of system under test. With configurable data emit rate, user can simulate different real-time data stream.

Data ingestion component of system under test receives messages and extract/transform/load messages to data storage component. Metrics of real-time data ingestion should involve two sides: throughput and latency. Throughput is to measure how many bytes are ingested in a unit time, and latency is the time from a message emitting by producer to be stored in data warehouse.

2. Extend to involve real-time benchmark
   Currently, total 30 queries of TPCx-BB are offline batch analytics, not including real-time data analytics which is a popular usage scenario of big data technology. It is convenient for TPCx-BB to cover real-time analytics by adding a real-time product recommendation engine into its benchmark suits, since it already contains a Web Click stream in its dataset. Web Click stream includes customers' profile and reviewed web pages, and real-time product recommendation engine can use the information to recommend product to customers,

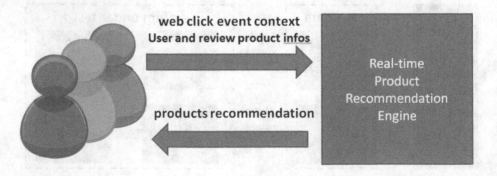

Fig. 10. Real-time analytics

as shown in Fig. 10. Now, it is common to use recommendation engine to promote products to potential customers for online retailers.

Recommendation algorithm is a typical category of machine learning. Recommending product based on customer's profile and product's features belongs to inference phase of machine learning. When TPCx-BB introduces product recommendation engine into its benchmark suits, it can represent not only real-time data analytics, but also inference phase of machine learning which is another hot direction of big data technology.

The metric of evaluating real-time analytics should also consider two sides: throughput and latency. Throughput is the number of web click event handled per second. Latency is response time of generating product recommendation information for each click event. For real-time processing, both metrics are very important.

As real time analytics is usually tightly coupled with real time ingestion, they can be merged together with the same data stream emit by producer. When web click events are inserted into data warehouse, product recommendation information is generated at the same time.

4   Related Work

TPC-DI is a data integration benchmark developed by TPC. The TPC-DI benchmark combines and transforms data extracted from a (fictitious) brokerage firm's On-Line Transaction Processing (OTLP) system along with other sources of data, and loads it into a data warehouse. But, TPC-DI only contains batch mode of data ingestion. The metric of TPC-DI only includes throughput not latency. So, TPC-DI couldn't help evaluate the performance of real-time mode of data ingestion.

Medvedev and Hassani [21] proposed benchmarking metrics to run a series of experiments to evaluate and test the ingestion and storage performance of the widely used open source platform - OpenIoT. They provide a detailed analysis of the experimental outcomes discussing OpenIoT's data ingestion and storage performance. So, they only focus on Data Ingestion and Storage Performance of IoT Platforms.

Yahoo Streaming Benchmarks [22] is a simple advertisement application. There are a number of advertising campaigns, and a number of advertisements for each campaign. The job of the benchmark is to read various JSON events from Kafka, identify the relevant events, and store a windowed count of relevant events per campaign into Redis. These steps attempt to probe some common operations performed on data streams. But, it is not end-to-end benchmark for big data framework, and just for real-time processing evaluation.

Numenta Anomaly Benchmark (NAB) [23] is a benchmark for streaming anomaly detection. NAB comprises two main components: a dataset with labeled, real-world time-series data, and a scoring system designed for streaming data. NAB repository now includes ten different anomaly detection algorithms. Overall, it is a standard open source framework for just evaluating real-time anomaly detection algorithms.

5   Future Work

In this paper, we only provide some very initial ideas about how to extend TPCx-BB covering real-time mode of data ingestion and analytics. For next step work, we will implement proof of concept and get some results from PoC to evaluate our ideas.

References

1. Kafka: https://kafka.apache.org/
2. Flume: https://flume.apache.org/
3. Kinesis: https://aws.amazon.com/documentation/kinesis/
4. Sqoop: https://sqoop.apache.org/
5. HDFS: https://hadoop.apache.org/
6. Cassandra: https://cassandra.apache.org/
7. MongoDB: http://camel.apache.org/
8. Kudu: https://kudu.apache.org/
9. MapReduce: https://hadoop.apache.org/
10. Spark: https://spark.apache.org/
11. Storm: https://storm.apache.org/
12. Tez: https://tez.apache.org/
13. Hive: https://hive.apache.org/
14. MLlib: https://spark.apache.org/mllib/
15. Mahout: https://mahout.apache.org/
16. GraphX: https://spark.apache.org/graphx/
17. TPCx-BB: http://www.tpc.org/tpcx-bb/default.asp/
18. Ghazal, A., Rabl, T., Hu, M., Raab, F., Poess, M., Crolotte, A., Jacobsen, H.-A.: BigBench: towards an industry standard benchmark for big data analytics. In: SIGMOD 2013, 22–27 June 2013, New York, New York, USA (2013)
19. TPC-DI: http://www.tpc.org/tpcdi/
20. Rabl, T., Frank, M., Sergieh, H.M., Kosch, H.: A data generator for cloud-scale benchmarking. In: Nambiar, R., Poess, M. (eds.) TPCTC 2010. LNCS, vol. 6417, pp. 41–56. Springer, Heidelberg (2011). https://doi.org/10.1007/978-3-642-18206-8_4
21. Medvedev, A., Hassani, A., Zaslavsky, A., Jayaraman, P.P., Indrawan-Santiago, M., Delir Haghighi, P., Ling, S.: Data ingestion and storage performance of IoT platforms: study of OpenIoT. In: Podnar Žarko, I., Broering, A., Soursos, S., Serrano, M. (eds.) InterOSS-IoT 2016. LNCS, vol. 10218, pp. 141–157. Springer, Cham (2017). https://doi.org/10.1007/978-3-319-56877-5_9
22. Chintapalli, S., Dagit, D., Evans, B., Farivar, R., Graves, T., Holderbaugh, M., Liu, Z., Nusbaum, K., Patil, K., Peng, B.J., Poulosky, P.: Benchmarking streaming computation engines: storm, flink and spark streaming. In: 2016 IEEE International Parallel and Distributed Processing Symposium Workshops
23. Lavin, A., Ahmad, S.: Evaluating real-time anomaly detection algorithms - the numenta anomaly benchmark. In: 2015 IEEE 14th International Conference Machine Learning and Applications (ICMLA)

JCC-H: Adding Join Crossing Correlations with Skew to TPC-H

Peter Boncz[1]([⊠]), Angelos-Christos Anatiotis[2], and Steffen Kläbe[3]

[1] CWI, Amsterdam, Netherlands
peter.boncz@cwi.nl
[2] EPFL, Lausanne, Switzerland
angelos.anadiotis@epfl.ch
[3] TU Ilmenau, Ilmenau, Germany
steffen.klaebe@tu-ilmenau.de

Abstract. We introduce JCC-H, a drop-in replacement for the data and query generator of TPC-H, that introduces Join-Crossing-Correlations (JCC) and skew into its dataset and query workload. These correlations are carefully designed such that the filter predicates on table columns in the existing TPC-H queries now suddenly can have effects on the value-, frequency- and join-fan-out-distributions, experienced by operators in the query plan. The query generator of JCC-H is able to generate parameter bindings for the 22 query templates in two different equivalence classes: query templates that receive "normal" parameters do not experience skew and behave very similar to default TPC-H queries. Query templates expanded with the "skewed" parameters, though, experience strong join-crossing-correlations and skew in filter, aggregation and join operations. In this paper we discuss the goals of JCC-H, its detailed design, as well as show initial experiments on both a single-server and MPP database system, that confirm that our design goals were largely met. In all, JCC-H provides a convenient way for any system that is already testing with TPC-H to examine how the system can handle skew and correlations, so we hope the community can use it to make progress on issues like skew mitigation and detection and exploitation of join-crossing-correlations in query optimizers and data storage.

1 Introduction and Motivation

The past four decades of research into data storage and indexing, query execution and query optimization have yielded many research contributions, but also impacted a wealth of systems in broad ICT use, whose reach significantly surpasses database systems alone, as shown by the popularity of big data frameworks, such as Spark, for data science, ETL, machine learning and stream processing, which at heart are also powered by these techniques.

Benchmarks have helped significantly to quantitatively evaluate the properties of such techniques and have arguably played an important role in maturing the state-of-the-art in systems. By now, a scalable data management system with a SQL-like query language needs to meet a high bar of user expectations,

© Springer International Publishing AG 2018
R. Nambiar and M. Poess (Eds.): TPCTC 2017, LNCS 10661, pp. 103–119, 2018.
https://doi.org/10.1007/978-3-319-72401-0_8

set by previous database systems, and also codified in a number of database benchmarks that it will be expected to be able to run. Significant benchmarks that have influenced the field of analytical database systems are TPC-H [1], TPC-DS [9], the Star Schema Benchmark [8] and BigBench [5].

Database benchmarks use synthetic data produced by data generators. This allows controlled generation of any desired dataset scale-factor (SF), which is useful for scalability analysis; yet regrettably so far this synthetic data has been rife with uniformity, in terms of (a) value distributions, (b) frequency distributions and (c) join fan-out distributions.[1] Any practitioner knows that in deployed use, as opposed to in benchmark tests, database systems face data that is typically skewed in all these aspects. To make matters worse, in real data, data tends to be highly correlated. A well known example of correlation would be a CAR(brand, model) table, where the predicate brand = Porsche and model = Panamera are correlated: after the selection on Panamera, there is 100% certainty that remaining tuples are Porsche. This type of correlations was long elusive for query optimizers using the independence assumption, but thanks to ample CPU power nowadays available, cardinality estimation is increasingly done by executing predicates on table samples, which catches any correlation within a single table. It was recently confirmed [7] that faulty cardinality estimation is the main problem for join-order optimization (which arguably is the most important query optimization problem), and as such the frontier for systems and for database research into this are correlations not within the same table, but across different tables. To continue the example, in a join of Panameras towards a SALES(date, price, brand, type) table, the optimizer would probably mis-estimate the cardinality of extract(year from date) between 2000 and 2010 because the Panamera was introduced only in 2009. Between different referenced items, there can be a hugely different number of join partners (e.g. Panamera vs Golf or iPhones vs. Nokia handsets, lately). These sales examples exemplify *Join-Crossing-Correlations* (JCC), which is as far as we know a poorly supported aspect of reality in current data management systems, and certainly unsupported in the current generation of database benchmarks.

In this paper we describe a non-invasive variant of the well-known TPC-H benchmark, that makes it a much harder benchmark to execute efficiently by introducing *join crossing correlations* and *skew* in its data and queries. As we explained above, a join-crossing-correlation means that values occurring in tuples from one table, can influence the behavior of operations (joins,filters,aggregations) involving data from other tables, in a query that joins these tables. Barring the recent Interactive Workload for the LDBC Social Network Benchmark (SNB [3]), which is focused on short-running graph traversal queries rather than ad-hoc OLAP queries, there do not exist database benchmarks that test join-crossing correlations; and none that contain join skew.

---

[1] The join fan-out distribution is the distribution of amount of join partners for values in a primary key (PK) column, towards a particular foreign key (FK) column.

The goals of JCC-H are as follows:

1. To be a drop-in replacement of TPC-H in terms of data generator and query generator. The only difference being a single flag -k, that when passed to dbgen generates skewed/correlated data, and for qgen generates the skewed query variants (see point 5). The advantage of being a drop-in replacement is that many existing products and research prototypes already have TPC-H testing suites that can be leveraged, and also, the nature of the TPC-H queries is already well-understood by their development teams [1].

2. To introduce severe skew in all foreign key joins: for each referencing table, 25% of all tuples refer to just a handful of PKs (typically: 5). Having a handful of very frequent values is a known practical issue and one of the effects it causes is that if table partitioning is used, then the partition in which such a frequent value happens to fall will be larger than others. Another effect is that when joining or aggregating in a shuffled fashion, the worker responsible for the frequent values will be overloaded (receive a lot of network traffic, and have a lot of CPU work), which will lead to poor load balancing, unless specific anti-skew measures are taken by the system. A deterioration of speedup when e.g. comparing single-core to parallel execution is a good indication of the adverse effects of skew.

3. To correlate the join-fan-out skew created by our modifications to the data generator to (join-crossing) filter-predicates in the query. The correlation is carefully generated to create as much effect as possible on the existing 22 query templates. This required a thorough understanding of all 22 TPC-H queries and drawing up a plan how each query, given its existing filter predicates, could be affected by join-crossing correlations.

4. To be able to generate different query parameters that cause the queries to touch different data but behave identically performance-wise. Having such multiple parameter bindings for usage in concurrent query stream tests is a useful benchmark feature, as it helps guard against inflating the score of an ad-hoc query benchmark using query result caching: a query variant can be executed multiple times in a (throughput) test run, with different parameter bindings, but with equivalent results in terms of performance, so the results remain comparable.

5. To create for all or most of the 22 TPC-H queries two *query variants*:[2] one **normal** variant whose behavior closely resembles the behavior of the query on **default** TPC-H and one **skewed** variant that causes the skew to surface during runtime.

6. To make the single-table statistics of the columns from which the query parameters are derived look innocuously uniform. That is, it should force the query optimizer to understand join-crossing-correlations for it to predict that a different parameter value leads to very different behavior, as the values (used in equi- or range-comparisons) have similar frequencies in the column accessed by the filter predicate.

---

[2] As in [6] the two variants stem from exactly the same query template: the only thing that makes them different are the parameters that get pasted into the template.

7. To design the "skewed" parameter bindings such that evaluating the query takes typically much more effort than for a "normal" parameter binding. It has been observed that for systems, workload scheduling could be eased if queries that affect very large volumes of data ("whale" queries, as opposed to normal "fish" queries) could be detected and handled differently. However, due to errors in cardinality estimation (which are often caused by join-crossing correlations and skew [7]) this is non-trivial.

A very important **non-goal** in JCC-H is to make TPC-H more "realistic", as has been done for instance in [2] by having the order-customer distribution over nations more real-life-like. While this may also interesting, we think that correlations that lead to unexpected and severe skew is a phenomenon that has been observed in practitioner lore so often that we consider introducing such correlation and skew a more important step in making TPC-H more "realistic" than trying to have the value and frequency distributions of it regions, nations, suppliers, customers, and orders to resemble real life more closely.

In order to fulfill all goals above, we must introduce skew and correlations primarily based on the predicates found in the 22 queries of TPC-H rather than on any overarching realism concerns.

This paper is organized as follows: in Sect. 2 we provide a detailed design of the JCC-H benchmark, while in Sect. 3 we describe our experiments we ran on multiple database systems, both single-server and MPP. In Sect. 4 we outline future work and conclude the paper.

2   Benchmark Design

In the remainder we assume the reader to be familiar with the TPC-H benchmark, and if not, advise the reader to first study its specification and/or [1].

In the JCC-H data generator we make use of *bijective permutation functions* based on a *linear permutation polynomial*, as also described in [4]. Given a key domain $K \in [0..N)$, and a fixed, chosen, prime number P, these functions find a number X where $X * P \bmod N = 1$. This number is easily found using linear search and leads to a hash function: $h(K) : K * P \bmod N$. This is a perfect hash in that it delivers an outcome $\in [0..N)$. Further, the function can be inversed simply using $h^{-1}(H) : H * X \bmod N$. The hash function can be made more random by adding and subtracting a constant: $h(K) : (K * P + C) \bmod N$ and $h^{-1}(H) : (H + N - C) * X \bmod N$. This is slightly different from [4], in that instead of $(H - C)$ we do $(H + N - C)$ and choose $C < N$ such that $(H + N - C)$ never underflows. This allows to use the fast C/C++ % operator (which is not a pure mod, but just a remainder).

We chose to modify the existing TPC dbgen, rather than to write a new data generator from scratch. The reason is that we want the tool to be an exact drop-in replacement, with exactly the same options and functionality. The TPC-H dbgen is arguably of a dated design, but it *can* generate data in parallel, or rather, it can generate all of its main tables in pieces, and thus with scripting that starts multiple data generators generating different pieces at the same time, parallelism is achieved (in a way that is independent of the parallelism framework).

In order to introduce correlations and skew, in the data generator we decide what to generate based on the identity of the tuple we are generating. The TPC-H dbgen does this by passing the primary key of the table to the routine that generates the record. This number fulfills a similar function as the random seed used in modern parallel data generators such as PGDF [4]. PDGF introduces the concept of hierarchical seeds that follow the schema as the seed of each table referenced by a parent table depends on the seed of the parent. The issue of table dependencies is only partially addressed in TPC-H, because dbgen generates the part and partsupp tables at the same time, as well as orders and lineitem. For our purposes, though, this does not generate enough context to insert all correlations, and therefore we designed an elaborate mechanism of dependencies that start with orderkey and propagate down to all other keys, as described next.

2.1 Join Skew and Aggregation Skew

In JCC-II we have introduced join skew in all major joins[3]:

c-n there are 25 nations, evenly divided in 5 regions. We identify for each region a "large" nation to which 18% of all customers belong, and 4 "small" nations to which 0.5% of customers belong ($5 * (18 + 4 * 0.5) = 100$). The $h(\text{c\_custkey})$ determines to which, by dividing the hash range in regions proportional to these percentages, as displayed in the left side of Fig. 1. Further, each large nation has one customer (the first in the hash range) that is a "populous customer": it will have very many orders. These populous customers have a special country nation code in their c_phone phone numbers (the first two digits have values 40,50,60,70,80 – normally country codes in TPC-H are <40), to make them recognizable in Q22.

s-n similar to customer, suppliers are mapped to nations based on $h(\text{s\_suppkey})$. There are also 5 populous suppliers, but they are not marked with a correlated column (which we did with c_phone).

o-c there are 5 populous orders, namely those with $h(\text{o\_orderkey}) < 5$; these orders will have very many lineitems. They are recognizable in that their o_comment contains the string "1mine2 3gold4". For the other orders, in 25% of the cases a populous customer key is chosen (the decision is made determined by $h(\text{o\_orderkey})$, in the other cases a normal customer is chosen). In all cases, the customer is chosen in such a way that $h(\text{o\_orderkey})$ determines in which region the customer is located. Thus, by knowing o_orderkey, the data generator knows from which region the customer stems. We choose the customers from only 100K * SF out of the total 150K * SF customers, because in default TPC-H, one third of customers also does not have any orders.

---

[3] In this paper, we abbreviate the foreign key joins of TPC-H (and JCC-H) using the first letters of the table name (ps for partsupp to distinguish it from p for part). For example, with l-o we mean the join between linetem and orders.

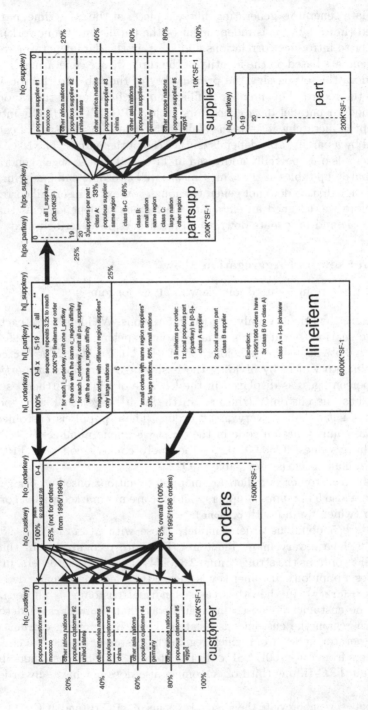

Fig. 1. JCC-H join connectivity

ps-p according to our targets, 25% of partsupp should refer (via `ps_partkey`) to only 5 distinct parts. This mean every such part must have many distinct suppliers. But even if we take *all* suppliers, this would give $5 * 10K * SF = 50K * SF$ different partsupps. Since (`ps_partkey`,`ps_suppkey`) must be unique, we use 20 populous parts, which link with all suppliers: $20 \times 10K * SF = 200K * SF$, i.e. 25% of partsupp (whose size is $800K * SF$).

ps-s For all non-populous parts, we generate three partsupps, i.e. choose three suppliers. This is done using a dependency of `ps_suppkey` on h(`ps_partkey`). We create an *affinity* between h(`ps_partkey`) and the supplier region. The three combinations are generated with three different formulas (called class-A, class-B and class-C suppliers), which guarantee that for a given `partkey`, class-A, B, C suppliers are distinct. To be exact, class A selects a populous supplier (which is always from a large nation) from the affinity region. Class-B selects a supplier from a small nation from the affinity region. Class C selects a supplier from a large nation from a distinct region. These three suppliers are evidently from different nations and therefore distinct.

l-o according to our target, 25% of the lineitem tuples have just 5 distinct `l_orderkey` values. For this, the 5 populous orders must consist of a lot of items $(300K * SF)$.[4] To generate these, we use the 15 higher populous parts, and generate all suppliers from a large nation in a *different* region. As this amounts to (15 parts) * (0.8 * 5 regions) * (0.8 * 0.2 * 10K * SF suppliers) = $96K * SF$, we fall short of the desired $300K * SF$ lineitems. Therefore, we repeat this sequence 3.2 times to get there. The skewed lineitems that we generate like this, have a few extra characteristics: `l_quantity` = 51 (just above the normal maximum value), `l_shipmode` = "REG AIR", `l_shipinstruct` = "DELIVER IN PERSON" and `l_returnflag` = R.

l-ps Given that 25% (i.e. $0.25 * 6000K * SF = 1500K * SF$) of the lineitems belong to populous orders, the other $1500K * SF-5$ orders must consist of 3 lineitems $(3 * 1500K * SF = 4500K * SF)$. For each of the 3 lineitems in an order, we must generate a partsupp reference. The two latter partsupps are so-called class-B partsupps, generated from a random partkey. The first partsupp in each non-populous order is the populous supplier matching the customer region, paired with one of the 5 populous parts (the one with matching region affinity). As such, all these first lineitems form just 5 different partsupp combinations, which is what we want for l-ps join skew.

Please note that when generating a table, we often choose a foreign key based on certain dependencies or conditions. These dependencies are computed in the hashed space of the parent key, and lead to choosing a hashed child key. For instance, as described above (o-c) in the generation of orders, we choose a customer such that from the orderkey we know the customer region (e.g. #region = h(`o_custkey`) mod 5). In order to actually generate a key (e.g. `o_custkey`) we use the inverse hash function $h^{-1}()$. This exploits the property in TPC-H that

---

[4] A huge order indeed, and realism is not our primary target. However, if one orders all parts of an entire airplane, or aircraft carrier, it might still be realistic ;-).

the key space is dense, so given any number H in $[0..N\rangle$ then $h^{-1}(H)$ must be a valid, existing key. The only exception to this rule are in fact orderkeys: there are holes in the space of orderkeys that TPC-H uses to generate inserts and deletes. However, JCC-H never needs to compute an orderkey as it is the root of the key hierarchy, therefore this is not an issue.

Finally, we introduce some correlated columns in the part table, for populous parts ($p(\text{p\_partkey}) < 20$). These have p_brand = "Brand#55", p_size = 1, p_container = "LG BOX", p_type = "SHINY MINED GOLD" and p_name = "shiny mined gold". Just doing this would introduce rather infrequent values for the latter two columns, as they would occur only 20 times. This would be easily picked up by the query optimizer in those TPC-H queries that have equality predicates on p_type and p_name. In order to hide these values in the statistics, we also give some non-populous parts these values, such that all individual column frequency distributions remain uniform. However, we guarantee that no non-populous parts have multiple of these values. Thus, only when selecting on a conjunction of these, the 20 populous parts will come out. This hiding of infrequent combinations is an example of a "simple" anti-correlated columns inside the same table. The fact that only 20 results come out, might be found by a multi-column histogram or using sampling (though likely the sample would be too small to contain a populous part). Still, even if query optimizers could detect this, this would only be stage one, as the second stage is to recognize the very different join-fan-out in the ps-p join that these populous parts have.

2.2   Filter Skew

In TPC-H the date dimension has a uniform value distribution. There is in fact a correlation between o_orderdate and the lineitem dates (the latter dates are within four months of the former). But, during the years, orders and lineitems are generated at the same pace.

JCC-H introduces a so-called Black Friday, which is one day in the year where there are many more orders. We actually chose to have this on Memorial Day, which is a fixed day (May 29), and on this day, 50% of all orders are placed. Please recall that absolute realism is a non-goal of JCC-H. But, we do want to test the effects of strong time skew in table generation. After generating o_orderdate we use the normal TPC-H mechanism to generate all lineitem dates based on it, so they follow after it within four months.

All 5 populous orders (25% of lineitem) are generated on Black Friday. Hence, even more than 50% of lineitems get ordered on Black Friday, because also 50% of the non-populous orders are from that date. This is done by moving a fraction of non-populous orders from their original random date to the Black Friday of that year. However, we do not do this in 2 out 7 the years, namely 1995 and 1996 (so $25\% + 5/7 * 50\%$ of 75% = 52% of lineitems was ordered on Black Friday). The reason is that 1995 and 1996 should be sanctuaries from join skew. These two years appear as constants (non-parameters) in default TPC-H Q7 and Q8. Recall that we want to generate two sets of parameter bindings: **skewed** bindings and **normal** bindings. By omitting generation of skew (i.e. class-A) in the lower 75%

of lineitem (the area labeled "small orders from same-region suppliers" in Fig. 1) during 1995–1996, we make it possible to avoid the o-c, l-c, and l-ps join skew by choosing date ranges from 1995 and 1996.

2.3 Query Parameter Generation

We now discuss how the JCC-H version of `qgen` substitutes parameter values into the 22 TPC-H query templates. We generate for each template parameters for two *query variants* [6]: one **normal** set of parameters where JCC-H tries to behave as close as possible to default TPC-H (no correlations, uniform distributions) and a **skewed** set of parameters, where all forms of correlation and skew come into play. Skewed variant generation is triggered using the -k flag of `qgen`.

Q1 because the query has no joins and is well-known for its full-scan behavior (it selects more than 95% of lineitem) and has few group-by values in the aggregation, there is no real opportunity for join-, aggregation- or filter-skew, so Q1 was left unmodified. Both normal and skewed queries use default parameters.

Q2 is a p-ps-s join with a `p_type` LIKE predicate. For the "skewed" query variant we set the parameter to suffixes of "SHINY MINED GOLD" (of at least 6 characters, e.g. "%INED GOLD". The "normal" parameters use default bindings. The effect of this is that skewed queries will select populous parts, and normal parameters non-populous parts.

Q3 has a date range that is lower-bounded on `o_orderdate` and upper-bounded on `l_shipdate`. Please recall that `l_shipdate` is always within four months of `o_orderdate`. Certain existing database systems that take join-crossing statistics into account and store the tables clustered or partitioned on date, will be able to unify these bounds on both lineitem and orders into bounded ranges in both tables (e.g. using MinMax indexes and noting which MinMax ranges of rows in orders and lineitem join with each other). This is the case already in TPC-H.

For the "skewed" query variants, we always choose a date range in 1993 around Black Friday. This will include the populous order from 1993[5], and thus join skew in l-o. For the "normal" variants, the date range lies in 1995. For orders from this date, there is no join skew in l-o and o-c. Please be aware that if a system uses table partitioning for lineitem, then the 5 partitions (or less) in which the populous orderkeys happen to fall will be larger than the rest. Therefore, the "normal" query variant will also experience scan-skew just for that reason, even if the tuples turn out to be not selected by the query. If additional measures are taken, such as clustering within the partition on a date, or sub-partitioning on date, then all other table areas than those corresponding to 1995 will be *skipped*, e.g. using partition pruning or by exploiting MinMax indexes. In that case, the "normal" variants of Q3 can avoid all skew.

---

[5] Because there are seven years (1992–1998) and 5 populous orders, there are two years without populous order and these are 1995 and 1996.

Q4 contains a 3-month range restriction on o_orderdate. For the "skewed" query variant, this range is picked from the years 1993 and 1994. For the "normal" variant from 1995 and 1996, which avoids the l-o join skew.

Q5 identical to Q4, except that the range is one year long.

Q6 identical to Q5, except that l_shipdate is involved.

Q7 in default TPC-H, there is a hard-coded (non-parametrized) two-year range restriction on l_shipdate. In JCC-H, the range boundaries become parameters, but for the "normal" query variant retain their old value (1995–1996). In the "skewed" variant the range is 1993–1994. The existing parameters are two nation names (between which trade is measured). In the "skewed" variant we pick two different large nations (from different regions, because there is only one large nation per region in JCC-H). For the "normal" variant, we pick two small nations from the same region. As has been described previously under l-ps join skew (and depicted in Fig. 1), the class-B partsupps match up suppliers from small nations with customers from the same region (10% of which are from a small nation, 2% out of 20%). Hence the two variants both produce results, but their joins traverse disjunct joined tuples, where the "skewed" variant will hit strong o-c, l-o, l-ps join skew, but the "normal" variant not.

Q8 similar to Q7, the hard-coded date restriction on 1995–1996 (on o_orderdate) was turned into a parameter that for the "normal" query variant remains 1995–1996 and for the "skewed" variant is 1993–1994. In that case, the p_type equi-restriction becomes "SHINY MINED GOLD". This will select populous parts, hence focus on join-skew. This skew is absent in 1995–1996.

Q9 contains all joins, and only has a p_name LIKE restriction. Similar to Q2, it is set to a suffix of "shiny mined gold", for the "skewed" query variant.

Q10 the "normal" variant selects a 3-month o_orderdate interval starting on a day in the first two months of 1995 (this means it misses Black Friday, which in JCC-H is on May 29), and there is no join skew. The "skewed" query variant uses other years than 1995–1996 (so there is join skew) and uses a week enclosing Black Friday.

Q11 the "normal" variant uses a small nation whereas the "skewed" variant uses a large nation.

Q12 the "normal" variant uses a 1-year l_receiptdate restriction of 1995 or 1996, whereas the "skewed" variant uses 1993–1994 and includes "REG AIR" in the l_shipmode restriction.

Q13 the "normal" variant in the o_comment NOT LIKE restriction uses a variation of "%1mine2%3gold4%" where any of the digits can be omitted. This will eliminate all populous orders. The "skewed" query variant uses the normal parameter bindings.

Q14 and Q15 the "normal" query variant uses a 3-month l_shipdate restriction in 1995 or 1996 that excludes the months May-August, whereas the "skewed" variant uses 1992, 1993, 1994, 1997 or 1998 where the range includes these four months (hence it experiences both Black Friday filter skew and join skew).

Q16 the "skewed" query variant makes sure that the p_size IN range includes 1, whereas the "normal" variant ensures it never includes it. In both cases, asking for p_brand in-equality on "Brand#55" is avoided. The result is that the "skewed" variant homes in on the populous parts, whereas the "normal" query variant only select non-populous parts.

Q17 the skewed variant ask for p_brand = "Brand#55" and p_container = "LG BOX" with an identical effect as in Q16.

Q18 this query cannot be easily parametrized, so a WHERE l_quantity < :2 parametrized restriction in the inner subquery was added, that in the normal case limits until 50 (which in default TPC-H is always the case) and in the skewed case until 100, so it will include the lineitems with join-skew (which have value 51 there).

Q19 the "skewed" variant restricts p_brand in the last disjunction to "Brand#55" and l_quantity to a range that includes 51. The effect is similar to Q16.

Q20 the "normal" variant uses a 1-year l_shipdate restriction of 1995 or 1996, whereas the "skewed" variant uses 1993–1994 and includes prefix of "shiny mined gold" in the l_name LIKE restriction.

Q21 the "normal" variant uses a small nation whereas the "skewed" variant uses a large nation.

Q22 the "skewed" variant include the c_phone area codes 30, 40, 50, 60, 70, 80 in the IN restriction, which selects populous customers. The "normal" variant uses the default parameter values which never will select such a customer.

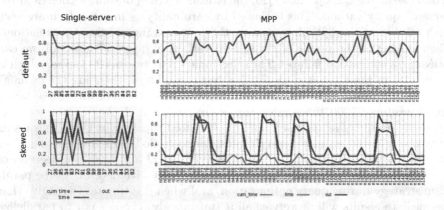

Fig. 2. Query 9: l-ps join load balance comparing JCC-H "skewed" with TPC-H "default" behavior on single-server and MPP systems (X-axis is workload per core).

3   Experiments

We ran experiments on Actian Vector (VectorWise) on a single-server machine and also using its MPP version VectorH (Vector on Hadoop) on a small cluster with relatively slow network. We also ran experiments on a faster cluster with Hive. The single-server machine is a dual-socket Intel Xeon E5-2650 v2 @ 2.60 GHz with in total 32 vCores (16 real), 256 GB RAM and four disks in RAID0. The disk configuration is not very relevant as all our results are with the data cached in-memory. The slow cluster consists of 16 nodes, each having a single-socket small machine i5-4590S CPU @ 3.00 GHz (4 vCores each), a single 1 TB magnetic disk and 16 GB of memory and 1 Gb ethernet. Actian Vector was version 5.1 and VectorH version 4.2. We used Hive 1.2.2 (Tez 0.8.5) and the fast cluster it ran on consisted of 8 nodes of each dual Intel Xeon X5660CPUs, 48 GB RAM, and 10 Gb ethernet. In all cases, the OS is Linux and both clusters ran Hadoop 2.7.3.

The Vector and VectorH results are listed in Table 2. Figure 3 summarizes the single-server numbers by normalizing query runtimes towards the default TPC-H query runtimes of the specific parallelism level (i.e. single-threaded or using 16 cores). We can observe at first that the green and blue bars, expressing runtimes of the 'normal" query variants, are always near 1, which means they behave very similar to the default TPC-H queries they are normalized to. This is an important requirement to fulfill goal 5.

Furthermore we can observe, comparing the "normal" queries with the "skewed" ones, that skewed query variants take significantly more effort to run than normal ones. One reason for this absolute difference is that indeed the skewed variant selects more data (goal 7: "whale" queries).

The disparity between normal and skewed gets worse when using all 16 cores. We have looked into detailed query profiles to establish the reasons for this. In certain cases, like Q2, Q17 and Q20, the reason is wrong optimizer choices in the "skewed" query variant. This is caused by cardinality estimates which are very much off due to the optimizer missing the join-crossing predicate correlations. When looking at the profile of the skewed variant of query 17 in detail, we can notice these estimation failures. The selection on part returns 20 tuples, which is about 0.1% of the estimated cardinality, but as we know, these are the "whale" tuples of the part relation. As a consequence, joining lineitem with these heavy hitters produces 1000 times more tuples than estimated. Aggregating on this join result produces again just 0.03% of estimated tuples, which is also a result of the wrong initial estimation on the part selection. So the used query plan does not seem to be the optimal one. Alternatively, in Q2 and Q20, the decision of query parallelization seem wrong. The system we test with determines the parallelism strategy during query optimization, and when it estimates (wrongly) that intermediate results will be very small it (mistakenly) chooses not to parallelize certain query subtrees anymore, because for small data volumes, the overheads of parallel execution tend not to pay off.

The second reason why the difference between skewed and normal gets bigger with more parallelism is indeed skew. The query profiles we examined had very strong scan skew, filter skew, aggregation skew and join skew. As an example, we have a more detailed look at query 9 in Fig. 2. These plots show various characteristics (time and output size) of the execution of the most expensive join operator (the l-ps join), per active core. On the single-server system as well as on the MPP system, the join in default TPC-H produces a balanced join fan-out, shown by the red lines. In contrast to that, the join of the skewed variant exhibits five peaks. While 5 threads return about 58 million tuples, the remaining 11 threads return only about 27 million results. The same can be observed in the MPP system: five nodes produce about 11 million tuples with

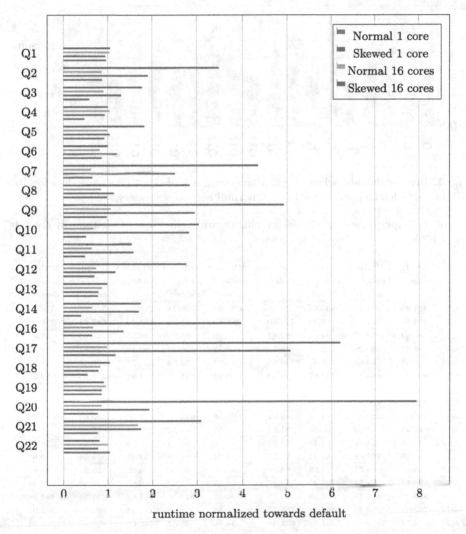

Fig. 3. Single-server Vector (Wise) experiments with JCC-H: runtime normalized towards default TPC-H with the same amount of cores (Color figure online)

116   P. Boncz et al.

each of their four threads, while the remaining 11 nodes return about 2 million results per thread. So, in the skewed query variants, the overall runtime of the join operator is dominated by the threads/nodes that process the parts with the peak cardinalities, causing the whole operator to run slower than in the default query variant. Overall, we observe in Fig. 3, that the impact of the skewed query variants on the parallel experiments (purple bar) is much higher than on the single-threaded runs (red bar).

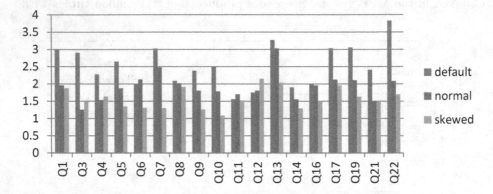

Fig. 4. Hive: scalability achieved when hardware is scaled ×4 (2 to 8 nodes) for 100 GB TPC-H (default) and JCC-H (resp. normal and skewed query sets).

Table 1. Experiments on the faster cluster with Hive: query runtime in seconds (SF = 100)

	TPC-H 2 nodes	JCC-H 2 nodes normal	JCC-H 2 nodes skewed	TPC-H 4 nodes	JCC-H 4 nodes normal	JCC-H 4 nodes skewed	TPC-H 8 nodes	JCC-H 8 nodes normal	JCC-H 8 nodes skewed
Q1	817.93	985.09	966.68	531.55	696.46	700.11	272.89	502.67	514.47
Q3	306.69	311.02	415.10	177.00	287.87	344.12	105.49	247.68	278.32
Q4	82.62	83.86	92.39	52.47	57.69	81.99	36.30	54.66	56.45
Q5	183.27	159.29	291.59	114.55	111.35	226.38	69.17	84.87	216.59
Q6	60.53	53.63	75.89	46.6	34.63	54.84	30.39	25.12	58.02
Q7	822.66	690.25	1237.07	530.13	410.23	1014.77	271.98	278.45	952.37
Q8	1306.56	1568.00	2402.17	882.11	1150.03	1667.44	624.6	776.87	1254.27
Q9	449.14	406.67	1945.30	371.25	278.72	1789.56	188.48	225.3	1540.54
Q10	243.05	232.23	448.57	191.21	168.56	414.79	97.40	130.04	413.74
Q11	41.27	29.52	68.58	31.92	24.05	49.37	26.47	17.34	45.08
Q12	37.48	34.49	42.33	84.04	25.35	24.53	21.35	19.07	19.67
Q13	139.15	137.98	142.43	95.27	74.26	97.69	42.57	45.58	69.85
Q14	58.73	39.73	82.54	68.38	33.86	58.68	30.85	25.57	63.88
Q16	74.17	73.14	126.20	51.28	44.11	104.99	36.95	37.32	84.34
Q17	855.21	815.78	909.09	438.17	501.61	622.31	281.64	384.19	464.98
Q19	1263.05	1332.35	1484.97	751.50	818.59	1041.23	413.44	632.50	908.99
Q21	1076.77	1023.01	1051.54	631.46	634.80	645.62	446.68	679.46	704.04
Q22	86.34	81.57	84.39	52.93	48.31	56.92	22.55	39.15	49.64

Table 2. Vector (left) and Vector-on-Hadoop (right) query runtime in seconds (SF = 100). Note: the Vector and VectorH results are not comparable in absolute terms (and this is not the point of these experiments), since the machines in the Hadoop cluster used for VectorH are older and slower than the single-server machine used for Vector. We can see that relatively, the skewed queries on MPP system VectorH bear a heavier performance and scalability penalty than on the single-server system.

	Vector, 16-core 256GB single-server						VectorH, 16x(2-core,4SMT 16GB) cluster					
	TPC-H 1 core	JCC-H 1 core normal	JCC-H 1 core skewed	TPC-H 16 cores	JCC-H 16 cores normal	JCC-H 16 cores skewed	TPC-H 16x1	JCC-H 16x1 normal	JCC-H 16x1s skewed	TPC-H 16x4	JCC-H 16x4 normal	JCC-H 16x4 skewed
Q1	14.96	14.40	14.11	1.12	1.16	1.18	0.95	1.36	1.37	0.30	0.91	0.96
Q2	3.23	2.80	6.13	0.87	0.75	3.04	0.62	0.66	33.45	0.59	0.46	29.18
Q3	1.17	0.68	1.52	0.39	0.35	0.69	1.43	1.72	1.21	0.57	2.36	2.57
Q4	0.73	0.34	0.69	0.23	0.24	0.23	0.06	0.10	0.08	0.06	0.05	0.07
Q5	3.53	3.24	3.66	0.66	0.65	1.20	1.49	1.08	4.62	1.09	1.51	3.91
Q6	0.94	0.81	1.13	0.27	0.22	0.27	0.14	0.10	0.23	0.07	0.07	0.22
Q7	3.54	2.29	8.90	0.64	0.40	2.78	1.74	0.69	4.97	1.02	0.79	6.66
Q8	3.94	3.86	4.46	0.69	0.58	1.96	0.67	0.79	29.43	0.62	1.45	48.02
Q9	18.80	18.23	54.32	2.10	2.22	10.34	6.64	5.98	39.68	3.85	5.67	39.02
Q10	2.62	1.31	7.40	0.55	0.37	1.67	1.43	3.36	20.75	4.63	5.48	20.47
Q11	1.84	0.89	2.89	0.38	0.24	0.58	0.49	0.12	0.44	0.10	0.10	0.55
Q12	1.88	1.29	2.18	0.33	0.24	0.91	0.55	0.21	0.60	0.10	0.10	2.78
Q13	19.42	15.04	15.17	1.27	1.09	1.24	1.69	2.18	3.23	1.93	3.99	4.05
Q14	2.44	0.96	4.13	0.45	0.29	0.78	0.70	0.28	3.06	0.26	1.06	2.44
Q16	6.27	3.99	8.41	0.82	0.54	3.25	1.01	0.74	7.73	1.02	2.58	8.75
Q17	4.33	5.04	21.9	0.58	0.56	3.39	0.56	0.54	19.81	0.72	1.39	18.24
Q18	5.43	2.89	4.21	0.60	0.49	0.62	0.76	0.46	0.73	0.25	0.40	0.39
Q19	11.48	9.72	9.73	1.05	0.99	0.95	1.01	1.00	0.70	1.06	0.92	0.81
Q20	4.45	3.39	8.53	0.60	0.51	4.76	3.88	1.91	77.34	4.77	2.08	75.72
Q21	16.21	12.33	27.85	1.18	1.96	3.65						
Q22	4.77	4.90	3.67	0.75	0.75	0.60	1.52	1.81	1.60	1.85	3.99	3.69

The most striking aspect of the VectorH results is that they show that the skewed queries relatively become much more expensive, with Q2, 8, 9, 10, 17, 20 running into tens of seconds. Also, scalability on these queries is fully gone and some even run slower on more hardware. We think this shows that when data movement over the network becomes a factor, the penalties for skew become higher. Further, MPP systems must do static partitioning of tables, and the fact that e.g. 5 of the lineitem partitions are much larger due to skew even makes queries without joins affected: even though Q1 on any database system tends to scale perfectly, the fact that 5 tasks must now scan a significantly bigger partition than the other tasks causes imperfect scaling.

The Hive results are in Table 1, where we tested scalability by running the JCC-H and TPC-H query sets on 2, 4 and 8 nodes. Figure 4 shows that while TPC-H scales reasonably from 2–8 nodes (though less than a factor 4), especially the JCC-H "skewed" query set scales very badly. The "normal" query set scales less badly, but still not so good. The fact that table partitioning is affected by skew, even affects queries with non-skewed query processing behavior, since the skewed partitions (read as Parquet files [6]) need to be scanned and this is an important factor in Hive performance.

4 Conclusion

In this paper, we have introduced a new variant of TPC-H, named JCC-H, that adds correlations and skew to TPC-H.[7] JCC-H was carefully designed to include very severe join skew as well as filter skew. Moreover, these skewed effects are observed by the original 22 TPC-H queries only if special parameters are given to them. That is, for each of the 22 queries there is a "skewed" query variant and a "normal" query variant (the normal variant is generated by default by qgen, and the skewed variant when passing -k). The decision to make JCC-H a drop-in replacement for TPC-H has a number of advantages, as JCC-H can be dropped into any existing benchmark testing pipeline, and its queries are well understood by practitioners.

A disadvantage of focusing on the existing 22 TPC-H queries is that there may be interesting and relevant query patterns where join-crossing correlations and related skew have even more significant effects. This belief is informed by the fact that access path selection for TPC-H is relatively straightforward. As such, it is also of immediate interest to devise additional query patterns for JCC-H where join-crossing correlation will affect the join execution order, or the (non-)use of unclustered indexes.

Acknowledgments. This paper is a result of the "Parallelism and Skew" working group at Dagstuhl seminar 17222 (Robust Performance in Database Query Processing). We would like to thank group members Johann-Christoph Freytag (HU Berlin), Alfons Kemper (TU Munich), Glenn Paulley (SAP Canada) and Kai-Uwe Sattler (TU Ilmenau) for their contributions. The research of A.C. Anadiotis was partially funded by the Swiss National Science Foundation, Project No.: 200021_146407/1 (FN-X-Core).

References

1. Boncz, P., Neumann, T., Erling, O.: TPC-H analyzed: hidden messages and lessons learned from an influential benchmark. In: Nambiar, R., Poess, M. (eds.) TPCTC 2013. LNCS, vol. 8391, pp. 61–76. Springer, Cham (2014). https://doi.org/10.1007/978-3-319-04936-6_5
2. Crolotte, A., Ghazal, A.: Introducing skew into the TPC-H benchmark. In: Nambiar, R., Poess, M. (eds.) TPCTC 2011. LNCS, vol. 7144, pp. 137–145. Springer, Heidelberg (2012). https://doi.org/10.1007/978-3-642-32627-1_10
3. Erling, O., Averbuch, A., Larriba-Pey, J., Chafi, H., Gubichev, A., Prat, A., Pham, M.-D., Boncz, P.: The LDBC social network benchmark interactive workload. In: SIGMOD (2015)

---

[6] We used the same DDL as in the VectorH SIGMOD paper: https://github.com/ActianCorp/VectorH-sigmod2016.

[7] The code for JCC-H can be downloaded from: http://github.com/ldbc/dbgen.JCC-H.

4. Frank, M., Poess, M., Rabl, T.: Efficient update data generation for DBMS benchmarks. In: Proceedings of the 3rd ACM/SPEC International Conference on Performance Engineering, pp. 169–180 (2012)
5. Ghazal, A., Rabl, T., Hu, M., Raab, F., Poess, M., Crolotte, A., Jacobsen, H.-A.: BigBench: towards an industry standard benchmark for big data analytics. In: SIGMOD (2013)
6. Gubichev, A., Boncz, P.: Parameter curation for benchmark queries. In: TPCTC, pp. 113–129 (2014)
7. Leis, V., Gubichev, A., Mirchev, A., Boncz, P., Kemper, A., Neumann, T.: How good are query optimizers, really? Proc. VLDB Endowment 9(3), 204–215 (2015)
8. O'Neil, P., O'Neil, E., Chen, X., Revilak, S.: The star schema benchmark and augmented fact table indexing. In: Nambiar, R., Poess, M. (eds.) TPCTC 2009. LNCS, vol. 5895, pp. 237–252. Springer, Heidelberg (2009). https://doi.org/10.1007/978-3-642-10424-4_17
9. Poess, M., Nambiar, R.O., Walrath, D.: Why you should run TPC-DS: a workload analysis. In: VLDB (2007)

TPCx-HS v2: Transforming with Technology Changes

Tariq Magdon-Ismail[1(✉)], Chinmayi Narasimhadevara[2],
Dave Jaffe[1], and Raghunath Nambiar[2]

[1] VMware, Inc., 4301 Hillview Ave, Palo Alto, CA 94304, USA
{tariq,djaffe}@vmware.com
[2] Cisco Systems, Inc., 275 East Tasman Drive, San Jose, CA 95134, USA
{cnarasim,rnambiar}@cisco.com

Abstract. The TPCx-HS Hadoop benchmark has helped drive competition in the Big Data marketplace and has proven to be a successful industry standard benchmark for Hadoop systems. However, the Big Data landscape has rapidly changed since its initial release in 2014. Key technologies have matured, while new ones have risen to prominence in an effort to keep pace with the exponential expansion of datasets. For example, Hadoop has undergone a much-needed upgrade to the way that scheduling, resource management, and execution occur in Hadoop, while Apache Spark has risen to be the de facto standard for in-memory cluster compute for ETL, Machine Learning, and Data Science Work-loads. Moreover, enterprises are increasingly considering cloud infrastructure for Big Data processing. What has not changed since TPCx-HS was first released is the need for a straightforward, industry standard way in which these current technologies and architectures can be evaluated. In this paper, we introduce TPCx-HS v2 that is designed to address these changes in the Big Data technology landscape and stress both the hardware and software stacks including the execution engine (MapReduce or Spark) and Hadoop Filesystem API compatible layers for both on-premise and cloud deployments.

Keywords: TPC · Big Data · Benchmark · Hadoop · Spark
Cloud · Performance

1 Introduction

Since its release on August 2014, the TPCx-HS Hadoop benchmark [1] has helped drive competition in the Big Data marketplace, generating 24 publications spanning 5 Hadoop distributions, 3 hardware vendors, 2 OS distributions, and 1 virtualization platform [2] (as of 2017/06/20). By all measures, it has proven to be a successful industry standard benchmark for Hadoop systems. However, the Big Data landscape has rapidly changed over the last three years. Key technologies have matured, while new ones have risen to prominence in an effort to keep pace with the exponential expansion of datasets. More-over, enterprises are increasingly considering cloud infrastructure for Big Data processing. What has not changed, however, is the need for a *straightforward*, industry standard way in which these current technologies and architectures can be evaluated with workloads and metrics that are well understood and easily relatable to the end user.

© Springer International Publishing AG 2018
R. Nambiar and M. Poess (Eds.): TPCTC 2017, LNCS 10661, pp. 120–130, 2018.
https://doi.org/10.1007/978-3-319-72401-0_9

In keeping with these important industry trends, we introduce TPCx-HS v2 for Hadoop and Spark that support not only traditional on-premise deployments but also cutting edge cloud deployments.

The rest of the paper is organized as follows. Section 2 briefly discusses the Hadoop ecosystem and the emergence of Spark. In Sect. 3, we present the changes made to TPCx-HS in version 2 of the benchmark specification and kit. Section 4 follows with an experimental comparison of Hadoop MapReduce and Spark. Finally, we conclude in Sect. 5.

2 Hadoop Ecosystem

At its core, Apache Hadoop is a software library that provides a framework for distributed processing of large datasets using a simple programming model. The popularity of Hadoop has grown in the last few years because it meets the needs of many organizations for flexible data analysis. Because of the increased deployment of Hadoop in production, a rich ecosystem of tools and solutions has developed around it. The number of official Apache open source projects alone, that are related to Hadoop, have increased from just 1 in 2008 [5] to 26 today [6]. Commercial Hadoop offerings are even more prolific and diverse, and include platforms and packaged distributions from vendors such as Cloudera, Hortonworks, and MapR, plus a variety of tools for specific Hadoop development, production, and maintenance tasks. Today, Apache Spark represents an increasingly important piece of this ecosystem.

2.1 Emergence of Spark

Apache Spark is an open source cluster computing framework that provides an interface for programming entire clusters with implicit data parallelism and fault-tolerance. It was developed to overcome some of the bottlenecks of Apache Hadoop, one of which is around the use of intermediate persistent storage. Spark provides an alternative to MapReduce that enables workloads to execute in memory, instead of on disk. Spark accesses data from HDFS but bypasses the MapReduce processing framework, and thus eliminates the resource-intensive disk operations that MapReduce requires. By using in-memory computing, Spark workloads typically run significantly faster compared to disk execution.

According to a Big Data survey report published by the Taneja Group [3], performance was cited as one of the main drivers of Spark adoption. Within the report, more than half of the respondents mentioned actively using Spark, with a notable increase in usage over the twelve months following the survey. Clearly, Spark is an important component of any Big Data pipeline today. Interestingly, but not surprisingly, there is also a significant trend towards deploying Spark in the cloud.

3 TPCx-HS v2

The TPCx-HS benchmark now stresses both the hardware and software stack including the execution engine (MapReduce or Spark) and Hadoop Filesystem API compatible layers for both on-premise and cloud deployments. The workload can be used to assess a broad range of system topologies and implementations of Hadoop/Spark clusters. In this new version of the kit, there have been changes made to support not only Spark but also Hadoop 2 APIs. The following sections discuss the need for these changes and describe what they are.

3.1   Hadoop 2 Support

With Hadoop 2, MapReduce from Hadoop 1 (MRv1) has been split into two components. The cluster resource management capabilities have become YARN (Yet Another Resource Negotiator) [11], while the MapReduce-specific capabilities remain MapReduce (MRv2)—albeit with a newer API. This is a significant upgrade to the way scheduling, resource management, and execution occur in Hadoop. It divides resource management and job lifecycle management into separate components.

The new YARN ResourceManager manages the global assignment of compute resources to applications, and the per-application ApplicationMaster manages the scheduling and coordination of an application. An application is either a single job (in the sense of Hadoop 1 MapReduce jobs) or a Directed Acyclic Graph (DAG) of such jobs. The ResourceManager and per-machine NodeManager daemon, which manages the user processes on that machine, form the computation unit of the job. The per-application ApplicationMaster is the framework-specific library and is tasked with negotiating resources from the ResourceManager and working with the NodeManager(s) to execute and monitor the tasks. One of the primary issues with MRv1 is that the Map and Reduce slot configuration is static. This inflexibility can lead to the underutilization of resources [10]. There is no slot configuration in YARN, allowing it to be more dynamic and hence more efficient [11]. Another limitation of MRv1 is that the Hadoop framework only supports MapReduce jobs. YARN supports both MapReduce and non-MapReduce applications.

3.1.1   MapReduce Kit Changes

While TPCx-HS v1 used the MRv1 API, the MapReduce code in the TPCx-HS v2 kit has been rewritten to conform to the MRv2 Java API. Since the MRv2 API is not backward compatible, a side effect of this change is that TPCx-HS v2 will not run on Hadoop 1. As before, job configuration options can be specified on the command line or in the mapred-site.xml file on the client. The vast majority of job configuration options that were available in MRv1 work in MRv2/YARN as well. For consistency and clarity, many options have been given new names. The older names are deprecated, but will still work for the time being. One more notable difference is the change in record format between TPCx-HS v1 and v2. The MRv1 code used a 64-bit Linear Congruential Generator (LCG) based random number generator, while the new MRv2 code uses a 128-bit LCG random number generator. As a result, keys now remain in the binary format. TPCx-HS v2 data is also less compressible as it was changed to reflect the changes in the GraySort benchmark [8] on which it is based [7]. Results of running the kit with the new API are detailed in Sect. 4.

3.2   Spark Support

Spark is a unified engine for distributed data processing. It enables batch, real-time, and advanced analytics on the Hadoop platform. Spark has a programming model similar to MapReduce but extends it with a data-sharing abstraction called "Resilient Distributed Datasets," or RDDs [9]. RDDs enable Spark to perform fault tolerant distributed in-memory computations.

Spark can be run in standalone mode or on YARN, both of which are supported by the TPCx-HS kit. In standalone mode, Spark manages its own cluster and uses a master/worker architecture. Here, a single driver (master) manages the workers on which the executors run. When run on YARN, YARN is responsible for allocating resources to Spark. Spark on YARN supports data locality for data residing in HDFS.

3.2.1   Spark Kit Changes

The TPCx-HS kit utilizes the Spark Scala API, for running the three phases of data generation, data sorting, and data validation required by the benchmark. The record generation in the Spark code is similar to the MRv2 code, so both of these results are comparable. The settings needed for Spark can be added to the Spark default configuration, for additional tuning. The kit supports running Spark using YARN or in standalone mode. The YARN configuration settings can be changed as needed for running Spark applications. The new jar file for Spark is also part of the kit and the user can choose to run with either Spark or MapReduce as the framework for running the benchmark. The results of the Spark framework tests are outlined in Sect. 4.

3.3   Cloud Support

The TPCx-HS specification now allows for cloud services to be part of the System Under Test. Moreover, the disclosure requirements have been amended to support public cloud environments where there is limited visibility into the underlying technology platform.

While there was nothing inherent in the workload or kit that prevented TPCx-HS from running on public or private cloud infrastructure, changes to the TPCx-HS specification were required in order to make the results compliant with the new TPC pricing policies outlined in the TPC Pricing Specification version 2.0 [4]. In particular, for a *measured configuration* the benchmark driver and the System Under Test must all reside in the same region and for a *priced configuration* the benchmark driver and the System Under Test must all reside in the same region. The region of the priced configuration may be different from the region of the measured configuration. The price of the priced configuration must include all hardware, software, cloud services, and maintenance charges over a period of 3 years.

4 Experimental Results

4.1 Configuration

The 13 HPE ProLiant DL 380 Gen 9 servers used in the test were configured identically, with two Intel Xeon E5-2683 v4 ("Broadwell") processors with 16 cores each and 512 GiB of memory. Hyper-Threading was enabled so each server showed 64 logical processors.

Each server was configured with two 1.2 TB spinning disks in a RAID 1 mirror for the server operating systems, as well as four 800 GB Non-Volatile Memory Express (NVMe) solid state disks connected to the PCI bus, and twelve 800 GB SAS Solid State Disks (SSDs) connected through the HPE Smart Array P840ar/2G raid controller.

Full server configuration details are shown in Table 1.

Table 1. Server configuration. In this document notation such as "GiB" refers to binary quantities such as gigibytes (2**30 or 1,073,741,824) while "GB" refers to gigabytes (10**9 or 1,000,000,000).

Component	Quantity/Type
Server	HPE ProLiant DL380 Gen 9
Processor	2× Intel Xeon CPU E5-2683 v4 @ 2.10 GHz w/16 cores each
Logical Processors (including HyperThreads)	64
Memory	512 GiB (16× 32 GiB DIMMs)
NICs	2× 1 GbE ports + 4 × 10 GbE ports
Hard Drives	2× 1.2 TB 12G SAS 10 K 2.5in HDD – RAID 1 for OS
NVMes	4× 800 GB NVMe PCIe – NodeManager traffic
SSDs	12× 800 GB 12G SAS SSD – DataNode traffic
RAID Controller	HPE Smart Array P840ar/2G Controller
Remote Access	HPE iLO Advanced

Three of the servers were virtualized with VMware vSphere 6.5 and ran virtual machines that managed the Hadoop cluster. On the first server, a VM hosted the Gateway node, running Cloudera Manager and several other Hadoop functions as well as the gateway for the Hadoop Distributed File System (HDFS), YARN, Spark, and Hive services. The second and third servers each hosted a Master VM, on which the active and passive HDFS NameNode and YARN ResourceManager components and associated services ran. ZooKeeper, running on all three VMs, provided high availability.

The other 10 servers ran only the worker services, HDFS DataNode, and YARN NodeManager. Spark executors ran on the YARN NodeManagers.

The full assignment of roles is shown in Table 2. Key software component versions are shown in Table 3.

Table 2. Hadoop/Spark roles.

Node	Roles
Gateway	Cloudera Manager, ZooKeeper Server, HDFS JournalNode, HDFS gateway, YARN gateway, Hive gateway, Spark gateway, Spark History Server, Hive Metastore Server, Hive Server2, Hive WebHCat Server, Hue Server, Oozie Server
Master1	HDFS NameNode (Active), YARN ResourceManager (Standby), ZooKeeper Server, HDFS JournalNode, HDFS Balancer, HDFS FailoverController, HDFS HttpFS, HDFS NFS gateway
Master2	HDFS NameNode (Standby), YARN ResourceManager (Active), ZooKeeper Server, HDFS JournalNode, HDFS FailoverController, YARN JobHistory Server,
Workers (10)	HDFS DataNode, YARN NodeManager, Spark Executor

Table 3. Key software components.

Component	Version
Operating System	Centos 7.3
Cloudera Distribution of Hadoop	5.10.0
Cloudera Manager	5.10.0
Hadoop	2.6.0+cdh5.10.0+2102
HDFS	2.6.0+cdh5.10.0+2102
YARN	2.6.0+cdh5.10.0+2102
MapReduce2	2.6.0+cdh5.10.0+2102
Hive	1.1.0+cdh5.10.0+859
Spark	1.6.0+cdh5.10.0+457
ZooKeeper	3.4.5+cdh5.10.0+104
Java	Oracle 1.8.0_111-b14
MySQL	5.6.35 Community Server

With the NVMe storage providing the highest random read/write IOs per second, the four NVMe devices in each server were assigned to handle the NodeManager temporary data, which consists of Hadoop map spills to disk and reduce shuffles. SAS SSDs provide very high speed sequential reads and writes, so the twelve SSDs in each server were assigned to the DataNode traffic, consisting of reads and writes of permanent HDFS data.

The Hadoop and Spark parameters used in the test are shown in Table 4. They fall into two categories. Parameters such as yarn.nodemanager.resource.cpu-vcores and yarn.nodemanager.resource.memory-mb assign the resources available to YARN (to provide to containers running Hadoop map or reduce tasks or Spark executors), while the rest are application-dependent parameters.

Table 4. Key Hadoop/Spark cluster parameters used in tests.

Parameter	Default	Configured
dfs.blocksize	128 MiB	1 GiB
dfs.replication	3	3
mapreduce.task.io.sort.mb	256 MiB	2047 MiB
yarn.nodemanager.resource.cpu-vcores		64
mapreduce.map.cpu.vcores	1	1
mapreduce.reduce.cpu.vcores	1	1
yarn.nodemanager.resource.memory-mb		448 GiB
mapreduce.map.memory.mb	1 GiB	6.25 GiB
mapreduce.reduce.memory.mb	1 GiB	6.25 GiB
Maximum map/reduce tasks per node		64/64
Number of map/reduce tasks used in tests		639/639
spark.executor.cores	1	4
spark.executor.memory	256 MiB	25 GiB
spark.driver.memory	1 GiB	10 GiB
spark.executor.instances		149
Maximum number of Spark executors per node		16
Log Level on HDFS, YARN, Hive	INFO	WARN

For yarn.nodemanager.resource.cpu-vcores, all 64 logical processors were assigned to YARN vcores. For yarn.nodemanager.resource.memory-mb, the 512 GiB server memory was reduced by about 12% to provide memory for the operating system, as well as the Java heap size required for the DataNode and NodeManager processes, resulting in 448 GiB usable for containers.

The dfs.blocksize was set at 1 GiB to take advantage of the large memory available to YARN, and the mapreduce.task.io.sort.mb was consequently set to the largest possible value, 2047 MiB, to minimize spills to disk during the map processing of each HDFS block.

The number of vcores assigned to map and reduce processes (mapreduce.map.cpu.vcores and mapreduce.reduce.cpu.vcores) were left at the default value of 1, meaning that a maximum of 64 map or reduce task containers could run at any one time on the 64-vcore cluster. It was found through experimentation that using all 64 vcores per server provided the fastest performance, but optimum performance was achieved by lowering the per-task memory (mapreduce.map.memory.mb and mapreduce.reduce.memory.mb) from the maximum sustainable by the 448-GiB cluster (7 GiB) down to 6.25 GiB. With each of the 10 nodes running 64 YARN containers, a maximum of 640 task containers could be run simultaneously. One YARN container was needed to run the YARN Application Master, leaving 639 for maps or reduces.

For Spark the calculations are similar: 16 Spark executors were enabled per node, each using 4 vcores (spark.executor.cores) and 25 GiB (spark.executor.memory). Spark automatically adds 10% of Spark executor memory overhead, so the total memory consumed by 16 Spark executors (16×27.5 GiB or 440 GiB) would fit within the 448-GiB cluster. However, it was found that the best Spark performance was obtained while allowing more free memory and vcores, so the final setup used 15 executors per node or 149 per cluster (again with one YARN container left over for the ApplicationMaster task).

Spark was run in yarn-client mode, meaning that the Spark master process ran on the Spark gateway on the Gateway VM. 10 GiB was assigned to this process (spark.driver.memory).

Finally, the log level of most Hadoop processes was lowered from INFO to WARN to reduce the amount of log traffic being written on each server.

4.2 Results

The results for the three versions of the code are shown in Table 5. Both the consolidated benchmark metric (HSph@3TB) in which larger is faster, and the elapsed times for the three TPCx-HS phases (smaller is better) are shown.

Table 5. Results

Test	TPCx-HS Performance Metric (HSph@3TB)	HSGen Elapsed Time (S)	HSSort Elapsed Time (S)	HSValidate Elapsed Time (S)
MRv1	7.8843	372	918	123
MRv2	7.2974	370	979	127
Spark	8.6281	368	799	79

Utilization of CPU, disks, and network are shown for the three tests in Figs. 1, 2, 3, 4, 5, 6, 7, 8 and 9. One can see how the various resources are utilized through the phases of the benchmark, as well as the small differences between the two MapReduce versions and the Spark version.

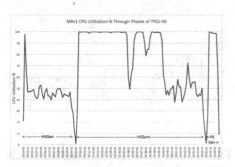

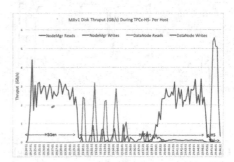

Fig. 1. MRv1 CPU Utilization on a single worker node.

Fig. 2. MRv1 Disk Throughput on a single worker node.

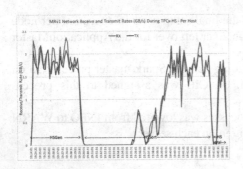

Fig. 3. MRv1 Network Receive and Transmit Rates on a single worker node.

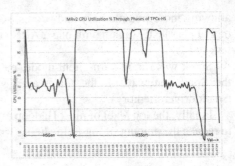

Fig. 4. MRv2 CPU Utilization on a single worker node.

Fig. 5. MRv2 Disk Throughput on a single worker node.

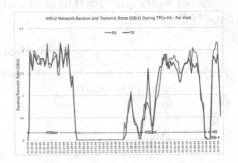

Fig. 6. MRv2 Network Receive and Transmit Rates on a single worker node.

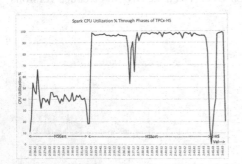

Fig. 7. Spark CPU Utilization on a single worker node.

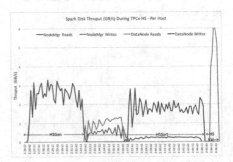

Fig. 8. Spark Disk Throughput on a single worker node.

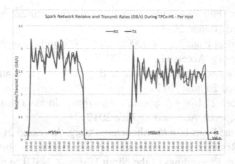

Fig. 9. Spark Network Receive and Transmit Rates on a single worker node.

5   Conclusion

The TPC has played a crucial role in providing the industry with relevant standards for total system performance, price-performance, and energy efficiency comparisons. TPC benchmarks are widely used by database researchers and academia. As Big Data became an integral part of enterprise IT, TPCx-HS was the TPC's first major step in creating a set of industry standards for measuring various aspects of hardware and software systems dealing with Big Data. It has helped drive competition in the Big Data marketplace and has proven to be a successful industry standard benchmark for Hadoop systems.

However, the Big Data technology landscape has rapidly changed since the benchmark's initial release, and in keeping with these changes TPCx-HS has also transformed. TPCx-HS v2 has advanced not only by supporting the significant leaps in technology, namely Hadoop 2 (MapReduce v2/YARN) and Spark, but also by accommodating major new infrastructure and deployment options such as the cloud.

Acknowledgements.   Developing a TPC benchmark for a new environment requires a huge effort to conceptualize, research, specify, review, prototype, and verify the benchmark. The authors acknowledge the work and contributions made by Da Qi Ren, David Grimes, Jamie Reding, John Poelman, Karthik Kulkarni, Matthew Emmerton, Meikel Poess, Mike Brey, Paul Cao, and Reza Taheri.

References

1. Nambiar, R., Poess, M., Dey, A., Cao, P., Magdon-Ismail, T., Ren, D.Q., Bond, A.: Introducing TPCx-HS: the first industry standard for benchmarking Big Data systems. In: Nambiar, R., Poess, M. (eds.) TPCTC 2014. LNCS, vol. 8904, pp. 1–12. Springer, Cham (2015). https://doi.org/10.1007/978-3-319-15350-6_1
2. TPCx-HS Results. http://www.tpc.org/tpcx-hs/results/tpcxhs_results.asp. Accessed 20 June 2017
3. Taneja Group Spark Market Adoption Report. https://www.cloudera.com/content/dam/www/marketing/resources/analyst-reports/taneja-group-spark-survey-exec-summary-Oct-2016.pdf.landing.html. Accessed 20 June 2017

4. TPC Specifications, http://www.tpc.org//tpc_documents_current_versions/current_specifi cations.asp. Accessed 20 June 2017
5. Apache Hadoop Project Page, 02 July 2008. http://web.archive.org/web/20080702015052/http://hadoop.apache.org. Accessed 20 June 2017
6. Apache Hadoop Ecosystem and Open Source Big Data Projects. https://hortonworks.com/ecosystems/. Accessed 20 June 2017
7. Getting MapReduce 2 Up to Speed. http://blog.cloudera.com/blog/2014/02/getting-mapreduce-2-up-to-speed/. Accessed 21 June 2017
8. Sort Benchmark Home Page. http://sortbenchmark.org. Accessed 21 June 2017
9. Zaharia, M. et al.: Resilient distributed datasets: a fault-tolerant abstraction for in-memory cluster computing. In: Proceedings of the Ninth USENIX NSDI Symposium on Networked Systems Design and Implementation, San Jose, CA (2012)
10. Guo, Z., Fox, G., Zhou, M., Ruan, Y.: Improving resource utilization in MapReduce. In: 2013 IEEE International Conference on Cluster Computing (CLUSTER) (2013)
11. Vavilapalli, V.K. et al.: Apache Hadoop YARN: yet another resource negotiator. In: Proceedings of the 4th Annual Symposium on Cloud Computing (SOCC), Santa Clara, CA (2013). Article No. 5

Performance Assurance Model for Applications on SPARK Platform

Rekha Singhal$^{(\boxtimes)}$ and Praveen Singh

Tata Consultancy Services Research, Mumbai, India
rekha.singhal@tcs.com

Abstract. The wide availability of open source big data processing frameworks, such as Spark, has increased migration of existing applications and deployment of new applications to these cost-effective platforms. One of the challenges is assuring performance of an application with increase in data size in production system. We have addressed this problem in our work for Spark platform using a performance prediction model in development environment. We have proposed a grey box approach to estimate an application execution time on Spark cluster for higher data size using measurements on low volume data in a small size cluster. The proposed model may also be used iteratively to estimate the competent cluster size for desired application performance in production environment. We have discussed both machine learning and analytic based techniques to build the model. The model is also flexible to different configurations of Spark cluster. This flexibility enables the use of the prediction model with optimization techniques to get tuned value of Spark parameters for optimal performance of deployed application on Spark cluster. Our key innovations in building Spark performance prediction model are support for different configurations of Spark platform, and simulator to estimate Spark stage execution time which includes task execution variability due to HDFS, data skew and cluster nodes heterogeneity. We have shown that our proposed approaches are able to predict within 20% error bound for Wordcount, Terasort, K-means and few TPC-H SQL workloads.

1 Introduction

The digitization wave has led to challenge of processing high volume and high velocity data in real time. Apache Spark is one of the commodity cluster platforms available in open source to address this need due to its in-memory processing capability. Application deployment on commodity cluster system has challenge of assuring its performance over time with increase in data size. Conversely, appropriate capacity sizing of production Spark cluster is needed for desired performance irrespective of increase in data size. This raises the need for a performance assurance model, which can estimate an application performance for larger data sizes and variable cluster sizes before deployment. Here, by performance we mean application *execution time*.

© Springer International Publishing AG 2018
R. Nambiar and M. Poess (Eds.): TPCTC 2017, LNCS 10661, pp. 131–146, 2018.
https://doi.org/10.1007/978-3-319-72401-0_10

One of the popular black box approaches is to use machine learning techniques to build performance prediction model. This requires identification of performance sensitive parameters (or relevant features) and collecting their values for multiple executions of application which may delay deployment. We have discussed this in detail in Sect. 3. An analytic or mathematical model based on few measurements is desirable to reduce cost and time to deploy.

An application deployed on Spark platform is executed as a sequence of Spark jobs. Each Spark job is executed as a directed acyclic graph (DAG) consisting of stages. Each stage has multiple executors running in parallel and each executor has set of concurrent tasks. This complexity cannot be handled by simple mathematics alone. We have proposed a hierarchical model for estimating Spark application execution time. Further, data skew and task execution variability have been handled by building a simulator for Spark jobs. Literature also has similar simulator but for Hadoop MR jobs [12]. We have focused on Spark parameters which can be changed during application execution and hence the proposed performance prediction model may be used with optimization techniques to get tuned value of Spark parameters for auto tuning. This paper has following contributions.

- Analysis of Spark's configurable parameters' sensitivity to application execution time with respect to increase in data size. Use of this analysis to define features to be used by machine learning algorithms for predicting application execution time on larger data sizes. We have compared accuracy of prediction models based on various ML techniques such as Multi Linear Regression (MLR), MLR-Quadratic and Support Vector Machine (SVM).
- Analytic based approach to predict an application execution time, on Spark platform, for larger data and cluster sizes using limited measurements in small size development environment. This has led to innovation in building simulator for estimating Spark job's stages' execution time. We have also built models for estimating task's JVM time, task's scheduler delay and task's shuffle time as function of input data size to support different configurations of Spark cluster. This capability of the model may also be used to build auto tuner.

The paper is organized as follows. Section 2 discusses the related work. The Spark platform performance sensitive parameters analysis and machine learning approach for building performance prediction model are discussed in Sect. 3. The analytic based performance prediction model is presented in Sect. 4. The experimental results for validation of the model are presented in Sect. 5. The extension of the performance prediction models to build auto tuner is formalized in Sect. 6. Finally, the paper is concluded in Sect. 7.

2   Related Work

Lot of work has been done in the area of performance prediction [5,7,14] and auto tuning of applications [4,6,8,9] on big data platforms. Majority of this work addresses Hadoop technology. [10,11] have concentrated on building performance prediction models, using limited measurements in small size development environment, for relational databases and Hive+Hadoop platforms respectively. However, [3,8,13] discuss performance analysis and tuning of Spark cluster. Ahsan [3] has shown that application performance degrades on large data size primarily due to JVM GC overheads. We have also built task's JVM prediction model as function of data size for estimating application execution time on larger data size, as discussed in Sect. 4.3. Machine learning techniques have also been used by big data community to build performance models [7,14]. We categorize the related work into two parts- Machine learning (ML) based approach and Cost based analytic approach.

2.1 ML Based Approach

Machine learning (ML) based approach is a black box method, which has been explored by big data community primarily to model performance of complex big data system. ML models are simple to build and are based on measurements collected during execution of actual workload on actual system. Kay et al. [7] has proposed generic ML approach with design of experiments and feature selection for analytic workload on big data platforms. [14] talks about tuning and performance prediction of Hadoop jobs using machine learning approach. They have focused on four performance sensitive parameters of Hadoop platform along with data size to build model. They have compared the accuracy of models built using different algorithms such as MLR, MLR-quadratic, SVM etc. We have customized this approach for Spark platform as discussed in Sect. 3.

2.2 Cost Based Approach

Cost based approach employs white box technique, which builds model based on deeper understanding of a system. However, it uses finite resources to build model unlike ML approach. Starfish [5] conducts instrumentation of Hadoop to collect performance measurements and build performance model to estimate a job execution time as function of various Hadoop platform parameters and data sizes. This method makes it adaptable for auto tuning by optimizing the model for different parameter settings. We have used similar methodology for Spark platform, but without instrumentation, by including Spark platform performance sensitive parameters as inputs to the prediction model as discussed in Sect. 4.

Panagiotis [8] proposes to tune a large number of Spark parameters using trial and error rule base created with few measurements. Their focus has been more on serialization and memory related parameters, however, we are interested in parallelism and memory related parameters in this paper. Shi et al. [9] has proposed Produce-Transfer-Consume (PTC) approach to model Hadoop job execution cost and used this to get optimal setting for Hadoop platforms. They have identified only few key parameters which are used to tune Hadoop system for a given job. We have also chosen only few performance sensitive parameters to build performance prediction model for Spark applications. The proposed model is formulated along the steps involved in an application execution on Spark platform. However, we do not perform white box instrumentation rather conduct our own experiments to collect the desired performance data for each such step. Wang et al. [13] has proposed an analytic based model for predicting Spark job performance and is closely related to our work discussed in Sect. 4. However, their model is restricted to same values for Spark parameters both in the sample and actual execution of an application. We could overcome this limitation by including sub models for estimating task JVM time, Shuffle time and Scheduler delay time. The heterogeneity at data, HDFS and hardware level for task execution has been handled by a simulator for estimating Spark stage execution time unlike the mathematical approach proposed in [13].

3   Machine Learning Based Model

Building a machine learning based model requires correct identification of features and choice of right machine learning algorithm. Spark platform has more than 100 parameters to configure [8]. The first challenge is to identify right set of parameters which impact an application execution time for varying data and cluster sizes and this set constitutes our feature set. We targeted only those parameters which could be changed during an application execution.

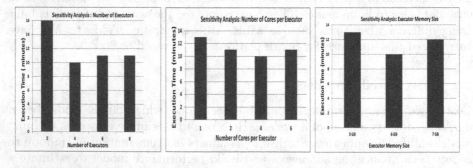

Fig. 1. Performance sensitivity analysis on 20 GB data size and 2 node cluster

We have conducted performance sensitivity analysis for number of parameters which are potential candidates for feature selection. The most sensitive parameters identified are the ones, whose changes led to variations in performance of the application. Our observed feature set in Spark 2.0 constitutes number of executors, number of cores per executor, executor memory size (this controls both shuffle memory and JVM heap size) and data size as shown in Fig. 1.

3.1   Experimental Set Up and Results

Our experimental setup consists of 5 nodes, each of Intel(R) Xeon(R) CPU X5365 @ 3.00 GHz, 8 cores and 16 GB RAM. The platform stack consists of Yarn,

Apache Spark 2.01 and HDFS 2.6. We have one master and maximum four slaves in these experiments. We have formulated set of experiments based on the hardware constraints of the system. For example, the product of 'number of cores per executor' and 'number of executors' can vary from 1 to maximum cores in the cluster. The experimental configurations to collect training data is given in Table 1. We have built and tested ML prediction models for three types of workloads – Wordcount, Terasort and K-means [1] for data sizes varying from 5 GB to 15 GB. A linux bash script executes each of the application for all combinations of the parameters settings given in Table 1. Few of the combinations are invalid due to resource mismatch and are skipped. In total we could collect around 400 data points, as training set, for each application to build ML model.

Table 1. Experimental setup configuration for machine learning model

Configuration parameter	Minimum value	Maximum value
Number of executors (–num-executor)	2	10
Number of cores per executor (–executor-cores)	1	8
Executor memory (–executor-memory)	1	12
Data size	1 GB	15 GB

Table 2. Accuracy of ML models for different algorithms

Wordcount		Terasort		K-Means	
Model	MAPE	Model	MAPE	Model	MAPE
Linear	0.2345	Linear	0.3049	Linear	0.2500
MLR-I	0.2445	MLR-I	0.21985	MLR-I	0.2900
MLR-Q	0.2310	MLR-Q	0.2998	MLR-Q	0.2508
SVM	0.2356	SVM	0.1701	SVM	0.2009
SVM tuning	0.2234	SVM tuning	0.0876	SVM Tuning	0.2152

Table 3. Performance tuning results for Applications on 20 GB data size with default settings on $(4 + 1)$ node cluster where, Ne: Number of executors, Nc: Number of cores per executor, Nm: Executor memory size in GB

Application	Default values	Execution time on default values	Parameter optimal values	Optimal execution time (Gain%)
Wordcount	Ne = 2, Nc = 1, Nm = 1	1165.1450	Ne = 10, Nc = 2, Nm = 4	377.02 (67%)
Terasort	Ne = 2, Nc = 1, Nm = 1	884.395	Ne = 4, Nc = 4, Nm = 1	664.81 (24%)
K-means	Ne = 2, Nc = 1, Nm = 1	14778.06	Ne = 8, Nc = 6, Nm = 12	875.479 (94%)

A statistical tool R is used to build performance prediction model using various algorithms such as Multiple Linear Regression (MLR), MLR with quadratic effect and SVM with and without tuning [14]. These ML model are used for predicting application execution time on 20 GB data size. As shown in Table 2, these algorithms are able to predict with Mean Absolute Percentage Error (MAPE) 22% on average. These performance prediction models are integrated with optimization algorithm in R and could yield up to 94% improvement in application performance as shown in Table 3. Machine Learning based prediction models requires lot of resources and time for data collection. Agile development framework does not allow time delay incurred in collecting training data for building performance assurance model. Therefore, we have built analytic model using one time measurements as discussed in the next section.

4   Measurement Based Analytic Performance Prediction Model

We assume a small size Spark cluster with application and its representative data sets available in development environment. The cluster is assumed to have atleast one instance of each type of heterogeneous nodes deployed in production system. The application is executed in this small cluster on small data size (*DevSize*). The application logs created by Spark platform are parsed to collect granular level performance data as given in Table 4. The problem statement is to estimate the application execution time for production environment, having larger data size (say *ProdSize*) and larger cluster size (say CS_{prod}) with different Spark parameter configurations, using the collected measurements. We will use notations given in Table 4 for further explanation of the model. An application is executed as a serial execution of a number of Spark jobs as shown in Fig. 2. Therefore, the application's predicted execution time is summation of the estimated execution time of its jobs launched one after another i.e.

$$ApplnExecutionTime = \sum_{i=0}^{i=N} pJobT_i \qquad (1)$$

A Spark job is executed in a form of directed acyclic graph (DAG), where each node in the graph represents a stage. A new stage is created whenever next operation requires data to be shuffled. A job's execution time is predicted as summation of the estimated execution time of all its stages i.e.

$$pJobT_i = JobSt_i + \sum_{k=0}^{k=SN_i} pStageT_i^k + JobCln_i \qquad (2)$$

Each stage is executed as set of concurrent executors with parallel tasks in each executor, depending on values of *number of executors* and *number of cores per executor* parameters. If executors allocated per node (i.e. $\frac{NE_p}{CS_p}$) can not be scheduled concurrently, due to non-availability of cores on the node (i.e. $\frac{NE_p}{CS_p} * NC_p <$ node's available cores), then the executors are serialized and executed one after another, and the stage's estimated execution time is increased by factor of the number of serialized executors. For simplification, we assume that Spark parameter configuration is such that executors are running concurrently at each node. Each executor spawns multiple threads, one for each task. All tasks launched in an executor share the same JVM memory. Each task processes a defined size of data set (i.e. block size). For a given data size, an executor may have multiple waves of such parallel tasks executions on each core. Since all tasks in a stage are identical and read same data size, therefore, execution time of stage 'j' of job 'i' may be estimated as:

$$pStageT_i^j = StgSt_i^j + Avg(pTskT_i^j) * \left\lceil \frac{pDS_i^j}{(BS_p * NE_p * NC_p)} \right\rceil + StgCln_i^j \quad (3)$$

However, variation in tasks' execution time may break the symmetry and number of tasks assigned per core (or wave count) may not be same at all cores. Variation in tasks' execution time could be due to data skew, heterogeneous nodes and/or variability in location of HDFS block(s) read by a task-local, same rack or remote. We have built a stage task execution simulator, using performance summary created in development environment (in Sect. 4.1), to capture this variability as discussed in Sect. 4.5. A task execution time constitutes scheduler delay, serialization time, de-serialization time, JVM overheads, compute time including IO read/write time in HDFS and shuffle IO time. Note that each task reads either shuffled data or input data and writes shuffled data or output data. Therefore execution time of a task in stage 'j' of job 'i' is estimated as:

$$pTskT_i^j = pTskSd_i^j + pTskSer_i^j + pTskCt_i^j + pTskJvm_i^j + pTskSf_i^j \quad (4)$$

A task's serialization and de-serialization time depends on amount of data processed by a task, which depends on the block size. Since this is a compute operation, it can be assumed to increase linearly with block size. For same block size in both the environments, $pTskSer_i^j = dTskSer_i^j$. A task's JVM time represents the overhead in garbage collection while managing multiple threads. The JVM time estimation depends on type of computation, hardware system and number of threads, which is discussed in detail in Sect. 4.3. For a given Spark cluster, an increase in input data size may increase a task's shuffle data such that it may not fit in the allocated memory. This results in spill over to disk and may increase shuffle time non-linearly because of additional disk read and write operations. We need a model to estimate shuffle read and write time as function of input data size, cluster size and shuffle memory as discussed in Sect. 4.4.

4.1 Performance Summary

We have observed that variation in task execution time also relates to its launch time on a core. To capture this variation, we divided a stage tasks into two types

Table 4. Notations used in the analytic model discussed in Sect. 4

Parameter	Development	Production
Block size	BS_{dev}	BS_{prod}
Number of executors	NE_d	NE_p
Number of cores per executor	NC_d	NC_p
Number of jobs in the application	N	N
Number of stages in job 'i'	SN_i	SN_i
Job 'i' execution time	$dJobT_i$	$pJobT_i$
Job 'i' start up time	$JobSt_i$	$JobSt_i$
Job 'i' clean up time	$JobCln_i$	$JobCln_i$
Job 'i' stage 'j' execution time	$dStageT_i^j$	$pStageT_i^j$
Job 'i' stage 'j' startup time	$StgSt_i^j$	$StgSt_i^j$
Job 'i' stage 'j' cleanup time	$StgCln_i^j$	$StgCln_i^j$
Job 'i', stage 'j', number of tasks	dNT_i^j	pNT_i^j
Job 'i', stage 'j', size of shuffled data	dDS_i^j	pDS_i^j
Job 'i', stage 'j', task Execution Time	$dTskT_i^j$	$pTskT_i^j$
Job 'i', stage 'j', task execution time in 'k'th wave	$dTskT_i^{jk}$	$pTskT_i^{jk}$
Job 'i', stage 'j', task serialization + de-serialization time	$dTskSer_i^j$	$pTskSer_i^j$
Job 'i', stage 'j', task JVM time	$dTskJvm_i^j$	$pTskJvm_i^j$
Job 'i', stage 'j', task shuffle IO time	$dTskSf_i^j$	$pTskSf_i^j$
Job 'i', stage 'j', task scheduler delay	$dTskSd_i^j$	$pTskSd_i^j$
Job 'i', stage 'j', first wave task compute time	$dFstTskCt_i^j$	$pFstTskCt_i^j$
Job 'i', stage 'j', first wave task scheduler delay	$dFstTskSd_i^j$	$pFstTskSd_i^j$
Job 'i', stage 'j', rest wave 'k'th bucket duration	$dRstTkBktDur_i^{jk}$	$pRstTkBktDur_i^{jk}$
Job 'i', stage 'j', number of rest wave tasks in 'k'th bucket	$dRstTkBktN_i^{jk}$	$pRstTskBktN_i^{jk}$
Job 'i', stage 'j', rest wave task compute time	$dRstTskCt_i^j$	$pRstTskCt_i^j$
Job 'i', stage 'j', rest wave task scheduler delay	$dRstTskSd_i^j$	$pRstTskSd_i^j$
Job 'i', stage 'j', rest wave task maximum compute time	$dRstTkMaxCT_i^j$	–
Job 'i', stage 'j', rest wave task minimum compute time	$dRstTkMinCT_i^j$	–

of tasks - first wave tasks and rest wave tasks as shown in Fig. 2 by emulating the task scheduling behaviour of Spark platform across $NE_d * NC_d$ cores. An application log is parsed to collect list of all $dTskT_i^j$ sorted in the order of their launch time. An array of data structure of size $NE_d * NC_d$ is allocated with each 'k'th element storing the 'k'th core current finish time. Initially all elements are initialized to zero. dNT_i^j tasks are scheduled on $NE_d * NC_d$ cores such that the next task in the list is scheduled on the core having minimum finish time, leading to a task allocation structure as shown in Fig. 2. Using the measurements collected from the Spark application log, $dFstTskCT_i^j$ and $dFstTskSd_i^j$ are computed as

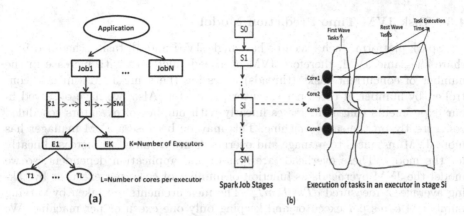

Fig. 2. (a) Application execution on Spark (b) Tasks execution in an executor for a stage Si with 4 cores

average of $(dTskT_i^j - dTskJvm_i^j - dTskSf_i^j - dTskSd_i^j)$ and average of $dTskSd_i^j$ respectively of all the tasks in the first wave. Similarly, $dRstTskSd_i^j$ is calculated as the average of scheduler delay of all tasks in the rest wave. $dRstTskCT_i^j$ is also computed as histogram of $(dTskT_i^j - dTskJvm_i^j - dTskSf_i^j - dTskSd_i^j)$ for all rest wave tasks, to capture variability in task execution time. The histogram has 'm' buckets each of size $BkSize_i^j$ such that

$$BkSize_i^j = \frac{(dRstTskMaxCT_i^j - dRstTskMinCT_i^j)}{m} \tag{5}$$

The 'k'th bucket duration is from $(k-1) * BkSize_i^j$ to $k * BkSize_i^j$. Each of the rest wave tasks is categorized into one of 'm' buckets such that $dRstTskCT_i^j$ falls into the duration of the bucket. $dRstTskBktDur_i^{jk}$ is computed as average of $dRstTskCT_i^j$ for all tasks in 'k'th bucket. Performance summary of stage 'j' of job 'i' consists of $dFstTskCT_i^j$ and 'm' buckets each with its average duration $dRstTskBktDur_i^{jl}$ and $dRstTskBktN_i^{jl}$ number of tasks in 'l'th bucket. Higher the value of 'm', more variation in task execution time can be captured. However, it may also increase the time taken to mimic scheduler for rest wave tasks, whose time complexity is O(n + m) for 'n' tasks.

4.2 Task Scheduler Delay Prediction Model

Scheduler delay is the delay incurred while scheduling a task. We have observed larger scheduler delay for first wave tasks due to task scheduling preparation overheads. Therefore,

$$pFstTskSd_i^j = dFstTskSd_i^j * \frac{pNT_i^j}{dNT_i^j} \tag{6}$$

$$pRstTskSd_i^j = dRstTskSd_i^j$$

4.3   Task JVM Time Prediction Model

On Spark platform, each executor has single JVM and all tasks scheduled in it share the same JVM, therefore JVM overheads increases with increase in the number of concurrent tasks (threads) accessing the same JVM which is controlled by number of cores per executor parameter. Also, we have observed in our experiments that it increases linearly with number of executors scheduled concurrently on the same machine. This may be because a JVM manager has more JVM instances to manage and overheads are assumed to increase linearly for the model. These overheads are system and application dependent, so we model the JVM overheads as function of number of cores per executor by taking average of measured $dTskJvmT_i^j$. The measurements are taken by varying number of cores per executor and keeping only one executor per machine. We use regression to estimate JVM overheads for NC_p cores per executor in the production environment. For example, Fig. 3 shows the JVM model used in our experimental setup for Wordcount and Terasort applications for one executor per machine. $pTskJVM_i^j$ is further extrapolated linearly to the number of concurrent executors per node.

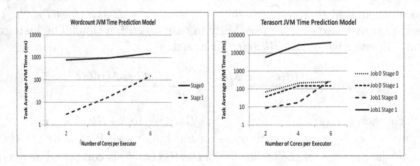

Fig. 3. JVM time estimation model for Wordcount and Terasort applications built on experimental set up given in Sect. 5

4.4   Task Shuffle Time Prediction Model

A naive approach to estimate a task shuffle time is linear extrapolation i.e.

$$pTskSf_i^j = \frac{\sum_{\forall tasks} dTskSf_i^j}{dNT_i^j} * \frac{pDS_i^j}{dDS_i^j} \qquad (7)$$

However, it may hold true only for those configurations of production system where a task's shuffle data size is small enough to fit in the allocated memory. Otherwise, shuffle operation leads to spill over to disk and incurs extra disk IO read/write operations for a task. We model this by estimating shuffle data size per task and predict if this will lead to spill over. If it does, we estimate the overheads of spill over and add that to a tasks shuffle time. Spill overheads are calculated at small data size by constraining the development environment to generate spurious disk spills. For simplicity, we assume that network is not a bottleneck here, so communication overhead increases linear to shuffle data size. Assuming block size unchanged, the size of shuffle data generated per task remains same.

Shuffle data size per executor is estimated as $(\frac{pDS_i^j}{NE_p})$. We have observed that shuffle data size in memory increases due to de-serialization. For an executor, if this increased size is more than allocated shuffle memory (i.e. storage memory fraction * executor memory size), the shuffle operation will spill over to disk for the executor tasks. Let say $OptS_i^j$ is the largest shuffle data size per executor which fits into allocated shuffle memory after serialization and does not spill over to disk, then for measured spill overheads as $Spill$ (in MB) per task in the development environment and $\frac{pDS_i^j}{NE_p} > OptS_i^j$,

$$pTskSf_i^j = \frac{\sum_{\forall tasks} dTskSf_i^j}{dNT_i^j} * \frac{pDS_i^j}{dDS_i^j} + \left(\frac{pDS_i^j}{NE_p} - OptS_i^j\right) * Spill$$

$$\text{where, } pDS_i^j = dDS_i^j * \frac{Prodsize}{DevSize}$$

(8)

4.5 Stage Task Execution Simulation

To estimate execution time of a stage, we need to estimate number of tasks, pNT_i^j, and their estimated execution time i.e. $pTskT_i^j$. pNT_i^j is estimated as $\frac{pDS_i^j}{BS_p}$ where, pDS_i^j is given in Eq. 8. As mentioned in Sect. 4.1, a stage tasks are divided into first wave and rest wave tasks, therefore we estimate average execution time for both the waves' task separately using the performance summary (Sect. 4.1) created in the development environment and prediction models discussed in Sects. 4.2, 4.3 and 4.4. Using Eq. 4, for first wave tasks,

$$pTskT_i^j = dFstTskCT_i^j + pFstTskSd_i^j + dTskSer_i^j + pTskJvm_i^j + pTskSf_i^j \quad (9)$$

Similarly, for rest wave tasks,

$$\forall_{l=(1,m)}, pRstTskBktDur_i^{jl} = dRstTskBktDur_i^{jl} + pRstTskSd_i^j +$$
$$dTskSer_i^j + pTskJvm_i^j + pTskSf_i^j$$

$$\forall_{l=(1,m)}, pRstTskBktN_i^{jl} = \frac{(pNT_i^j - NE_p * NC_p)}{(dNT_i^j - NE_d * NC_d)} * dRstTskBktN_i^{jl}$$

(10)

Stage execution is simulated by scheduling pNT_i^j tasks across $NE_p * NC_p$ number of cores. The simulator maintains an array of data structure of size $NE_p * NC_p$ with each 'k'th element storing the 'k'th core current finish time. $NE_p * NC_p$ tasks are allocated as the first wave tasks of duration given in Eq. 9 to each of the cores. Then, all the rest wave tasks are scheduled from each of 'm' buckets of duration given in Eq. 10 in round robin fashion such that a task is scheduled on the core having minimum finish time so far. Therefore,

$$pStageT_i^j = StgSt_i^j + \text{Max on } T \text{ cores} \sum_{\text{`}k\text{'}thCoreTasks} pTskT_i^{jk} + StgCln_i^j \tag{11}$$
$$where, \quad T = NE_p * NC_p$$

5   Experimental Results and Analysis

Our experimental setup consists of 5 nodes, each of Intel(R) Xeon(R) CPU X5365 @ 3.00 GHz, 8 cores and 16 GB RAM. Each node has disk capacity of 30 GB. The platform stack consists of Yarn, Apache Spark 2.01, Hive 1.2.1 and HDFS 2.6. We have one master and maximum four slaves in these experiments. We have kept executor memory as 4 GB across all experiments in both the development and production environments. However, model supports different executor memory size as well. The different experimental configuration are shown in Table 5. We have tested the prediction model for four types of workloads- Wordcount, Terasort, K-means [1], two SQL queries from TPC-H [2] benchmarks, for data sizes varying from 5 GB to 20 GB. The development environment consists of 1 + 2 node cluster with 5 GB data size. We have executed each application on 1 node cluster by varying –executor-cores parameter to build JVM model for each application as shown in Fig. 3. Each workload listed in Table 5 is executed in the development environment to build the model as discussed in Sect. 4. The analytic model is built in Java. It has two components - Parser for parsing the Spark application log and Prediction module for building the prediction models which takes input from the parser to build the model. Equation 1 is used to predict each application execution time for different production environments created by possible combinations of parameters listed in Table 5.

Table 5. Production system configuration for model validation

Configuration parameter	Values
Number of executors (–num-executor)	2, 4, 6
Number of cores per executor (–executor-cores)	2, 4, 6
Executor memory size	4 GB
Cluster size	2, 4
Data size	10 GB, 20 GB
Workload	Wordcount, Terasort, Kmeans
SQL1	select sum(l_extendedprice * (1 – l_discount)) as revenue from Lineitem
SQL2	select sum(l_extendedprice * (1 – l_discount)) as revenue from Lineitem, Order where l_orderkey = o_orderkey

5.1 Discussions

We have validated the model for around 15 production configurations for each of the workloads. Prediction error is calculated as the ratio of the absolute difference in the actual execution time and the model's estimated execution time, to the actual execution time. We have observed an average 15% prediction error for each application as shown in Fig. 4 with maximum 30% error. We have observed that large prediction errors are due to gaps in capturing variations in tasks execution time i.e. $pTskCt_i^j$ in Eq. 4. The analytic model accuracy has been compared with that of the machine learning model proposed in Sect. 3 for 20 GB data size on 4 nodes cluster for four different configurations of Spark platform parameters. Figure 5 shows that prediction accuracy of the analytic model is better than that of the machine learning model. This is because the ML model uses black box techniques while the analytic model is based on Spark internal job processing details. Figure 6 shows the actual execution time vs. predicted execution time for different production environments for Wordcount, Terasort and K-means applications.

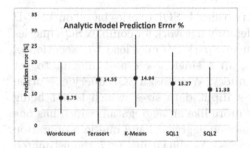

Fig. 4. Analytic model average prediction error(%)

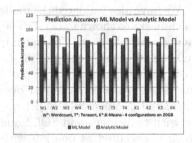

Fig. 5. ML vs analytic model accuracy

Wordcount application has only one job with two stages. It is a simple map-reduce application, where the proposed model's estimations are very close to the actual execution time. We have observed an average accuracy of 91%. Terasort is a sorting application with two jobs and two stages in each job. For most of the test cases we observed an accuracy of atleast 80%, however there is one outlier on 4 node cluster with 4 executors and 4 cores per executor, where the estimated execution time is 30% more than the actual. This is because for stage 4, where partially sorted data sets are merged and written back to disk, the model estimates more number of tasks with larger execution time than the actual. This is due to uniform extrapolation of number of tasks in each bucket which may need to be refined using data distribution. K-means application has around 20 jobs, each job with 2 stages. Here, we observed accuracy of 85% percent. Few outliers with at most error of 23% are due to the variation in task execution time which may not be captured in the histogram for few jobs. The proposed

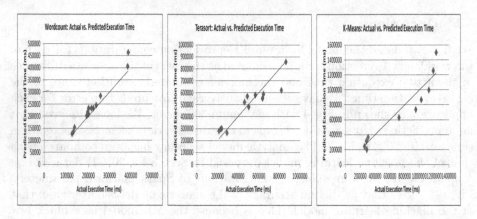

Fig. 6. Model validation for Wordcount, Terasort and K-Means applications: Better accuracy for points closer to the line

simulator uses only four buckets irrespective of type of job or stage- this may need to be tuned for better accuracy.

We have also validated the model for two simple SQL queries based on TPC-H benchmarks as shown in Fig. 7. The model may not work for complex SQL queries having multiple joins. The optimization in Spark 2.0 may lead to execution of multiple steps of a complex SQL query in a single stage and difficult to get performance data for each step of SQL query. Whereas, a SQL query execution time is sensitive to each join operator's input data sizes, which is not being considered in our model. SQL1 query is more like an aggregation which has one job with two stages and SQL2 query has one aggregate and one join operation which is executed as one job with 4 stages. As shown in Fig. 7 the estimated values for both SQL queries are closer to the actual value with accuracy of 90%.

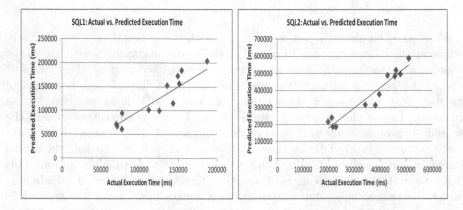

Fig. 7. Model validation for TPC-H SQL queries: Better accuracy for points closer to the line

6 Auto Tuning of Application Execution on Spark

The performance prediction model presented in Sect. 4 can be used iteratively in an optimization algorithm to get Spark parameters values for an optimal performance (i.e. minimum execution time) on a given cluster and data size as given in Fig. 8. The parameters we have considered for tuning are number of executors, number of cores per executors and executor memory size. Note that, there is a scope to include more performance parameters as discussed in [8], however, we have restricted the model for these three parameters only in this paper.

```
OptimizationModule(Input: DataSize, ClusterSize)
{
Optimal_time = 9999;

For Numexecutor = 1 to max cores in the Cluster do
For Numcore_Executor = 1 to max cores on node do
For Executormemory =  Min Size to RAM size on node do

If ValidConfiguration(cluster size, numexecutor, numcoreExecutor, Executormemory)
{
  Time = PredictTimeModel(DataSize, ClusterSize, Numexecutor, NumcoreExecutor, Executormemory)
  if Time < optimal_time
  {
     optimal_Numexecutor = Numexecutor
     optimal_NumcoreExecutor = NumcoreExecutor
     optimal_Executormemory = Executormemory
     optimal_time = Time;
  }
}
Done
Done
Done
Return (optimal_Numexecutor, optimal_NumcoreExecutor, optimal_Executormemory)
}
```

Fig. 8. Auto tuner: Optimization of application execution using prediction model

7 Conclusions and Future Work

Spark is a widely deployed commodity based parallel processing framework. The challenge is to assure performance of applications on Spark cluster for larger data size before deployment. In this paper, we have presented a model to predict application execution time for larger data size using finite measurements in small size development environment. We have presented both machine learning based approach and analytic model. The analytic model handles data skew and node heterogeneity by building a simulator for estimating Spark's stage execution time. The analytic model is flexible to different Spark configurations since it also estimates execution time of all components of Spark's task as function of the Spark production cluster's configuration. This capability of the model may be harnessed to build auto tuner for applications deployed on Spark platform. The proposed model shows prediction accuracy of atleast 80% for different workloads. There is scope to extend the model to support more parameters as discussed in [8]. Further work is needed for extensive validation of the model for different applications, more combinations of Spark parameters, larger data size, larger cluster size and also for cloud deployments. We also plan to create synthetic benchmarks which can be matched to a given applications to enhance the model's prediction capability for an unknown application.

References

1. SparkBench: Spark performance tests. https://github.com/databricks/spark-perf
2. TPC-H benchmarks. https://www.tpc.org/tpch
3. Awan, A.J., Brorsson, M., Vlassov, V., Ayguade, E.: How data volume affects spark based data analytics on a scale-up server. arXiv:1507.08340 (2015)
4. Awan, A.J., Brorsson, M., Vlassov, V., Ayguade, E.: Architectural impact on performance of in-memory data analytics: apache spark case study. arXiv:1604.08484 (2016)
5. Herodotou, H., Babu, S.: Profiling, what-if, analysis, and cost-based optimization of mapreduce programs. In: The 37th International Conference on Very Large Data Bases (2011)
6. Jia, Z., Xue, C., Chen, G., Zhan, J., Zhang, L., Lin, Y., Hofstee, P.: Auto-tuning spark big data workloads on POWER8: prediction-based dynamic SMT threading. In: Proceedings of the 2016 International Conference on Parallel Architectures and Compilation (2016)
7. Ousterhout, K., Rasti, R., Ratnasamy, S., Shenker, S., Chun, B.: Making sense of performance in data analytics frameworks. In: Proceedings of the 12th USENIX Symposium on Networked Systems Design and Implementation (NSDI 2015) (2015)
8. Petridis, P., Gounaris, A., Torres, J.: Spark parameter tuning via trial-and-error. arXiv:1607.07348 (2016)
9. Shi, J., Zou, J., Lu, J., Cao, Z., Li, S., Wang, C.: MRTuner: a toolkit to enable holistic optimization for mapreduce jobs. PVLDB 7(13), 1319–1330 (2014)
10. Singhal, R., Nambiar, M.: Predicting SQL query execution time for large data volume. In: ACM Proceedings of IDEAS (2016)
11. Singhal, R., Sangroya, A.: Performance assurance model for HiveQL on large data volume. In: International Workshop on Foundations of Big Data Computing in conjunction with 22nd IEEE International Conference on High Performance Computing (2015)
12. Singhal, R., Verma, A.: Predicting job completion time in heterogeneous mapreduce environments. In: Proceedings of IPDPS: Heterogeneous Computing Workshop, IPDPS (2016)
13. Wang, K., Khan, M.M.H.: Performance prediction for apache spark platform. In: IEEE 17th International Conference on High Performance Computing and Communications (HPCC) (2015)
14. Yigitbasi, N., Willke, T., Liao, G., Epema, D.: Towards machine learning-based auto-tuning of mapreduce. In: IEEE 21st International Symposium on Modelling, Analysis and Simulation of Computer and Telecommunication Systems (2013)

Benchmarking and Performance Analysis for Distributed Cache Systems: A Comparative Case Study

Haytham Salhi[1]($\boxtimes$), Feras Odeh[1]($\boxtimes$), Rabee Nasser[1]($\boxtimes$), and Adel Taweel[1,2]($\boxtimes$)

[1] Birzeit University, Birzeit, Palestine
hsalhi89@gmail.com, ferasodh@gmail.com, rabinasser@gmail.com,
ataweel@birzeit.edu
[2] King's College, London, UK

Abstract. Caching critical pieces of information in memory or local hard drive is important for applications' performance. Critical pieces of information could include, for example, information returned from I/O-intensive queries or computationally-intensive calculations. Apart from such, storing large amounts of data in a single memory is expensive and sometimes infeasible. Distributed cache systems come to offer faster access by exploiting the memory of more than one machine but they appear as one logical large cache. Therefore, analyzing and benchmarking these systems are necessary to study what and how factors, such as number of clients and data sizes, affect the performance. The majority of current benchmarks deal with the number of clients as *"multiple-threads but all over one client connection"*; this does not reflect the real scenarios where each thread has its own connection. This paper considered several benchmarking mechanisms and selected one for performance analysis. It also studied the performance of two popular open source distributed cache systems (Hazelcast and Infinispan). Using the selected benchmarking mechanism, results show that the performance of distributed cache systems is significantly affected by the number of concurrent clients accessing the distributed cache as well as by the size of the data managed by the cache. Furthermore, the conducted performance analysis shows that Infinispan outperforms Hazelcast in the simple data retrieval scenarios as well as most SQL-like queries scenarios, whereas Hazelcast outperforms Infinispan in SQL-like queries for small data sizes.

Keywords: Benchmarking · Performance analysis
Distributed cache systems · Hazelcast · Infinispan
Retrieval operations

1 Introduction

Studying the performance of distributed cache systems has received much attention in recent years due to their wide usage in improving latency and throughput

© Springer International Publishing AG 2018
R. Nambiar and M. Poess (Eds.): TPCTC 2017, LNCS 10661, pp. 147–163, 2018.
https://doi.org/10.1007/978-3-319-72401-0_11

significantly for various applications. In computing, cache is a software component that stores portions of datasets which would otherwise either take a long time to calculate, process, or originate from an underlying back-end system [16,21]. Caching is used mainly to reduce additional request round trips and sometimes to reduce database querying time for frequently used data [16,21].

A typical methodology for analyzing the performance of distributed cache systems is often done by performing a controlled- and an unbiased-study to investigate these systems' factors of influence. There have been extensive empirical studies conducted by researchers [13,24] and industry [2,7,8] that attempt to look into the performance of these systems. For example, Zhang et al. [24] analyzed the performance of three systems: Memcached, Redis, and the Resilient Distributed Datasets (RDD). More recently, Das et al. [13] studied the performance for Hazelcast only. Nevertheless, although some of these studies have studied more than one factor (such as number of client threads) and targeted many types of cache operations, they studied *multiple threads over one client connection*, and little attention has been paid to study *number of client connections*, where each client opens its own connection to distributed cache server, as well as the behavior when varying the data sizes.

Thus, this paper presents the performance analysis of retrieval operations (including *get* and *SQL-like* queries) of two popular open source distributed cache systems, namely Hazelcast (version 3.6.1) and Infinispan (version 8.1.2.Final), with a focus on two factors: *different number of concurrent clients* for *different sizes of data* managed by the cache. In other words, to be able to understand some of the intrinsic properties of distributed cache, the paper studies the performance behavior of the two systems by varying the number of concurrent client connections for different data sizes, through a controlled study, which is the main objective of this paper. In addition, the paper considers several potential benchmarking frameworks and identifies a suitable one, namely Yardstick. Yardstick is a benchmarking tool usually intended for general distributed systems and captures the behavior of performance as a function of time (i.e., the duration of benchmark) only, which is not sufficient to understand the exact performance behavior of distributed cache systems for our factors of interest. To overcome, an additional mechanism has been developed and integrated into Yardstick to benchmark distributed caches to capture the varying number of clients and data sizes to ensure proper synchronization of run-times.

The evaluation results show that there is a clear relationship between the performance of data retrieval operations and number of concurrent clients as well as data sizes. In addition, the performance behavior of the two selected systems can significantly be influenced by other implementation factors such as *data serialization, object formats*, and *indexing*. The rest of this paper is structured as follows: Sect. 2 presents related work. Section 3 describes the used study design and setup. Section 4 shows the conducted study results. Section 5 discusses the results and the drawn interpretations. Finally, Sect. 6 draws the conclusion and future work.

2   Related Work

Das et al. [13] studied the performance degradation of Hazelcast and suggested to spawn fewer number of threads that process number of client requests in order to improve the performance. While this study aimed to perform a controlled study and add a capability to Yardstick for conducting a performance comparison in the context of multi-client connections, some studies added utilities to ease the process of performance analysis, such as an emulator e.g., *InterSense*, to aid the performance analysis of distributed big-data applications and to facilitate the sensitivity analysis of complex distributed applications [22], and other studies have performed empirical performance analysis on distributed systems like SQL engines [23]. Several papers proposed different methods for conducting performance analysis for general distributed systems [11,14,19,20]. However, our approach focuses on distributed cache systems that use both virtual and physical configurations, which introduce additional factors that need to be taken into consideration when conducting performance analysis.

Zhang et al. [24] analyzed the performance for in-memory data management of three systems: Memcached, Redis, and Resilient Distributed Datasets (RDD) implemented by Spark. The authors performed a thorough performance analysis of object operations such as *set* and *get*. The results show that none of the systems handles efficiently both types of workloads. The CPU and I/O performance of the TCP stack were the bottlenecks for Memcached and Redis. On the other hand, due to a large startup cost of the *get* job, RDD does not support efficient *get* operation for random objects.

Industry, on the other hand, especially the companies that offer distributed cache systems, whether open-source or commercial, usually build benchmarks to show the performance of their system or to compare it with another and publish their results as white papers or on their web sites, which may carry some bias. Hazelcast company [7], for example, built benchmark for *get* and *put* operations only, to compare their distributed cache (3.6-SNAPSHOT) with Red Hat Infinispan 7.2 (a version supported by Red Hat), using Radar-Gun benchmarking framework[1]. Based on their results, they claim that they are up to 70% faster than Infinispan [7]. However, this comparative study performed did not take into account the number of concurrent clients (where each client opens its own connection to the cluster) nor did consider other retrieval operations, such as SQL-like queries.

The Hazelcast company built other benchmarks comparing their distributed cache system to other systems, such as Redis [8], using Radar-Gun framework. In this study, the Hazelcast company investigated the effect of very small number of clients (1 and 4) with different number of threads and showed Hazelcast outperform Redis for the *get* operation [8]. In another comparison between Grid Gain and Apache Ignite [2] performed by Hazelcast, they studied the performance of several operations including *put/get* and *SQL-like* queries, using Yardstick framework. Others like Grid Gain company [1] built benchmarks, comparing

---

[1] https://github.com/radargun/radargun/wiki.

between their system and Hazelcast for several operation types such as *get, put, SQL-like* as well as transactional operations. In addition, they did the same for Apache Ignite and Hazelcast [4].

All the above mentioned studies, except the one done by Zhang et al. [24], show the performance behavior of cache operations as a function of time with a fixed number of clients, a fixed number of threads per client, and a fixed data size. These may be sufficient in some cases, but do not, however, reflect real-life performance behavior, where number of concurrent clients dynamically varies over the period of system run-time. To address this issue, the authors developed a mechanism to maintain varying number of concurrent clients and data sizes, along with the function of time, maintained by Yarkstick.

While other efforts have developed the "Yahoo! Cloud Serving Benchmark" (YCSB)[2] [12] into other extensions like YCSB+T [15] in order to produce metrics for database operations within transactions and detect anomalies from any workload, Yardstick[3] was chosen. Yardstick is a powerful framework, well-documented and intended for benchmarking distributed operations. Its benchmarks can be developed faster than other frameworks, such as Java Microbenchmarking Harness (JMH)[4], Radar Gun, and YCSB [12]. Moreover, Yardstick is open source, written in Java and allows contributions to enhance and enrich its framework.

3   Study Design and Setup

This section discusses the main aspects of the study design on which the setup relies. First, it presents the investigated key factors of interest that may have greater effect on the performance of retrieval operations for distributed cache systems. Second, it lists the queries that were used, with their specifications and complexities.

Finally, it describes the used topology of machines, their setup, and the mechanism of benchmarking.

3.1   Factors of Interest

The performance of a distributed cache system depends on several different factors including number of concurrent clients [10,18], data sizes [9], type of operations, complexity of queries, number of distributed caches, and so forth. Since the dependent variable of interest is *the performance of data retrieval operations*, this study is particularly concerned with the effect of two key factors as follows:

– **Number of concurrent clients:** The more the number of concurrent clients a system can handle efficiently, the more efficient the application is [10,18]. To achieve reasonable performance system outlook, the study is run against eight

---

[2] https://github.com/brianfrankcooper/YCSB/wiki.
[3] https://github.com/yardstick-benchmarks/yardstick.
[4] http://tutorials.jenkov.com/java-performance/jmh.html.

variations of concurrent client numbers which includes: **1, 2, 4, 8, 16, 32, 64, and 128** clients to log the performance change as the number of clients grows.
- **Data size:** As the data size increases in the cache, a distributed cache system needs to maintain the maximum number of entries it can store [9]. To achieve, this study examines five variations of data sizes as shown in Table 1. One million data size (or records) was tested in all cases, except in benchmarking SQL-like queries due to the huge number of records returned to the clients which caused memory heap exceptions in some cases.

Variables that may affect the performance of data retrieval operations in a distributed cache systems, such as those related to the environment (like CPU, RAM, etc.) or related to the cache itself, were controlled and made similar as much as possible for both systems. Systems' internal configurations were kept on default configurations. Furthermore, indexing on both systems was enabled.

Table 1. Data size variations used in initializing the distributed cache.

Number of entries	Size (B)
100	9 KB
1000	89.8 KB
10,000	898 KB
100,000	8.8 MB
1,000,000	87.7 MB

3.2   Queries Specifications

In this study, the *map* data structure was used as data representation in both systems. Two main types of queries on this data structure were investigated. The first, is a basic query type, the *get* operation, a popular operation on map. The second, is an SQL-like type, which can be used to retrieve a collection of objects. In addition, we formulated four SQL-like queries, each with a different complexity level. The reason behind choosing SQL-like queries is that they are very useful for retrieving complex data from caches. Table 3 summarizes the queries with their complexities. The complexity is generally defined as follows: *"The greater the query, in terms of SQL operations (i.e., the number of logical and comparison operations), the higher the complexity value"*. The metric for calculating the value of a query complexity is described below.

The complexity is computed based on the number of logical operations (e.g., AND, OR, LIKE, etc.) and comparison operations ($=, >, <$, etc.). The defined metrics assign a complexity value to each query based on the type and the number of its operations. The complexity value for each query in Table 3 below is computed by aggregating the complexity values for each operation appearing in the query. Table 2 shows the complexity value for each operation. The higher the complexity value, the greater its computation needs in terms of CPU and memory.

Table 2. Complexity definitions for each SQL operation.

SQL operation	Complexity value
>, <, =	1
AND	1
OR, LIKE	2

In order to be close to a real world scenario, two entities (Employee and Organization) were used as objects to hold data. *Employee* entity has four attributes: *id, name* (indexed), *age* (indexed), *password*, and *organization*, whereas *Organization* has five attributes: *id, name* (indexed), *acronym*, and *numberOfEmployees*. The relationship between the two entities is a one-to-many association. The single-attribute index was used for both systems. Moreover, in Hazelcast, non-ordered index was used in order to make the index settings as much neutralized as possible to match Infinispan's index settings.

Table 3. Retrieval queries used in benchmarking with their complexities.

Label	Query	Complexity
get	get(i) where i is a random number	N/A
SQL-like0	SELECT employee FROM Employee WHERE age >50	1
SQL-like1	SELECT employee FROM Employee WHERE age >25 AND age <75	3
SQL-like2	SELECT employee FROM Employee WHERE age <25 OR age >75	4
SQL-like3	SELECT employee FROM Employee WHERE age >50 AND name like 'A%' AND organization.name LIKE '%tum%'	7

3.3 Topology and Mechanism

As shown in Fig. 1, the study setup included five machines and one switch to conduct experiments within a local isolated network, to eliminate external networking issues. Out of the five, four machines, named host 1, 2, 3, and 4 were used to run the client benchmarks. The nodes of cache cluster were set up on the fifth machine, named workstation. The specifications for the machines are detailed below.

In this study, HP Z230 Tower Workstation was used as the server machine. Table 4 lists the specification of the server machine.

For clients, four machines were used, three of them with equal specifications. The fourth machine has a different CPU (Intel(R) Core(TM) i7-3770 CPU @ 3.40 GHz) tough. Table 5 lists the specifications of the client machines. One host (host 1) was used to manage the running of benchmark clients, and the usage of the other hosts is described in the algorithms below.

Table 6 lists the network switch specifications used during the study to enable the networking between the four hosts and the workstation.

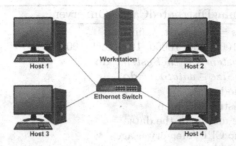

Fig. 1. Topology of experimental setup.

Table 4. Server machine specifications

Environment variable	Specs
Operating system	Ubuntu 14.04 (64 bit)
Platform	Java 1.8 (64 bit)
CPU	Intel(R) Xeon(R) CPU E3-1241 v3 @ 3.50 GHz
RAM	16 GB

Table 5. Client machines specifications

Environment variable	Specs
Operating system	Ubuntu 14.04 (64 bit)
Platform	Java 1.8 (64 bit)
CPU	Intel(R) Core(TM) i7-4770 CPU @ 3.40 GHz
	Intel(R) Core(TM) i7-3770 CPU @ 3.40 GHz
RAM	8 GB

Table 6. Network specifications

Environment variable	Specs
Switch	Cisco Catalyst 3560-X Series WS-C3560X-24P-S 24 PoE+ 715W
Switching Fabric	160 Gbps
DRAM	256 MB (51 2 MB for 3750X-12S and 3750X-24S)
Flash	64 MB (128 MB for 3750X-12S and 3750X-24S)
Total VLANs	1005
VLAN IDs	4 K

In order to set up and run the experiments, a cluster of distributed cache nodes were set up on the workstation, and a script that generates clients for requesting cache data on the clients machines (namely host 1, 2, 3, and 4). The purpose of these four hosts is to run the client drivers. The steps to run the cache cluster on the workstation are described in Algorithm 1.

Algorithm 1. RunningDistrbutedCachesOnServer

1: Let *cacheSystems* =[Hazelcast, Infinispan]
2: Let *dataSizes* =[100, 1000, 10000, 100000, 1000000]
3: **for each** *cacheSystem* ∈ *cacheSystems* **do**
4:     **for each** *dataSize* ∈ *dataSizes* **do**
5:         Run four nodes
6:         Create a distributed map
7:         Initiate the map with the data
8:         Monitor the CPU/memory usage
9:         Invoke Algorithm 2   ▷ client benchmarks run here
10:        Wait until client benchmarks finish
11:    **end for**
12: **end for**

After the cache cluster was started and run in a stable mode, the four hosts ran the client benchmarks. Each benchmark started generating requests for a period of 180 s (the first 30 s are for warm-up). The benchmark recorded the throughput (operations/sec) for the 150 s period. Each benchmark resulted in a CSV file containing the throughput over 150 s for a specific number of concurrent clients and a specific data size.

The generated results were then taken and further analyzed to produce an overall throughput for each number of concurrent clients. To record throughput with a varying number of clients and data sizes, managing the runs of benchmarks is achieved through Algorithm 2, as shown below.

Algorithm 2. RunningBenchmarksOnClients

1: Let *clientsNumbers* =[1, 2, 4, 8, 16, 32, 64, 128]
2: Let *queries* =[get, SQL-like0, SQL-like1, SQL-like2, SQL-like3]
3: **for each** *clientsNumber* ∈ *clientsNumbers* **do**
4:     **for each** *query* ∈ *queries* **do**
5:         **if** *clientsNumber* = 1 or 2 **then**
6:             Monitor the CPU/memory usage on host 1
7:             Run benchmarks of *clientsNumber* concurrently on host 1
8:         **else**
9:             Let $n = clientsNumber/4$ ▷ Number of client benchmarks on each host
10:            Monitor the CPU/memory usage on host 1
11:            Run benchmarks of n concurrently on host 1 asynchronously
12:            Monitor the CPU/memory usage on host 2
13:            Run benchmarks of n concurrently on host 2 asynchronously
14:            Monitor the CPU/memory usage on host 3
15:            Run benchmarks of n concurrently on host 3 asynchronously
16:            Monitor the CPU/memory usage on host 4
17:            Run benchmarks of n concurrently on host 4 asynchronously
18:        **end if**
19:        Wait until all benchmarks finish
20:    **end for**
21:    Aggregate data and covert results into throughput per number of clients
22: **end for**

All required benchmarks were implemented in Java using Yardstick framework. Algorithms 1 and 2, described above, were implemented using both Java and Shell programming languages. The project including the benchmarks as well as shell scripts used in this study can be found on a public Github repository. Here is the link[5].

This design was developed and enhanced over many iterations of dry-runs and trials. During the wet-run of the study, CPU/memory usage was also monitored to ensure high fidelity of the study and make sure that systems' performance is not affected by machine limitations.

4 Study Results

The obtained study results are shown formatted below so that the relevant performance results of both systems are brought together to compare between the two systems. Each chart below contains more than one curve, each representing the behavior of performance for a specific system and a specific data size, where the Y-axis is the throughput (ops/sec), and the X-axis represents the number of concurrent clients. Since readings were taken for only a subset of concurrent clients (i.e., 1, 2, 4, 8, 16, 32, 64, 128), a linear approximation between points was used.

4.1 Performance of *get* Query

As shown in Fig. 2, the throughput increases for both systems starting with 1 client increasing to 64 concurrent clients, for which Infinispan obviously does better in this range. However, the throughput of Hazelcast drops down when moving from 64 client to 128 clients, while Infinispan throughput keeps increasing. It is worth noting that Infinispan did not reach a maximum throughput in this case.

When increasing the data size from 100 to 1000000, the behaviour remains the same over all concurrent client variations. Throughput, on the other hand, drops down by around 19% on average for Hazelcast, whereas Infinispan drops down by around 0.2%, as shown in Fig. 2. The average, minimum, and maximum throughput for each data size for Hazelcast and Infinispan are shown in Tables 7 and 8, respectively. Each color in the leftmost column indicates a curve in Fig. 2.

4.2 Performance of *SQL-like* Queries

For *SQL-like* queries, which are more complex than the primitive *get* query, the throughput of both systems is significantly small compared to what the case is in the *get* query, as shown next. Moreover, it is clear that there is a significant drop in throughput for both systems for a shift from 100 to 100000 data size. The results also show that the effect of the number of concurrent clients becomes less significant on larger data sizes.

---

[5] https://github.com/ferasodh/Distributed-Caches-Benchmarking-Experiment.

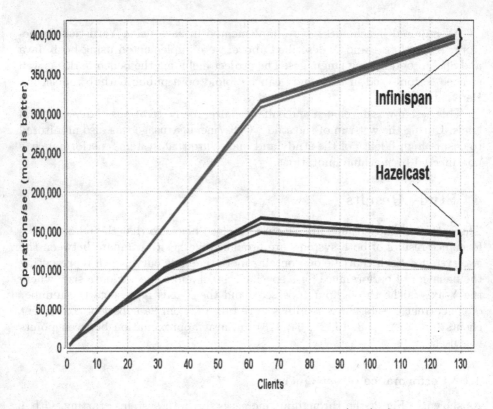

Fig. 2. Behavior of *get* performance in terms of throughput (ops/sec) as a function of number of clients. Each color in the leftmost column of Tables 7 and 8 indicates a curve in this figure. (Color figure online)

Table 7. Per data size average, minimum, and maximum throughput (in thousands ops/sec) for *Hazelcast*.

- Data Size	Avg	Min	Max
100	63.33	3.33	159.76
1000	59.48	3.37	147.36
10000	64.21	3.33	166.52
100,000	64.13	3.37	165.68
1,000,000	51.33	3.39	124.33

Performance of *SQL-like0* Query: For *SQL-like0* query, the number of rows returned is directly proportional to data size. Hazelcast outperforms Infinispan for 100 data size by 39.8%, as shown in Fig. 3. The throughput increases for both systems for the range 1 to 64 clients. However, Infinispan outperforms Hazelcast for all bigger data sizes. Moreover, it clearly shows Infinispan has more average

Table 8. Per data size average, minimum, and maximum throughput (in thousands ops/sec) for *Infinispan*.

- Data Size	Avg	Min	Max
100	126.51	4.80	397.97
1000	127.04	4.82	399.33
10000	125.39	4.79	390.36
100,000	124.62	4.74	389.51
1,000,000	126.25	4.73	395.70

throughput than Hazelcast by 34.6%, 64.7%, and 43% in 1000, 10000, and 100000 data sizes, respectively.

Performance of *SQL-like1* Query: For *SQL-like1* query, the throughput increases for both systems as number of clients increases for 100 data size, while for bigger data sizes the maximum throughput is reached at 16 clients. For this, Hazelcast outperforms Infinispan for 100 data size by 57.9%, as shown in Fig. 4. However, Infinispan outperforms Hazelcast for all bigger data sizes. Moreover, it shows that Infinispan has a better average throughput than Hazelcast by 51%, 66.3%, and 66.9% at 1000, 10000, and 100000 data sizes, respectively.

However, with large data size at 10000, there is a drop in Infinispan performance for the range of 16 to 64 clients, while Hazelcast achieves minimum throughput at 100000 data size and 128 clients.

Performance of *SQL-like2* Query: None of the systems reach the maximum throughput in *SQL-like2* query for 100 data size, while for bigger data sizes the maximum throughput is reached with 32, 16, and 8 clients. In this case, Hazelcast outperforms Infinispan for 100 data size by 55.9%, as shown in Fig. 5. However, Infinispan outperforms Hazelcast for all bigger data sizes.

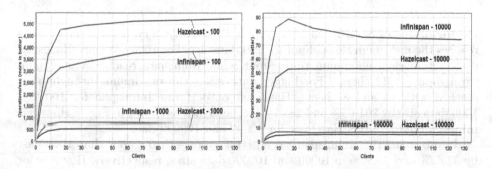

Fig. 3. Behavior of *SQL-like0* performance in term of throughput (ops/sec) as a function of number of clients (1, 2, 4, 8, 32, 64, 128) for all data sizes.

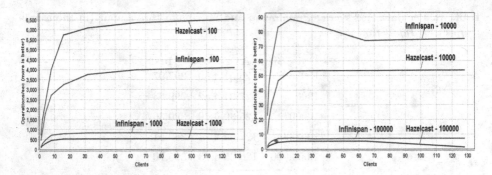

Fig. 4. Behavior of *SQL-like1* performance in term of throughput (ops/sec) as a function of number of clients (1, 2, 4, 8, 32, 64, 128) for all data sizes.

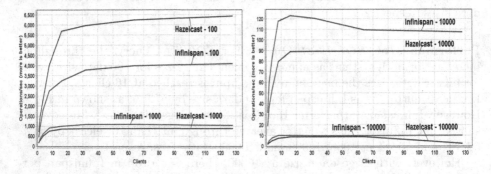

Fig. 5. Behavior of *SQL-like2* performance in term of throughput (ops/sec) as a function of number of clients (1, 2, 4, 8, 32, 64, 128) for all data sizes.

Moreover, the results also show Infinispan has a better average throughput than Hazelcast by 20.5%, 37.6%, and 40.9% at 1000, 10000, and 100000 data sizes, respectively. For 10000 data size, there is a drop in Infinispan performance for 16 to 64 clients, and Hazelcast achieves minimum throughput at 100000 data size and 128 clients.

Performance of SQL-like3 Query: For *SQL-like3* query, none of the systems reaches the maximum throughput for 100 data size. For 1000 data size Hazelcast does not reach a maximum throughput while Infinispan reaches a maximum throughput at 32 clients. For bigger data sizes, the maximum throughput is reached with 16 and 8 clients. Hazelcast outperforms Infinispan for 100 and 1000 data size by 261.65% and 285.7%, respectively, as shown in Fig. 6. However, Infinispan outperforms Hazelcast for 10000 and 100000 data sizes.

It also shows that Infinispan has a better average throughput than Hazelcast by 37.62% and 40.86% in 10000 and 100000 data sizes, respectively. However for 10000 data size, there is a drop in Infinispan performance for 16 to 64 clients. Hazelcast achieves minimum throughput on 100000 data size and 128 clients.

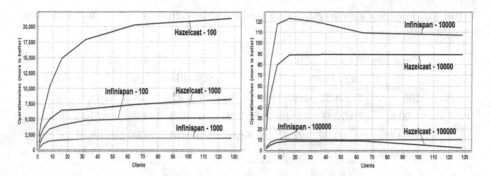

Fig. 6. Behavior of *SQL-like3* performance in term of throughput (ops/sec) as a function of number of clients (1, 2, 4, 8, 32, 64, 128) for all data sizes.

Table 9. Per data size average, max, and min throughput (ops/sec) for each query for *Hazelcast.*

Data size	Avg	Min	Max	Avg	Min	Max
	SQL-like0			SQL-like1		
100	3,485.25	650.43	5,224.75	4,157.87	741.37	6,531.27
1,000	401.24	114.05	538.07	406.09	112.15	541.37
10,000	40.18	11.08	53.30	40.36	10.89	53.77
100,000	4.06	1.12	5.47	3.60	1.13	5.46
	SQL-like2			SQL-like3		
100	4,101.74	731.26	6,428.29	12,154.58	2,177.01	2,177.01
1,000	651.77	175.98	874.01	5,099.81	1,260.55	8,203.85
10,000	68.24	19.40	89.20	68.24	19.40	89.20
100,000	5.80	1.81	8.81	5.80	1.81	8.81

Tables 9 and 10 summarize results for the SQL-like queries showing the average, minimum, and maximum throughput for each query and for each data size for Hazelcast and Infinispan, respectively.

5   Discussion

As shown above, Infinispan outperforms Hazelcast in all benchmarks except in SQL-like queries at small data sizes. There are several factors that affect the performance of Infinispan and Hazelcast and could be reasons for performance bottlenecks; some of these factors are discussed below:

– **Data serialization:** In order to transfer cache objects across a network between clients and a cache cluster or between cache cluster peers, objects need to be serialized into bytes. When read by the application, those bytes

Table 10. Per data size average, max, and min throughput(ops/sec) for each query for *Infinispan*.

Data size	Avg	Min	Max	Avg	Min	Max
	SQL-like0			SQL-like1		
100	2,493.22	449.31	3,875.48	2,633.41	480.84	4,103.19
1,000	612.90	140.89	827.48	613.40	149.24	829.77
10,000	66.20	22.35	88.85	66.44	23.09	88.61
100,000	5.81	2.07	7.27	6.01	2.11	7.59
	SQL-like2			SQL-like3		
100	2,631.53	479.09	4,077.35	3,360.91	667.01	5,242.86
1,000	785.25	182.37	1,085.06	1,322.45	282.71	1,899.73
10,000	93.91	31.86	122.82	93.91	31.86	122.82
100,000	8.17	2.92	10.10	8.17	2.92	10.10

need to be converted back to objects or deserialized. Whenever a request comes to a cache system, about 20% of the processing time is spent in serialization and deserialization in most configurations [5]. Obviously, data serialization is one of the key factors that affects cache performance. However, the default Java implementation, which is the used implementation for Hazelcast, is slow in terms of CPU cycles and produces unnecessarily large bytes [3,5]. On the other hand, Infinispan uses Jboss marshalling framework[6] as its default serialization scheme.

Jboss marshalling framework do not write full class definitions to the stream, instead each known type is represented by a single byte by using magic numbers [5]. Moreover, Infinispan forces developers of applications to register an "externalizer" for their application types to make use of Jboss marshalling [5,6]. Based on this, serialization has a significant impact on both systems' throughput and explains why Infinispan has a better performance in most cases.

– **In-memory objects format:** When objects are stored in Hazelcast or Infinispan they are serialized to byte arrays and deserialized when they are read. In Hazelcast, the default format is the binary format. However, this format is not efficient if the application is doing a lot of SQL-like queries where serialization/deserialization happens on the server side. Moreover, Hazelcast provides other formats like object and native format. One drawback of Object format is that it adds an extra serialization/deserialization step for *get* and *put* operations, while native format is only available for Hazelcast Enterprise HD version [17]. This study used the default Hazelcast binary format which explains the low performance of Hazelcast on SQL-like queries, especially with large data sizes.

Even though the cost of serialization/deserialization maybe small for smaller

---

[6] http://jbossmarshalling.jboss.org/.

data sizes, it will become large for larger data sizes especially in the SQL-like queries where the returned result set is large.

- **Indexing:** One of the most significant factors in query performance is indexing. Although indexes were added to both systems, Hazelcast and Infinispan, it may be possible that the engine for Infinispan, which is based on hibernate search and Apache Lucene, is more optimized than Hazelcast default indexing mechanism.

6   Conclusion and Future Work

Changing the number of concurrent clients and varying processed data sizes affect the performance of data retrieval operations of distributed cache systems. In this study, all known variables that can affect the performance of the two systems except the factors of interest (i.e., number of concurrent clients and data size) were as much as possible considered and neutralized.

Results show that studying performance analysis of systems with dynamically varying number of concurrent clients and data sizes is critical in determining a more accurate performance readings. Measuring performance with static independent variable or factors may provide misleading results, particularly in systems where cache is a critical part of a system function or design. These require building benchmarking tools that consider such dynamically changing variables to reflect and replicate real-life usage of systems. The other significant factors that may well affect cache systems' performance are data serialization, in-memory object formats and indexing, which their exact chosen implementation may improve a system's performance over another. However, these need further study and investigation in how best to address the implication of these varying variables or factors.

In addition, results show that Infinispan (version 8.1.2.Final) outperforms Hazelcast (version 3.6.1) in all tested cases except in SQL-like queries with small data sizes. Moreover, the study shows that the concurrent clients, where each client opens its own connection, has a considerable impact on the performance of *get* and *SQL-like* queries. The data size, on the other hand, has very small impact on the performance of *get* query but large impact on the performance of *SQL-like* queries.

Further, based on the mechanism followed in this study, a more integrated benchmarking framework, as proposed above, need to be developed that takes into account the varying number of concurrent clients and data sizes for distributed caches. There are several other interesting issues to consider, first, it would be interesting to study the effect of different data storage formats such as compressed and uncompressed. Second, understanding the effect of larger data sizes and cache access patterns would shed light on performance variations. Future work may also include developing new techniques that improve the performance with respect to data representations and communication protocols.

References

1. Gridgain vs. hazelcast benchmarks. http://go.gridgain.com/Benchmark_GridGain_vs_Hazelcast.html. Accessed 28 May 2016
2. Gridgain/apache ignite vs hazelcast benchmark. https://hazelcast.com/resources/benchmark-gridgain/. Accessed 28 May 2016
3. Hazelcast documentation. http://docs.hazelcast.org/docs/3.6/manual/html-single/index.html#distributed-query. Accessed 28 May 2016
4. Ignite vs. hazelcast benchmarks. http://www.gridgain.com/resources/benchmarks/ignite-vs-hazelcast-benchmarks/. Accessed 28 May 2016
5. Infinispan. http://www.aosabook.org/en/posa/infinispan.html#fn10. Accessed 25 June 2017
6. Infinispan documentation. http://infinispan.org/docs/8.2.x/index.html. Accessed 01 May 2016
7. Red hat infinispan vs hazelcast benchmark. https://hazelcast.com/resources/benchmark-infinispan/. Accessed 28 May 2016
8. Redis 3.0.7 vs hazelcast 3.6 benchmark. https://hazelcast.com/resources/benchmark-redis-vs-hazelcast/. Accessed 28 May 2016
9. Agrawal, S., Chaudhuri, S., Das, G.: Dbxplorer: a system for keyword-based search over relational databases. In: Proceedings of 18th International Conference on Data Engineering, 2002, pp. 5–16. IEEE (2002)
10. Chen, S., Liu, Y., Gorton, I., Liu, A.: Performance prediction of component-based applications. J. Syst. Softw. **74**(1), 35–43 (2005)
11. Chen, X., Ho, C.P., Osman, R., Harrison, P.G., Knottenbelt, W.J.: Understanding, modelling, and improving the performance of web applications in multicore virtualised environments. In: Proceedings of the 5th ACM/SPEC International Conference on Performance Engineering, pp. 197–207. ACM (2014)
12. Cooper, B.F., Silberstein, A., Tam, E., Ramakrishnan, R., Sears, R.: Benchmarking cloud serving systems with YCSB. In: Proceedings of the 1st ACM Symposium on Cloud Computing, pp. 143–154. ACM (2010)
13. Das, A., Mueller, F., Gu, X., Iyengar, A.: Performance analysis of a multi-tenant in-memory data grid. In: 2016 IEEE 9th International Conference on Cloud Computing (CLOUD), pp. 956–959. IEEE (2016)
14. Denaro, G., Polini, A., Emmerich, W.: Early performance testing of distributed software applications. In: Proceedings of ACM SIGSOFT Software Engineering Notes, vol. 29, pp. 94–103. ACM (2004)
15. Dey, A., Fekete, A., Nambiar, R., Röhm, U.: YCSB+T: benchmarking web-scale transactional databases. In: Proceedings of 2014 IEEE 30th International Conference on Data Engineering Workshops (ICDEW), pp. 223–230. IEEE (2014)
16. Engelbert, C.: White paper: caching strategies. Technical rep., Hazelcast Company. https://hazelcast.com/resources/caching-strategies
17. Evans, B.: White paper: an architect's view of hazelcast. Technical rep., Hazelcast Company. https://hazelcast.com/resources/architects-view-hazelcast/
18. Fedorowicz, J.: Database performance evaluation in an indexed file environment. ACM Trans. Database Syst. (TODS) **12**(1), 85–110 (1987)
19. Khazaei, H., Misic, J., Misic, V.B.: Performance analysis of cloud computing centers using $m/g/m/m+r$ queuing systems. IEEE Trans. Parallel Distrib. Syst. **23**(5), 936–943 (2012)
20. Klems, M., Anh Lê, H.: Position paper: cloud system deployment and performance evaluation tools for distributed databases. In: Proceedings of the 2013 International Workshop on Hot Topics in Cloud Services, pp. 63–70. ACM (2013)

21. Paul, S., Fei, Z.: Distributed caching with centralized control. Comput. Commun. **24**(2), 256–268 (2001)
22. Wang, Q., Cherkasova, L., Li, J., Volos, H.: Interconnect emulator for aiding performance analysis of distributed memory applications. In: Proceedings of the 7th ACM/SPEC on International Conference on Performance Engineering, pp. 75–83. ACM (2016)
23. Wouw, S.V., Viña, J., Iosup, A., Epema, D.: An empirical performance evaluation of distributed SQL query engines. In: Proceedings of the 6th ACM/SPEC International Conference on Performance Engineering, pp. 123–131. ACM (2015)
24. Zhang, H., Tudor, B.M., Chen, G., Ooi, B.C.: Efficient in-memory data management: an analysis. Proc. VLDB Endowment **7**(10), 833–836 (2014)

A Comparison of ARM Against x86 for Distributed Machine Learning Workloads

Sebastian Kmiec[1], Jonathon Wong[1], Hans-Arno Jacobsen[1(✉)], and Da Qi Ren[2]

[1] University of Toronto, Toronto, ON, Canada
jacobsen@eecg.toronto.edu
[2] Futurewei Technologies, Santa Clara, CA, USA

Abstract. The rise of Machine Learning (ML) in the last decade has created an unprecedented surge in demand for new and more powerful hardware. Various hardware approaches exist to take on these large demands motivating the need for hardware performance benchmarks to compare these diverse hardware systems. In this paper, we present a comprehensive analysis and comparison of available benchmark suites in the field of ML and related fields. The analysis of these benchmarks is used to discuss the potential of ARM processors within the context of ML deployments. Our paper concludes with a brief hardware performance comparison of modern, server-grade ARM and x86 processors using a benchmark suite selected from our survey.

Keywords: Machine learning · Distributed · Benchmark · ARM
x86

1 Introduction

As distributed workloads become more common with the advent of Machine Learning (ML) and Big Data, energy and cost concerns become more of a burden on datacentres. Currently, server operation costs account for roughly 57% of all monthly datacentre operational costs [23]. Moreover, the energy consumed by servers is not proportional to workload intensity [22]. Although power consumption and workload intensity are related, a large amount of power efficiency is lost with the exception being intense workloads that stress servers to their limits [22]. As it stands, the largest sources of energy consumption for servers are CPUs (up to 45% of a server's energy consumption) and cooling systems [4]. To address these new demands, our solution proposes use of power efficient ARM processors. In order to come up with a definitive answer as to which processor is most suitable for the problem, we survey available benchmarks for evaluating hardware performance and benchmark an ARM processor against the lower power x86 Xeon processor commonly used in datacentres.

In this paper, we will refer to a benchmark as a standard methodology for testing the performance of hardware platforms, primarily in the field of ML. Benchmarks of interest provide implementations of commonly used algorithms/models

© Springer International Publishing AG 2018
R. Nambiar and M. Poess (Eds.): TPCTC 2017, LNCS 10661, pp. 164–184, 2018.
https://doi.org/10.1007/978-3-319-72401-0_12

with varying degrees of parallelism and instruction mixes. Our definition of a benchmark is not to be confused with the more popular definition used in the field of ML: a standard methodology of evaluating and/or comparing a model's problem specific performance. An example of such a benchmark is MNIST, a database of images of handwritten digits that are centred, size-normalized and commonly used for the evaluation of pattern recognition methods.

Although our initial focus is a survey of hardware evaluation benchmarks in the field of ML, many benchmark suites are geared towards high performance GPUs. This is a consequence of the fact that the hardware market for improving processing delays of training neural networks is largely dominated by high-performance GPUs, as operations like matrix multiplications are highly parallelizable, hence, they are suitable for GPUs with specialized libraries. The focus of this paper, however, will be to emphasize the role of server-grade processors in the field of ML.

The market for server-grade processors is largely dominated by Intel x86-64 architecture processors, which will be referred to as x86 processors. With the popularity of ARM processors in low-power applications, such as mobile devices, the question arises as to whether ARM can meet the computational demands of datacentres, in exchange for superior power efficiency. Since the development of the ARM Server Base System Architecture (SBSA) standard three years ago, semiconductor manufacturers have entered the server market with ARM processors. At a minimum, this standard provides support for 64-bit architectures, virtual memory, popular Linux distributions and software development environments.

There are many fundamental aspects of ARM that make it a power efficient processor with the potential to become the new standard for server-grade processing. ARM itself is a Reduced Instruction Set Computer (RISC) architecture, as opposed to the more common Complex Instruction Set Computer (CISC) x86 architectures. For an average program on a CISC architecture, 25% of available instructions make up 95% of execution time [13]. As such, it is possible to reduce instructions available (a RISC architecture) at the expense of infrequently incurring extra cycles for a single CISC instruction, trading power efficiency for performance. Although instruction set alone does not decide energy efficiency, ARM processors incorporate many power saving implementation design points over x86 [6]. For instance, ARM processors have more fine-grain control of frequency (including sleep states) to help minimize power consumption [3].

The recent rise of ARM can also be attributed to ARM's business model. Any semiconductor company can become a licensee of ARM and produce a System on a Chip (SoC). SoCs integrate application specific hardware accelerators with the ARM CPU on a single die, improving performance and saving power by avoiding bridges [3]. ARM server-grade processors have already begun introducing hardware accelerators for common datacentre use cases, such as Web Serving and Big Data storage [7].

The remainder of this paper attempts to answer the question of whether up and coming ARM processors can provide similar levels of performance as existing x86 Xeon processors, specifically for distributed machine learning workloads.

Section 2 provides a survey of available hardware evaluation benchmarks that we considered in our efforts to compare ARM and x86 processors. From this survey, we select a benchmark suite and describe workload characteristics in Sect. 3, along with experimental details. In Sect. 4, we provide an experimental comparison between a state-of-the-art ARM processor against an x86 Xeon processor in a similar performance range. We discuss related ARM versus x86 benchmarks in Sect. 5 and conclude in Sect. 6.

2   Benchmark Survey

Our primary motive is to obtain a benchmark suite with features that are desirable for benchmarking ARM processors against x86 processors for distributed machine learning workloads. In this section, we provide a survey of open-source benchmarks for evaluating hardware performance, specifically for Machine Learning applications. Our goal is to distill the large pool of available benchmarks into a set of unique benchmarks, rather than provide a full list of benchmarks with overlapping features.

2.1   Benchmark Survey Overview

PARSEC, released in 2008, is a benchmark suite developed to help guide researchers in designing multi-core processors [5]. Part of this effort is embodied in the diversity of the parallelism benchmark programs created. The benchmark programs have applications ranging from enterprise storage to media processing.

CortexSuite, released in 2008, is a benchmark suite developed to help guide research in designing system architectures and compilers for computer vision oriented applications [24]. In particular, the programs within the Cortex benchmark were selected by determining the most commonly used algorithms (kernels) in image processing and image understanding [24].

Tonic Suite, released in 2015, is a benchmark suite developed to guide research into future warehouse scale computing (WSC) and server platforms specialized for Deep Neural Networks (DNN). The Tonic suite provides image processing, speech recognition and natural language processing benchmarks, which all rely on DijiNN. The purpose of DijiNN is to provide DNN as a service. Tonic suite clients make requests to DijiNN servers. These servers then load trained DNNs into memory and then perform inference to return the expected result [14].

Fathom, released in 2016, is a collection of state-of-the-art DNN models and input datasets intended to help guide research in hardware acceleration of DNNs [1].

Rllab, released in 2016, is a benchmark suite developed to address the lack of comprehensive benchmarks in reinforcement learning algorithms, particularly in the continuous control domain [10]. Rllab provides basic, locomotive, partially observable and hierarchical tasks implemented in physics simulators. Rllab also provides benchmarks for state-of-the-art policy optimization algorithms.

KITTI Vision Benchmark Suite, released in 2012, is a project intended to bring more challenging benchmarks to the computer vision community, via data gathered from "Annieway", an autonomous driving platform with a high resolution video camera [12]. KITTI also provides a leader board for submission of experimental results on algorithms utilized on these standard datasets.

Rodinia Benchmark Suite, released in 2009, is a benchmark suite developed to address the lack of benchmarks for heterogeneous systems (i.e., systems with CPUs and accelerators, such as GPUs and FPGAs) [8]. PARSEC, discussed earlier, is a well-known general purpose, multicore processor benchmark suite. Use of Principal Component Analysis (PCA) determined that PARSEC and Rodinia benchmarks cover similar spaces in terms of their instruction mix, input working sets and memory sharing behaviours [8], despite their different target hardware platforms.

Scalable HeterOgeneous Computing (SHOC), released in 2009, provides benchmarks for general purpose heterogeneous systems that can be run on a cluster using the Message Passing Interface (MPI) library [9].

Model Zoo, released in 2013, is a large collection of pre-trained, state-of-the-art, deep learning models gathered by the open source community, intended to help reproduce research.

HiBench, released in 2012, is a benchmark suite intended to benchmark new Hadoop-based Big Data deployments. At the time of development of HiBench, Hadoop was entering the Big Data storage and processing scene (roughly in April 2010) [15]. HiBench provides programs for common use cases of MapReduce (e.g., Web Search, ML) and has since added new workloads and adapted to new software stacks.

SparkBench, released in 2015, is a benchmark suite intended to address the lack of comprehensive Spark benchmarks for user applications [20]. SparkBench provides benchmarks for ML, graph computing, SQL querying and streaming applications.

BigDataBench, released in 2013, is a benchmark suite developed to address the lack of Big Data benchmarks with a diverse set of real-world datasets and workloads [25]. The suite covers applications from streaming social network workloads to offline analysis of multimedia (all using real-world datasets).

DeepBench, released in 2016, is a benchmark suite developed to allow optimization of hardware and software for deep learning applications. DeepBench uses hardware dependent neural network libraries utilized by deep learning frameworks such as Caffe, to benchmark fundamental operations such as matrix multiplication.

OpenDwarfs, released in 2010, is a benchmark suite intended to help guide development of hardware requirements on heterogeneous platforms for parallel scientific computation [11]. OpenDwarfs is a collection of kernels (frequently used algorithms and operations) that operate on OpenCL compatible hardware platforms. This collection ranges from dense linear algebra operations to graphical model operations, relevant to higher-level ML and artificial intelligence applications.

2.2   Benchmark Comparison

A set of criteria has been selected to provide insights on the difficulties of extending these benchmark suites, as well as, their suitability for the various hardware platforms that exist. An overview of the benchmark comparison can be found in Tables 1 and 2.

Table 1. A comparison of benchmarks surveyed - Part 1 of 2

Benchmark suite	License	Maturity	Target hardware	Programming languages
PARSEC	– PARSEC framework license – Package specific licenses	Mature and well-adopted	Multicore processors	C, C++
CortexSuite	Benchmark specific licenses (BSD style)	Mature and moderately well-adopted	Computer vision architectures	C, Matlab
Tonic Suite	BSD 3-clause	Immature and poorly adopted	DNN Server platforms	Caffe (C++, Python)
Fathom	MIT License	DNN hardware accelerators	Multicore processors	Python 2.6+
Rllab	MIT License	Immature and poorly adopted	N/A	Python 3.5+
KITTI	Creative Commons Attribution-NonCommercial-ShareAlike 3.0 License	Mature and well-adopted	N/A	Python, Matlab
Rodinia	Rodinia License	Mature and moderately well-adopted	Heterogeneous systems	C, C++
SHOC	BSD License	Mature and poorly adopted	Clusters of heterogeneous systems	C, C++
Model Zoo	BAIR License	Mature and well-adopted	N/A	Caffe, Tensorflow (Python, C++)
HiBench	Apache License, Version 2.0	Moderately mature and well-adopted	Hadoop-based clusters	Java (Hadoop) Java, Python, Scala, R (Spark)
SparkBench	Apache License, Version 2.0	Immature and poorly adopted	Spark-based clusters	Java, Python, Scala, R (Spark)
BigDataBench	Apache License, Version 2.0	Moderately immature and well-adopted	Big Data related hardware	Java (Hadoop) Java, Python, Scala, R (Spark) And more
DeepBench	Apache License, Version 2.0	Immature and poorly adopted	Nvidia GPUs Intel CPUs	C++
OpenDwarfs	GNU Lesser General Public License v2.1	Mature and poorly adopted	Heterogeneous systems	OpenCL (C, C++)

Table 2. A comparison of benchmarks surveyed - Part 2 of 2

Benchmark suite	Threading models	Parallelization models	Distributed	Other features and details
PARSEC	Pthreads OpenMP TBB	Data parallel pipelining	X	Instruction mix and synchronization primitive use analysis available [5]
Cortex Suite	Multi-threaded	Instruction level data level thread level	X	Benchmark programs have a heavy focus on arithmetic operations (eg. matrix multiplication)
Tonic Suite	NVIDIA's multi-process service	CUDA (Caffe)	✓	Optimizations for DNN as a service available [14]
Fathom	Multi-threaded (Tensorflow)	Multi-layer pipeline data parallelism	✓	Workload characteristics analysis available (eg. instruction mix) [1]
Rllab	Multi-threaded (Tensorflow)	N/A	X	Compatible with OpenAI Gym
KITTI	N/A	N/A	X	Datasets and development kits are provided. There are no benchmark programs implemented
Rodinia	Multi-threaded	CUDA OpenMP OpenCL	X	PARSEC and Rodinia cover similar workloads despite different hardware targets [8]
SHOC	Multi-threaded	CUDA OpenCL	✓	Provides benchmarks from simple throughput testing to complex scientific computation kernels
Model Zoo	Multi-threaded	CUDA (Caffe)	X	N/A
HiBench	N/A	Hadoop spark	✓	– EnhancedDFSIO: Provides low-level system metrics and high-level Hadoop job metrics – Many software stacks available
Spark Bench	N/A	Spark	✓	Workload characteristics analysis available [20]
BigDataBench	N/A	Hadoop spark and many more	✓	– Allows scaling of real-world datasets – Many software stacks, workload types and application domains available
Deep Bench	Multi-threaded (MKL)	OpenMP (MKL) cuDNN	X	N/A
Open Dwarfs	Multi-threaded	OpenCL	X	N/A

Licenses, **maturity** and **adoption** help develop an understanding of the potential difficulties of extending these benchmark suites. Licenses determine whether these benchmark suites can be modified, among other legal details such as commercial use, liability and copyright details. Mature and well-adopted benchmark suites are more likely to be stable. **Target hardware** and **programming languages** are intended to provide quick understanding of what class of hardware is targeted by these benchmarks. These criteria may also affect the difficulty of extending these benchmarks.

Threading models and **parallelization models** are highly specific to a given benchmark suite. These criteria help indicate the application scope of benchmark suites, given their target hardware. The ´distributed and **other features** criteria, found in Table 2, are auxiliary criteria that demonstrate key features of the benchmark suites, as well as readiness for distributed workloads.

3   Benchmark Selection and Experiment Setup

3.1   A Benchmark Suite Selection: BigDataBench

For the purposes of benchmarking the performance of ARM processors against x86 processors, we chose the BigDataBench (BDB) benchmark suite over HiBench. Both BDB and HiBench provide implementations for a variety of software stacks and a diverse set of relevant Machine Learning applications. They both also provide distributed workloads without delving into low-level operations seen in benchmarks that utilize OpenCL and GPU libraries. It is worth noting that HiBench is more mature and well-adopted than BDB, but we choose BDB as it provides a larger assortment of workload types and benchmarks overall.

BDB is a benchmark suite that addresses the lack of Big Data benchmarks by employing a diverse set of real-world datasets. The BDB benchmark suite provides the following workload types: Offline Analytics, Graph, Data Warehouse, Streaming, Online Services and Cloud workloads. These workloads cover the following application domains: Search Engines, Social Media, E-commerce, Multimedia, and Bioinformation.

3.2   Hardware Selection

After surveying benchmark suites and selecting BDB, the next crucial step in comparing ARM and x86 processors is to select hardware that would allow for a fair comparison, while representing the strengths of current ARM and x86 processors. A criticism of the ARM vs. x86 benchmark paper by Indian Institute of Science (IISc) [18] is their choice of processors. The ARM AMD Opteron A1170 and the x86 AMD Opteron 3380 are both fairly weak processors and it is unlikely that their results will carry over to the state-of-the-art, non-HPC (high-performance computing) ARM and x86 processors that exist. Hence, an effort was made to survey state-of-the-art and upcoming ARM processors, notably: Cavium's ThunderX CN8890, Adapteva's Epiphany-V, AMD's K12, and AppliedMicro's X-Gene 3.

The dual socket Cavium ThunderX CN8890 is the most powerful ARM processor currently available for sampling. Given the price point of this new processor and its lack of availability, we used Packet's bare metal service, at the expense of not being able to measure its power consumption. We then chose to use a local x86 server with similar hardware specifications in order to provide a fair benchmark comparison, as shown in Table 3.

Table 3. Selected ARM and x86 hardware platforms

Criteria	ARM (Packet - Option 2A)	x86 (local)
OS Kernel	CentOS Linux release 7.3.1611 4.5.0-22.el7.aarch64	CentOS release 6.6 (final) 2.6.32-504.el6.x86_64
Memory	128 GB (8 ×16 GB) DD4 ECC 2400 MHz	128 GB (8 × 16 GB) DD4 ECC 2400 MHz
Disk	**340 GB Intel® SSD (DC S3500 Series)** 480 MB/s, 355 MB/s (Sequential Read, Write) 67000 IOPS, 14500 IOPS (Random Read, Write)	**512 GB SAMSUNG SSD (PM871)** 540 MB/s, 520 MB/s (Sequential Read, Write) 97000 IOPS, 90000 IOPS (Random Read, Write)
CPU	**2 x Cavium ThunderX: CN8890**: 48 Cores (96 total) 48 Threads (96 total) Max Frequency: 2000 MHz Base Speed: 2000 MHz	**2 x Intel® Xeon® Processor E5-2620 v4**: 8 Cores (16 total) 16 Threads (32 total) Max Frequency: 3100 MHz Base Speed: 2100 MHz
	Caches: 32 KB L1 Data Cache 78 KB L1 Instruction Cache 16 MB Shared L2 Cache No L3 Cache	Caches: 256 KB L1 Data Cache 256 KB L1 Instruction Cache 256 KB L2 Cache Per Core 20 MB Shared L3 Cache
	Cavium Processor Interconnect: 240 Gb/s (raw bit rate) [21] TDP: 80 W (160 W total) [16] SPEC_INT: 700 (Dual Socket) [16]	Intel QuickPath Interconnect: 384 Gb/s (raw bit rate) [21] TDP: 85 W (170 W total) [2] SPEC_INT: 684 (Dual Socket) [2]
Swap	Disabled	Disabled

3.3 Experimental Setup

Despite the large variety of workloads provided by BDB, our initial experimental focus is strictly the Spark and Hive workloads provided. These workloads best represent the types of processing performed in the fields of ML and Big Data. Below, in Table 4, we provide Spark and Hadoop configurations and software versions used in our experiments. Although pre-built software is readily available for x86 processors, it is necessary to build software from source for ARM.

Table 4. Spark and Hadoop configurations

Spark configuration property	ARM server	x86 server
SPARK_EXECUTOR_INSTANCES	7	7
SPARK_EXECUTOR_CORES	13	4
SPARK_EXECUTOR_MEMORY	16 GB	16 GB
SPARK_DRIVER_MEMORY	8 GB	8 GB
SPARK_WORKER_CORES	95	31
SPARK_WORKER_MEMORY	120 GB	120 GB
SPARK_WORKER_INSTANCES	1	1
mapred.tasktracker.map.tasks.maximum	92	31
mapred.tasktracker.reduce.tasks.maximum	92	31

By default, the *spark.dynamicAllocation.enabled* Spark configuration property is set to false, enforcing a static number of workers and executors, as well as resources allocated per worker, executor and driver.

3.3.1   ARM LSE Atomic Instructions

As part of the recent Large System Extension (LSE) update to the ARMv8.1 architecture, ARM architectures now provide support for new atomic instructions. Since Linux kernel v4.3, support has been added for these new atomic instructions. Accordingly, software such as JDK 8 also make use of these new atomic instructions by default. These new atomic instructions can cause unstable system behaviour under heavy loads. This results in repeated crashes when processing Spark or Hadoop jobs, due to the heavy use of these instructions by JVMs. One solution is to use a kernel that does not advertise support for LSE instructions, or to avoid software that makes use of these instructions by default. We disable the use of LSE atomic instructions in all JVMs spawned by Hadoop and Spark in our experimentation and determined that this does not significantly alter performance results.

3.3.2   BigDataBench Spark Workloads

The Spark benchmarks utilize the Big Data Generator Suite (BDGS) to generate data scaled from real-world datasets. A benchmark program starts a job in the Spark cluster that processes the generated data stored on Hadoop's Distributed File System (HDFS). We vary the inputs up to 130 GB to demonstrate the effect of data scaling, as well as the characteristics of Spark with moderate disk usage. Below, we detail Spark workloads that follow this benchmark process. In terms of instruction mix, all workloads are representative of common Big Data applications (high amount of loads and stores compared to other instructions) [25], (Table 5).

Table 5. Experimental software stack

Software package/framework	Version - source
Hive	v0.9.0
Hadoop	v1.2.0
Spark	v1.3.0
Java (for ARM)	jdk8-server-release-1603
Java (for x86)	JDK/JRE 8u131
BigDataBench	v3.2.5 for Spark

The **Word Count** workload is an Offline Analytics workload that consists of an input dataset of Wikipedia Entries. Word Count is a simple microbenchmark that sorts and outputs the frequency of unique words in these Wikipedia Entries.

The **Naive Bayes** workload is an Offline Analytics workload that consists of an input dataset of Amazon Movie Reviews. The Naive Bayes benchmark trains a Naive Bayes classifier model in one job, then classifies the remaining data in a second job. The integer/floating point operation intensity of this workload is relatively high [25], thus, it is representative of machine learning workloads. Moreover, learning a generative graphical model and performing classification are fundamental machine learning tasks.

The **Page Rank** workload is an Offline Analytics workload that consists of an input dataset of Google Web Graphs. Page Rank is a benchmark that performs iterations of the Page Rank algorithm, it ultimately ranks the relative importance of web pages, represented by nodes. Our disk sizes currently limit the scaling of our benchmarks, due to the size of intermediate files created.

3.3.3 BigDataBench Hive Workloads

The Hive benchmarks also utilize the Big Data Generator Suite (BDGS) to generate data scaled from real-world E-commerce transaction data. The BDGS generates a set of structured text files and subsequently creates tables using Hive that we name *order*, *item*, and *item_temp*. A benchmark program starts a job in the Hadoop cluster via the Hive interface, this job processes the generated data stored on the HDFS. We are limited to scaling the input up to 80 GB, due to the size of intermediate files generated.

As previously mentioned, all BDB benchmarks, including the Hive benchmarks are representative of Big Data applications (due to the instruction mix). More specifically, the Hive benchmarks are also highly relevant to ML applications, as large amounts of data are typically pre-processed and/or stored in a cluster in the form of relations (tables). In fact, Spark is currently migrating towards a DataFrame based API, as this idea is commonly employed. Below, we detail Hive workloads that follow the aforementioned benchmark process.

In order to describe the benchmarks, we first describe the tables created. The external *order* table consists of: buyer_id, order_id, and date. The external *item* table consists of: item_id, order_id, goods_id, goods_number, goods_price, and goods_amount (product of goods_number and goods_price). The internal *item_temp* table is the order_ids found in *item*.

Aggregate averaged (or **AV**) refers to the average of four benchmarks, that individually acquire the average/sum/maximum/minimum of goods_number from *item*. **Union** selects rows from *item* with two separate sets of criteria and creates a table as the union of these results. **Aggregate** creates a sorted table of goods_id from *item* and calculates the sum of goods_number. **Select** creates a table of goods_price and goods_amount for rows in *item* that match a criteria. **Order By** creates a table of all rows in *item* sorted by item_id. **Cross Project** creates a table with order_id from *item* joined to matching rows in *order*. **Projection** creates a table of order_id from *order*. **Filter** creates a table of rows in *item* that meet a criteria. **Join** creates a table of buyer_id and the sum of goods_amount from *item*, and joins this with the *order* for up to 10 matching order_ids (a limit), all while sorting by buyer_id. **Difference** creates a table of order_id from *order* and performs a left outer join on *item_temp* on the order_ids.

3.3.4   Metrics

The Spark and Hive benchmarks provided by BDB do not report any metrics other than execution time. For further analysis, we use *perf* and *sysstat*. The *perf* tool is capable of reporting hardware counters for the overall execution of a program. For the ARM hardware platform, we record the number of instructions, data and instruction TLB load and store misses, as well as L1 data and instruction cache, store, load, and prefetch misses. *Sysstat* provides tools such as *sar* that provide the capabilities to record key system performance parameters relating to CPU, memory, disk and network traffic.

4   Spark Experimental Results

In this section, x86 and ARM processors are compared with respect to system metrics recorded for BDB Spark workloads. We begin our discussion of experimental results with the execution times of the benchmark workloads in Fig. 1.

Our results differ from previous benchmarks of ARM and x86 for Big Data workloads [18]. In our results, the performance of the ARM processor did not improve relative to the x86 processor with larger datasets. Moreover, we find that the performance of ARM is not superior to x86 for all input sizes of Naive Bayes and Page Rank benchmarks. With the exception of Page Rank, ARM consistently has slightly worse performance than x86. An interesting observation can be made, however, with the extremely poor performance of ARM for the Page Rank benchmark, relative to x86. This is likely because a single x86 core provides superior floating point performance to that of a single ARM core, as Spark only recruits a small number of cores for small Page Rank workloads.

A closer look at the CPU usage of ARM and x86 processors under a heavy load, in Fig. 2, demonstrates idling when the number of cores waiting for I/O increases. This is further demonstrated in the disk statistics of Fig. 3.

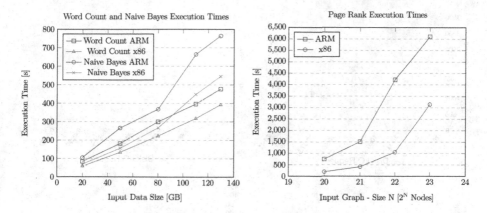

Fig. 1. Execution times for Word Count and Naive Bayes (left), and Page Rank (right).

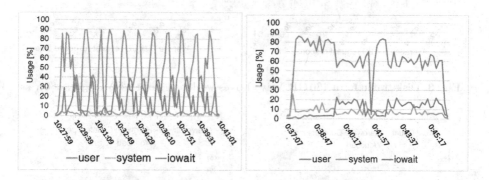

Fig. 2. CPU usage for a 130 GB Naive Bayes benchmark (left: ARM, right: x86)

In Fig. 3, we present a side by side comparison of disk statistics of the ARM and x86 servers. The x86 server is able to make more disk I/O requests per second, while maintaining lower response times. Although it is not shown, this also translates into roughly 60% higher sector reads and writes per second for the x86 server. Moreover, the timings of high I/O requests coincide with CPU idling in Fig. 2, for both ARM and x86. An explanation for this is that the x86 server's random read and write disk speeds are significantly faster than the ARM server in Table 3. Another possibility is that the ARM processor is ineffective in scheduling requests to the disk, causing large I/O request response times. It is plausible that the ARM processor is unable to simultaneously keep the hard disk heavily utilized while performing demanding Naive Bayes floating point operations (as indicated by the erratic spikes in I/O requests in Fig. 3).

Figure 4 shows hardware counters recorded for every Spark benchmark performed on the ARM processor. Misses are recorded in units of PKI (per thousand instructions executed) and are displayed on a logarithmic scale. There is a very large amount of data L1 cache store misses, regardless of the benchmark or

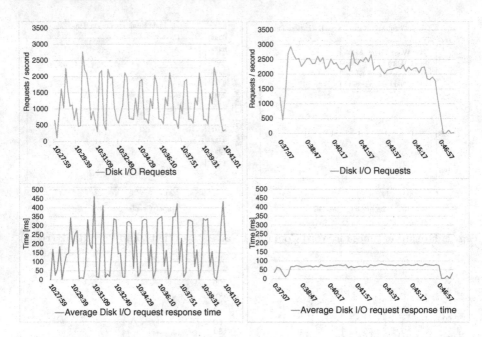

Fig. 3. Disk traffic for a 130 GB Naive Bayes workload (left: ARM, right: x86).

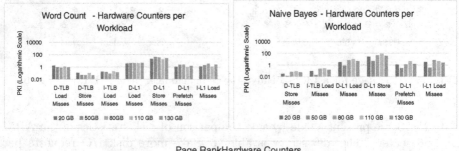

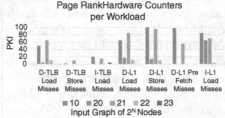

Fig. 4. ARM - Hardware counters recorded per benchmark

input size. By looking at all plots, it is apparent that Page Rank has the largest number of L1 cache misses, followed by Naive Bayes and Word Count, which matches previous results made on x86 processors [25]. Although these patterns match previous findings, the magnitude of L1 cache misses for the ARM processor is far greater than the x86 processor. The significance of this is that the L1 cache is paramount for Big Data related workloads [25], this may partially explain ARM's lagging performance for Spark workloads. The TLB behaviour of the ARM and x86 processors is similar.

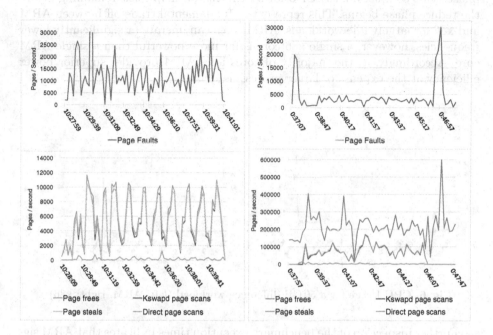

Fig. 5. Memory management for a 130 GB Naive Bayes workload (left: ARM, right: x86). Note the difference in y-axis scales in the bottom graphs.

In Fig. 5, a side-by-side comparison is made between the ARM and x86 server memory management statistics. The ARM server is unable to effectively manage memory, as it has far more page faults per second (this may also explain the large I/O wait of the ARM server). This behaviour is likely due to the ARM server scanning, stealing and freeing far fewer memory pages per second. The superior x86 server memory management is also embodied in the amount of time spent by the kernel in Fig. 2.

We found that patterns relating to network traffic such as packets per second, number of context switches per second, and memory usage patterns (memory used and cached) between the servers are highly similar.

4.1 Hive Experimental Results

In this section, x86 and ARM processors are compared with respect to system metrics recorded for BDB Hive workloads. We begin our discussion of experimental results with the execution times of the benchmark workloads in Fig. 7.

It is first worth noting ARM's extremely poor performance in the Difference benchmark, as demonstrated in the bottom right of Fig. 7. This poor performance is identical to the Page Rank benchmark seen previously. By comparing the CPU usage of the x86 and ARM server in Fig. 6, it is clear that as the map phase nears completion, the CPU idles with the few map tasks remaining before the reduce phase begins. This represents a fundamental trade-off between ARM and x86 for largely idle workloads. ARM cores can operate at significantly lower frequencies, however, a single x86 core is far more powerful than a single ARM core. Accordingly, as the majority of cores idle, ARM provides superior power efficiency at the expense of larger processing delays.

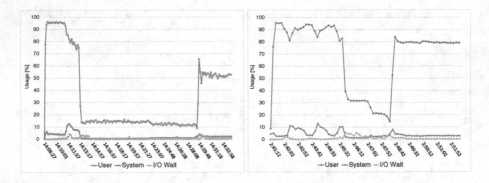

Fig. 6. CPU Usage for a 50 GB difference workload (left: ARM, right: x86)

Further inspection of the benchmark execution times indicates that ARM significantly outperforms x86 in Select, Aggregate and Projection, as demonstrated in Fig. 7. What these benchmarks have in common is that the entire input dataset and intermediate files created are able to fit in memory, hence, deferring the need to spill to the disk (refer to Fig. 10). This alone does not explain ARM's success, as ARM only performs on par with x86 for Filter, Union, and AV workloads, which all have moderate memory usage.

Using sysstat, we record instantaneous pages/second measurements over the course of the benchmarks. In order to determine the total number of pages from the disk and to the disk, we use a crude trapezoidal approximation, evaluated as the product of the sum of instantaneous measurements with the interval of the measurements (as seen in Fig. 8). This alone is misleading, as some benchmarks vary in execution time by an order of magnitude, and will have more disk pages to/from the disk over the whole period of the benchmark. Accordingly, we scale the total number of pages by the execution time per benchmark and normalize across benchmarks to determine which workloads are particularly heavy on page writes and reads. In Fig. 9, we see that Select, Aggregate and Projection have significantly more page writes than Union, Filter and AV. This leads us to conclude that ARM has superior performance over x86 for write heavy Hive workloads, particularly the creation of tables and intermediate files necessary to compute the final resultant table.

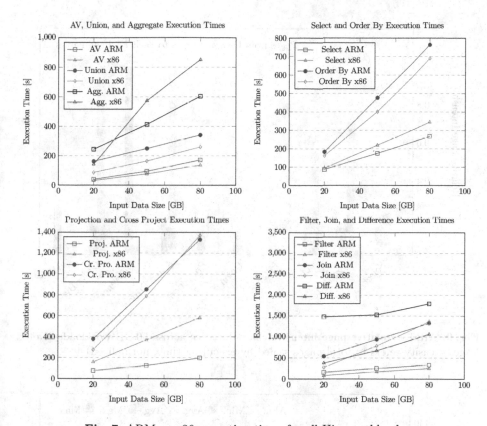

Fig. 7. ARM vs x86 execution times for all Hive workloads

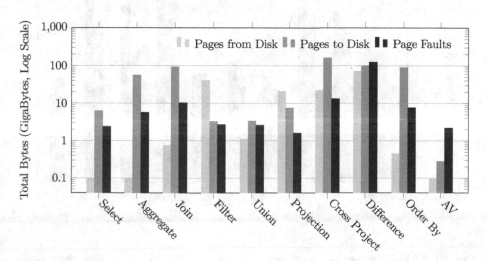

Fig. 8. ARM - Paging characteristics across 50 GB workloads via trapezoidal rule approximation

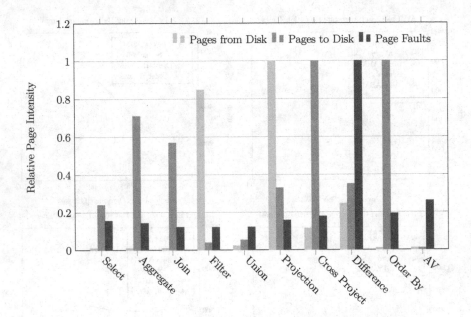

Fig. 9. ARM - Relative page intensity characteristics across 50 GB workloads (Note: Page intensity refers to total pages scaled by execution time, normalized)

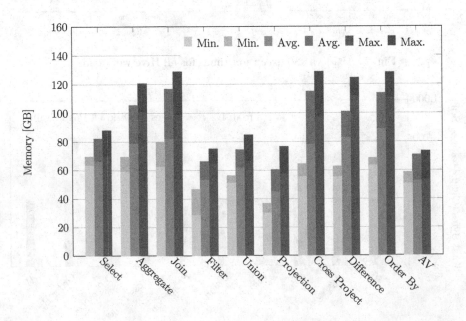

Fig. 10. ARM - Memory usage characteristics across all workloads (Note: green refers to memory cached, the addition of red and green refers to total memory used) (Color figure online)

Another point worth discussing is the scaling of ARM versus x86 for Aggregate, Cross Project, and Join, and how this ties into ARM's lagging performance in Union, Filter, Order By, and AV benchmarks. From previous experimentation, namely Web Serving, the expectation is that ARM would excel for the simplest of workloads. However, by looking at the execution times of Union, Filter and AV it seems as if the ARM server incurs a constant delay associated with the time spent preparing before progress is made in the map phase. Otherwise, the performance of the two servers is roughly on par.

Furthermore, the superior scaling of ARM in the aforementioned workloads suggests that the large number of cores on the ARM processor excels for workloads with components that can be computed in parallel. For instance, the Aggregate benchmark consists of a select, an order by and a sum, which can progress concurrently, as opposed to only a single select query in the Filter benchmark, or a single sum query in the AV benchmarks.

5 Related Work

Previous experimentation of ARM processors against x86 processors already exists [3, 6, 17–19, 23]. The common theme in these works is that x86 processors generally outperform ARM processors in terms of execution times. The key strength of ARM, however, lies in its performance per watt. For instance, in a Web Server application, ARM processors serve more web requests per watt when compared to x86 processors [3]. Another nuance of ARM processors is that they are strictly application dependent. For CPU-bound applications, specifically those that are heavy in integer or floating point operations, ARM processors not only result in longer execution times, but may also have worse performance per watt [3, 17].

Moreover, a recent benchmark of ARM processors against x86 processors, by the IISc [18], used the HiBench benchmark suite. This suite was originally intended for benchmarking new Hadoop-based Big Data deployments, but has since been adapted for other software stacks, such as Spark and Apache Storm. The group strictly employed Hadoop workloads with the intention to demonstrate the potential for Big Data workloads on ARM processors. The authors found that not only was performance per watt improved (typically measured by Energy Delay Product), but it also became possible for ARM processors to match or improve performance over x86 processors under certain workloads.

6 Conclusions

In this paper, we presented a survey of existing hardware performance benchmark suites that range from evaluation of heterogeneous systems to distributed ML workloads for clusters of servers. From the survey, we selected BigDataBench in order to compare the performance of server-grade ARM and x86 processors for a diverse set of workloads and applications, using real-world datasets that are scalable. We benchmarked a state-of-the-art dual socket Cavium ThunderX CN8890 ARM processor against a dual socket Intel®Xeon®processor E5-2620 v4 x86-64 processor. Initial results demonstrated that ARM generally had slightly worse performance compared to x86 processors for Spark Offline Analytics workloads, and on par or superior performance for Hive workloads. We determined that the ARM server excels over x86 for write heavy workloads. It is worth noting the apparent disk I/O bottleneck of the ARM server when comparing performance results to the x86 server. There are many other BigDataBench workloads that have yet to be tested on ARM, many of which may lead to promising results when provided with larger amounts of disk and network I/O. Moreover, recording the CPU temperatures and power consumptions of these servers may yield even more fruitful results, further promoting the use of ARM in server-grade processing for ML and Big Data applications.

Acknowledgements. This work was supported by the Data Center Technology Lab of Huawei.

References

1. Adolf, R., Rama, S., Reagen, B., Wei, G., Brooks, D.M.: Fathom: reference workloads for modern deep learning methods. CoRR abs/1608.06581 (2016). http://arxiv.org/abs/1608.06581
2. The Linley Group Analyst: Thunderx rattles server market. Technical report, The Linley Group, June 2014. http://www.cavium.com/pdfFiles/ThunderX_Rattles_Server_Market.pdf
3. Aroca, R.V., Gonçalves, L.M.G.: Towards green data centers: a comparison of x86 and ARM architectures power efficiency. J. Parallel Distrib. Comput. **72**(12), 1770–1780 (2012). http://www.sciencedirect.com/science/article/pii/S0743731512002122
4. Barroso, L.A., Hölzle, U.: The case for energy-proportional computing. Computer **40**(12), 33–37 (2007)
5. Bienia, C.: Benchmarking modern multiprocessors. Ph.D. thesis, Princeton University, Princeton (2011). aAI3445564
6. Blem, E., Menon, J., Sankaralingam, K.: Power struggles: revisiting the RISC vs. CISC debate on contemporary ARM and x86 architectures. In: 2013 IEEE 19th International Symposium on High Performance Computer Architecture (HPCA), pp. 1–12, February 2013
7. Cavium: ThunderX® ARM processors. http://www.cavium.com/ThunderX_ARM_Processors.html
8. Che, S., Sheaffer, J.W., Boyer, M., Szafaryn, L.G., Wang, L., Skadron, K.: A characterization of the Rodinia benchmark suite with comparison to contemporary CMP workloads. In: Proceedings of the IEEE International Symposium on Workload Characterization (IISWC 2010), pp. 1–11. IEEE Computer Society, Washington, DC (2010). http://dx.doi.org/10.1109/IISWC.2010.5650274
9. Danalis, A., Marin, G., McCurdy, C., Meredith, J.S., Roth, P.C., Spafford, K., Tipparaju, V., Vetter, J.S.: The scalable heterogeneous computing (SHOC) benchmark suite. In: Proceedings of the 3rd Workshop on General-Purpose Computation on Graphics Processing Units (GPGPU-3), pp. 63–74. ACM, New York (2010). http://doi.acm.org/10.1145/1735688.1735702

10. Duan, Y., Chen, X., Houthooft, R., Schulman, J., Abbeel, P.: Benchmarking deep reinforcement learning for continuous control. CoRR abs/1604.06778 (2016). http://arxiv.org/abs/1604.06778
11. Feng, W.C., Lin, H., Scogland, T., Zhang, J.: OpenCL and the 13 dwarfs: a work in progress. In: Proceedings of the 3rd ACM/SPEC International Conference on Performance Engineering (ICPE 2012), pp. 291–294. ACM, New York (2012). http://doi.acm.org/10.1145/2188286.2188341
12. Geiger, A.: Are we ready for autonomous driving? The KITTI vision benchmark suite. In: Proceedings of the 2012 IEEE Conference on Computer Vision and Pattern Recognition (CVPR 2012), pp. 3354–3361. IEEE Computer Society, Washington, DC (2012). http://dl.acm.org/citation.cfm?id=2354409.2354978
13. George, A.D.: An overview of RISC vs. CISC. In: Proceedings of the Twenty-Second Southeastern Symposium on System Theory, pp. 436–438, March 1990
14. Hauswald, J., Kang, Y., Laurenzano, M.A., Chen, Q., Li, C., Mudge, T., Dreslinski, R.G., Mars, J., Tang, L.: Djinn and Tonic: DNN as a service and its implications for future warehouse scale computers. In: Proceedings of the 42nd Annual International Symposium on Computer Architecture (ISCA 2015), pp. 27–40. ACM, New York (2015). http://doi.acm.org/10.1145/2749469.2749472
15. Huang, S., Huang, J., Dai, J., Xie, T., Huang, B.: The HiBench benchmark suite: characterization of the MapReduce-based data analysis. In: 2010 IEEE 26th International Conference on Data Engineering Workshops (ICDEW), pp. 41–51. IEEE (2010)
16. Intel: Intel® Xeon® processor e5-2620 v4. https://ark.intel.com/products/92986/Intel-Xeon-Processor-E5-2620-v4-20M-Cache-2_10-GHz
17. Jundt, A., Cauble-Chantrenne, A., Tiwari, A., Peraza, J., Laurenzano, M.A., Carrington, L.: Compute bottlenecks on the new 64-bit ARM. In: Proceedings of the 3rd International Workshop on Energy Efficient Supercomputing (E2SC 2015), pp. 6:1–6:7. ACM, New York (2015). http://doi.acm.org/10.1145/2834800.2834806
18. Kalyanasundaram, J., Simmhan, Y.: ARM wrestling with big data: a study of ARM64 and x64 servers for data intensive workloads. CoRR abs/1701.05996 (2017). http://arxiv.org/abs/1701.05996
19. Laurenzano, M.A., Tiwari, A., Jundt, A., Peraza, J., Ward, W.A., Campbell, R., Carrington, L.: Characterizing the performance-energy tradeoff of small ARM cores in HPC computation. In: Silva, F., Dutra, I., Santos Costa, V. (eds.) Euro-Par 2014. LNCS, vol. 8632, pp. 124–137. Springer, Cham (2014). https://doi.org/10.1007/978-3-319-09873-9_11
20. Li, M., Tan, J., Wang, Y., Zhang, L., Salapura, V.: SparkBench: A comprehensive benchmarking suite for in memory data analytic platform Spark. In: Proceedings of the 12th ACM International Conference on Computing Frontiers (CF 2015), pp. 53:1–53:8. ACM, New York (2015). http://doi.acm.org/10.1145/2742854.2747283
21. Morgan, T.P.: Intel lines up ThunderX ARM against Xeons. Technical report, The Next Platform, May 2016. https://www.nextplatform.com/2016/05/31/intel-lines-thunderx-arms-xeons/
22. Saponara, S., Fanucci, L., Coppola, M.: Many-core platform with NoC interconnect for low cost and energy sustainable cloud server-on-chip. In: 2012 Sustainable Internet and ICT for Sustainability (SustainIT), pp. 1–5, October 2012

23. Svanfeldt-Winter, O., Lafond, S., Lilius, J.: Cost and energy reduction evaluation for ARM based web servers. In: Proceedings of the 2011 IEEE Ninth International Conference on Dependable, Autonomic and Secure Computing (DASC 2011), pp. 480–487. IEEE Computer Society, Washington, DC (2011). http://dx.doi.org/10.1109/DASC.2011.93

24. Venkata, S.K., Ahn, I., Jeon, D., Gupta, A., Louie, C., Garcia, S., Belongie, S., Taylor, M.B.: SD-VBS: The San Diego vision benchmark suite. In: Proceedings of the 2009 IEEE International Symposium on Workload Characterization (IISWC 2009), pp. 55–64. IEEE Computer Society, Washington, DC (2009). http://dx.doi.org/10.1109/IISWC.2009.5306794

25. Wang, L., Zhan, J., Luo, C., Zhu, Y., Yang, Q., He, Y., Gao, W., Jia, Z., Shi, Y., Zhang, S., Zheng, C., Lu, G., Zhan, K., Li, X., Qiu, B.: BigDataBench: a Big Data benchmark suite from internet services. CoRR abs/1401.1406 (2014). http://arxiv.org/abs/1401.1406

Author Index

Printed in the United States
By Bookmasters